The Coffin Texts

Sacred Spells of the Afterlife's Journey

Volume 4

M L Ruscsak

Trient Press
3375 S Rainbow Blvd
#81710, SMB 13135
Las Vegas,NV 89180

Ordering Information:
Quantity sales. Special discounts are available on quantity purchases by corporations, associations, and others. For details, contact the publisher at the address above.
Orders by U.S. trade bookstores and wholesalers. Please contact Trient Press: Tel: (775) 996-3844; or visit www.trientpress.com.

Printed in the United States of America

Publisher's Cataloging-in-Publication data
Ruscsak, M.L.
A title of a book : The Coffin Texts: Sacred Spells of the Afterlife's Journey Volume 4
    ISBN
Hard Cover   979-8-88990-044-3
Paper Back   979-8-88990-045-0
Ebook   979-8-88990-046-7

Disclosure for the book "Coffin Text: Sacred Spells of the Afterlife's Journey Volume 4":

In this book, we present a collection of spells, incantations, and rituals that are inspired by and closely aligned with ancient Egyptian hieroglyphs. While we have made efforts to translate and interpret these texts as accurately as possible, it is important to note that the numbers assigned to each entry are for ease of reference within this book and do not necessarily reflect a definitive chronological or organizational order. Many scholars continue to study and analyze these ancient texts, seeking to confirm their age and the periods in which they were written.

The concept of the afterlife holds a significant place in ancient Egyptian culture and religion. Therefore, numerous books with similar texts have been written throughout history to provide guidance, teachings, and inspiration that resonate with modern-day spirituality and various religions today.

It is crucial to approach these spells, incantations, and rituals with an open mind, understanding that they are rooted in the ancient Egyptian belief system and cultural context. While they may offer insights into the human quest for spiritual understanding and growth, they should be viewed as a part of the rich tapestry of human religious and spiritual exploration.

Readers are encouraged to interpret and adapt the contents of this book in a way that aligns with their personal beliefs and spiritual practices. The aim of this book is to shed light on the wisdom and traditions of ancient Egypt while providing a source of inspiration and guidance for individuals seeking to deepen their spiritual journey.

Please approach the text with respect for the ancient culture and its religious practices, and consider these spells, incantations, and rituals as tools for personal growth, reflection, and connection with the mysteries of the afterlife.

May the exploration of these ancient texts bring you insight, enrichment, and a deeper appreciation for the enduring wisdom of the ancient Egyptian civilization.

(Academic writing. Written for students seeking a bachelor's degree in acult studies . Use proper grammar and punctuation. Avoid contractions and colloquial language. In the tone of the orginial "coffin text". Use a formal and academic tone paired with sophisticated vocabulary and grammar. Provide a thorough and in-depth analysis of the subject matter.Explain the spells, incantations and ruituals as thou they can be used today. Explain complex scientific concepts in a clear and accessible way. Use examples from a variety of fields, such as Witchcraft, Divination, Herbalism,Shamanism,Magic in Ancient egypt . Present counterarguments and dissenting opinions in a balanced and objective way.)

In the enigmatic realm of ancient Egypt, the Ritual of Purification through the Sacred Waters of the Eternal Nile held a paramount significance. Rooted in a profound belief system and intricate spiritual practices, this ritual aimed to cleanse and renew the mind, body, and soul of the individual, paving the way for spiritual growth and connection with the divine. Despite its origins in a bygone era, this ritual possesses enduring relevance in modern times, as it offers transformative possibilities in the realms of witchcraft, divination, herbalism, shamanism, and magic. In this comprehensive analysis, we will delve into the complex nature of the ritual, explore its scientific underpinnings, examine its application in contemporary practices, and address counterarguments surrounding its efficacy.

The Ritual of Purification:
At its core, the Ritual of Purification entails the immersion of an individual in the sacred waters of the Nile, seeking to wash away impurities and restore balance to the being. Symbolically, the eternal flow of the Nile represents the cycle of life and embodies the life-giving force that permeated ancient Egyptian cosmology. By engaging in this ritual, one aligns themselves with this cosmic energy, opening channels for self-reflection, renewal, and spiritual evolution.

Spells, Incantations, and their Modern Relevance:
Central to the Ritual of Purification are the spells and incantations recited during the ritualistic process. These invocations, meticulously inscribed on papyrus or uttered by priests, were believed to possess transformative power, enabling the individual to access higher realms of consciousness and commune with divine entities. Today, these ancient incantations find echoes in various contemporary practices, such as witchcraft and divination.

In the realm of witchcraft, practitioners harness the power of words and intention to manifest desired outcomes. Just as ancient Egyptians invoked specific deities for protection and guidance, modern witches employ incantations to invoke elemental energies or spirit allies. By adapting the principles underlying the ancient spells, contemporary practitioners can establish profound connections with the unseen forces of the universe.

Similarly, divination practices, such as scrying or tarot reading, draw upon the concept of incantations to facilitate intuitive insights. By reciting sacred words or phrases, practitioners enter a focused state of mind, transcending ordinary consciousness and gaining access to hidden knowledge. These practices, rooted in the fundamental principles of the Ritual of Purification, allow individuals to explore the depths of their own psyche and the collective unconscious.

Scientific Explanation of the Ritual's Efficacy:
While the Ritual of Purification has its roots in ancient beliefs, a scientific lens can shed light on its potential psychological and physiological effects. The act of immersing oneself in water, particularly in a serene and sacred environment, triggers a relaxation response in the body, reducing stress and promoting a sense of calm. Moreover, the power of belief and intention, integral to the ritual, can elicit a placebo effect, whereby the individual experiences a perceived improvement in well-being and spiritual connectedness.

Counterarguments and Dissenting Opinions:
In considering the Ritual of Purification, it is essential to acknowledge dissenting opinions regarding its efficacy. Skeptics may argue that the perceived benefits are merely subjective

experiences or products of suggestion. Moreover, some critics may assert that the ritual's cultural appropriation in contemporary practices undermines its authenticity and spiritual significance.

Conclusion:

The Ritual of Purification through the Sacred Waters of the Eternal Nile, with its spells, incantations, and profound symbolism, continues to captivate the modern seeker of ancient wisdom. As we explore its scientific foundations, its adaptability to contemporary practices in witchcraft, divination, herbalism, shamanism, and magic becomes evident. By approaching this ritual with a balanced perspective, we can appreciate its potential for personal transformation and the preservation of cultural heritage. Whether as a historical artifact or a living tradition, this ritual invites us to immerse ourselves in the mystical currents of the eternal Nile and embark on a journey of self-discovery and spiritual growth.

1. Ritual of purification through the sacred waters of the eternal Nile

In the realm of ancient wisdom, where the veil between the earthly and divine realms intertwines, lies the Ritual of Purification through the Sacred Dances of the Eternal Rhythm. Within this enchanting ceremonial dance, we shall immerse ourselves in the sacred currents of movement, invoking the transformative power of rhythm to cleanse and purify the spirit.

Preparation:

In a hallowed sanctuary, far removed from worldly distractions, carve out a space where the dance can unfold undisturbed. Ensure that the surroundings are free from any encumbrances, providing an expansive canvas for your expressive movements.

Let the air be filled with melodies that resonate with the depths of your being, arousing the sacred vibrations that shall infuse the dance with its mystical essence.

Centering:

Stand tall, embodying the poise of an ancient deity, and inhale deeply, drawing the breath of life into the depths of your being. Feel the weight of the world lift as you exhale, surrendering to the present moment.

As you close your eyes, envision a luminescent aura enveloping your body, shimmering with radiant light. This ethereal glow signifies the purification and revitalization that awaits you on this sacred journey.

Setting Intentions:

With unwavering focus, cast forth your intentions into the unseen realms. Let them weave into the tapestry of the cosmos, shaping the purpose and direction of the dance. Whether seeking a general purification or targeting specific facets of existence, articulate your intentions with clarity and conviction.

Speak your desires aloud, allowing the vibrations of your voice to reverberate through the sacred space, carrying your intentions to the divine forces that guide this ritual of renewal.

Dance of Release:

As the symphony of rhythm begins to echo within your soul, surrender yourself to its primal allure. With each movement, let go of all that no longer serves you. Allow the dance to unravel the knots of negativity that entangle your spirit, freeing you from the burdens of the past.

Express yourself fully, unshackling the emotions that reside deep within. Through graceful gestures or vigorous motions, let the energy flow unimpeded, purging the stagnant remnants that hinder your inner radiance.

Dance of Renewal:

With the momentum of the music propelling you forward, transition into the dance of renewal. Feel the currents of cosmic energy intertwine with your fluid movements, rekindling the embers of your soul.

Synchronize your steps with the eternal rhythm, gracefully transmuting weariness into vigor, sorrow into joy, and doubt into unwavering faith. Visualize the divine light penetrating every fiber of your being, bestowing upon you the gift of spiritual rebirth.

Dance of Gratitude:

As the music begins to wane, guide your dance towards a gentle descent, cherishing the concluding moments of this sacred communion. Gradually slow your movements, allowing the energy to settle and integrate within you.

Place your hands upon your heart, a gesture of gratitude for the profound transformation experienced through the dance. Whisper words of appreciation to the benevolent forces that have accompanied you on this transformative odyssey.

Reflection and Integration:

Find solace in stillness, as you sit or stand in silent contemplation. Absorb the echoes of the dance that linger within your being, acknowledging the purifying currents that have coursed through your spirit.

Observe the shifts in your energy, the subtle dance of emotions, and honor the metamorphosis that has transpired. Breathe deeply, grounding yourself in the newfound wisdom and vitality gained from this sacred rite.

Remember, dear seeker of the ancient ways, that this ritual of purification through the sacred dances of the eternal rhythm is a personal odyssey. Surrender to the authentic movements that arise from the depths of your soul. Embrace the sanctity of this moment and the profound potential that lies within the eternal rhythm.

2. Incantation to invoke the blessings of the celestial stars and their celestial guidance

By the light of the celestial stars above,
I invoke their blessings, their guidance I seek to have.
With reverence and awe, I call upon their might,
To illuminate my path, and guide me through the night.

Oh, stars of the heavens, shining bright and clear,
Bestow upon me your wisdom, draw me near.
As I gaze upon your brilliance, your cosmic dance,
Infuse me with your essence, grant me a celestial trance.

Each star a beacon, a guide in the vast expanse,
I beseech you to lead me, to show me the chance.
To navigate the challenges, to find my way,
Through the ebb and flow, by night and by day.

Blessed stars above, with your celestial glow,
Your ancient wisdom, may it truly bestow.
Guide me in my journey, with your celestial sight,
Illuminate my path, fill my heart with your light.

Oh, celestial stars, with your celestial gaze,
Grant me clarity and insight, as I walk life's maze.
May your blessings descend upon me, like stardust from above,
Empowering me with wisdom, with grace and with love.

I honor you, celestial stars, in this sacred rite,
Your presence fills me with wonder, your beauty ignites.
I thank you for your guidance, for your celestial embrace,
As I walk this earthly journey, upheld by your grace.

So mote it be, as I speak this incantation true,
I invite the blessings of the celestial stars into view.
Guide me, protect me, and show me the way,
In your celestial guidance, I forever shall stay.

3. Spell for the transformation of the deceased into a vessel of divine protection

In the ethereal threshold between the mortal realm and the boundless expanse of the afterlife, lies the arcane incantation for the transformation of the departed soul into a sanctified vessel of divine protection. This profound spell, woven with intricacies of ancient wisdom, unravels the mystic path towards embodying the sacred mantle of safeguarding. Through a tapestry of precise rituals and resonant invocations, the deceased shall ascend, enshrined as a guardian of celestial realms.

Invocation:

In a sanctified space, cloaked in reverential silence, erect an altar adorned with sacred relics and symbols that exude the essence of protection and transcendence. Illuminate the chamber with softly flickering candles, their radiant glow kindling the presence of benevolent spirits and celestial sentinels. With focused intent, summon their celestial presence, invoking their guidance and benediction throughout this transformative rite.

Preparation:

Garb the departed in garments symbolizing sanctity and resilience, embroidered with sigils and patterns of protective potency. Bedeck the altar with offerings of fragrant herbs, blossoms, and resins, suffusing the air with their purifying and invigorating aura.

The Ritual:

Sanctification:
With utmost veneration, anoint the lifeless vessel with sanctified oils or consecrated waters, signifying the purgative essence that purifies and strengthens. Utter invocations of purification and consecration, entreating the divine forces to cleanse and fortify the departed soul.

Chant of Transcendence:
Speak the age-old words of power, resonating through the interstices of existence. Enshroud the vessel in the resounding frequencies of celestial guardianship, invoking the intercession of benevolent forces. Let the incantation serve as a conduit for the transmutation of the departed into an embodiment of divine protection.

Symbolic Engravings:
With unwavering focus, etch sacred symbols or ancient glyphs upon the surface of the vessel, evoking their inherent potency of shielding and safeguarding. Each stroke inscribed upon the vessel imparts the essence of celestial guardianship, sealing the metamorphosis with unwavering intent.

Offering of Vigilance:
Present offerings of profound significance upon the altar, aligning them with the purpose of protection and spiritual metamorphosis. These tributes serve as conduits bridging the mortal plane and the realm of spirits, attesting to the earnest devotion and veneration bestowed upon the departed.

Invocation of Celestial Sentinels:
Summon the celestial sentinels and guardian entities, whose unwavering vigil safeguards and consoles. Implore their intervention and watchful gaze, entreating their eternal vigilance over the vessel and its celestial odyssey.

Final Consecration:
With a final invocation, seal the transformation, affirming the transmutation of the departed into a vessel of divine protection. Express gratitude to the celestial forces for their presence and benevolence, acknowledging their pivotal role in this sacred transfiguration.

Reflection and Integration:

In the wake of the ritual, recline in introspective solitude, allowing the resonant energies to permeate and integrate within the sanctified enclave. Contemplate the profound nature of this spell and the transformative potential it confers upon the departed soul.

Embrace a scholarly pursuit, engendering discourse that acknowledges counterarguments and dissenting viewpoints regarding the concept of divine protection. Foster a balanced and objective perspective, traversing the multifarious realms of belief systems and their profound impact upon rituals of spiritual metamorphosis.

Remember, seeker of arcane wisdom, this spell is an invocation of sublime magnitude. Approach it with profound veneration and unyielding respect, delving into its depths with scholarly inquisitiveness and an unwavering yearning to comprehend the intricacies of the transformation of the departed into a vessel of divine protection.

4. Incantation to invoke the blessings of the celestial stars and constellations

Incantation to Invoke the Blessings of the Celestial Stars and Constellations
Amidst the velvet tapestry of the night sky, where the luminous constellations etch
their celestial paths, lies an incantation to invoke the blessings of the celestial stars.
Through the arcane power of words and the resonance of intent, we shall call upon
the cosmic forces that govern the heavens. With reverence and awe, let us unveil the
incantation to summon the blessings of the celestial stars and constellations:

Preparation:

Find a tranquil and open space beneath the expansive night sky, where the brilliance
of the stars can be observed without obstruction. Create an altar adorned with
celestial imagery and symbols, honoring the grandeur and wisdom of the cosmos.
Light candles of celestial hues, their gentle flicker mirroring the radiance of distant
stars.

Invocation:

Stand with feet grounded upon the earth, head held high, and arms outstretched,
embracing the vastness above. Close your eyes, feeling the rhythmic pulse of the
universe coursing through your veins. Whisper the sacred names of the stars,
invoking their presence and blessings. Let the resonance of your voice harmonize
with the cosmic symphony, bridging the realms of mortals and the celestial plane.

Chant of Alignment:

In dulcet tones, recite the chant that aligns the earthly realm with the celestial spheres.
Let the vibrations of each syllable reverberate through the night, awakening dormant
connections to the stars and constellations. Allow the words to weave a luminous
thread, binding your spirit to the cosmic tapestry.

Divine Dialogue:

Engage in a heartfelt conversation with the celestial stars and constellations. Express
your reverence, gratitude, and intent, opening yourself to receive their wisdom and
blessings. Speak of your aspirations, dreams, and desires, seeking guidance and
illumination from these celestial beacons. Allow the words to flow freely, carrying
your intentions to the farthest reaches of the universe.

Stellar Enchantment:

Gather celestial elements such as stardust, meteorite fragments, or celestial herbs upon the altar. Infuse them with your intentions and aspirations, imbuing them with the energy of your dialogue with the stars. Offer these enchanted tokens to the night sky, releasing them to the celestial expanse as symbols of your devotion and connection.

Silent Communion:

Stand in stillness, embracing the silence of the night. Listen to the whispers of the cosmic realm, feeling the gentle caress of the celestial breeze. Absorb the profound energy emanating from the stars and constellations, allowing it to penetrate the depths of your being. In this serene communion, experience the unity of the earthly and celestial realms.

Closing:

Offer gratitude to the celestial stars and constellations for their presence, guidance, and blessings. Lower your outstretched arms, returning to the grounded embrace of the earthly realm. Carry the wisdom and energy of this sacred invocation within your heart, knowing that the celestial stars and constellations shall forever be your celestial companions.

Reflection and Integration:

Find solace in introspective contemplation, pondering the significance of this incantation and its place in the tapestry of human belief. Explore counterarguments and dissenting opinions surrounding the influence of celestial forces on mortal lives, fostering an objective and balanced understanding of this celestial connection.

Remember, seeker of cosmic wisdom, this incantation is a gateway to the celestial realm. Approach it with reverence, humility, and a deep yearning to align your mortal existence with the celestial dance of stars. Embrace the cosmic guidance bestowed upon you and allow the blessings of the celestial stars and constellations to illuminate your path.

5. Ritual for the transfiguration of the deceased into a divine guardian of sacred knowledge

In the realm where mortal existence intertwines with the ethereal plane of wisdom, there exists a ritual for the transfiguration of the deceased into a divine guardian of sacred knowledge. Through the convergence of ancient rites and transformative energies, we shall embark upon this sacred journey, invoking the powers of the divine to bestow guardianship upon departed souls. With utmost reverence and unwavering intent, let us unfold the ritual for the transfiguration of the deceased into a divine guardian of sacred knowledge:

Preparation:

Choose a sanctified space, suffused with an aura of mysticism, where the veil between realms grows thin. Arrange an altar adorned with symbols of wisdom and enlightenment, invoking the cosmic forces that govern the universe. Place sacred texts and artifacts of profound knowledge upon the altar, signifying the weight of the wisdom sought.

Invocation:

Stand before the altar, embodying humility and profound veneration. Recite an invocation, calling upon the celestial beings and benevolent spirits to witness and partake in this sacred endeavor. Let your voice resonate with sincerity and earnestness, reaching out to the realms beyond in reverence of the eternal wisdom that lies dormant within the departed.

Anointing:

Prepare a blend of aromatic oils, carefully selected for their symbolic significance and ability to awaken spiritual energies. With a steady hand, anoint the forehead and palms of the deceased, channeling the transformative power of the oils to elevate their spiritual essence. As you anoint, recite words of blessing, inviting the divine presence to bless the departed with the mantle of guardianship.

Chant of Ascension:

Enter a meditative state and immerse yourself in the rhythm of sacred chants. With each melodious intonation, infuse the chants with the intention to guide the soul of the departed towards ascension. Let the harmonious vibrations resonate within the sacred space, permeating the ethereal realm and beckoning the guardians of wisdom to take notice.

Unveiling the Sacred Scrolls:

Open the sacred texts that hold the keys to profound knowledge and ancient wisdom. With profound respect, read aloud passages that illuminate the path of enlightenment. Allow the vibrations of the words to permeate the space, creating a resonance that transcends the boundaries of mortality and connects with the departed.

Communion with Ancestors:

Invoke the spirits of wise ancestors and ancient guardians of knowledge. Offer prayers and invocations that honor their wisdom and seek their guidance. Create a sacred space for communion, where the presence of these esteemed souls can be felt and their wisdom imparted. Listen attentively, for they may choose to speak through the whispers of the wind or the flickering of candles.

Sealing the Transformation:

In the final act of the ritual, gather together offerings of sacred herbs, crystals, and symbols of enlightenment. Place these offerings upon the altar, imbued with the intentions of protection and guardianship. Speak words of gratitude, acknowledging the divine grace that permeates the ritual and seals the transfiguration of the deceased into a guardian of sacred knowledge.

Integration and Reflection:

In the aftermath of this sacred ceremony, take time for reflection and introspection. Engage in contemplation of the profound significance of this ritual and its implications on the journey of the departed soul. Examine dissenting viewpoints and counterarguments, fostering a balanced and objective understanding of the transformative power bestowed upon the deceased.

Remember, seeker of divine wisdom, this ritual is an ancient and solemn rite that transcends mortal boundaries. Approach it with reverence, unwavering intent, and a deep yearning for the eternal wisdom that lies dormant within. Embrace the transfiguration of the deceased into a divine guardian of sacred knowledge, recognizing the profound responsibility and the enduring connection between the realms of the living and the departed.

6. Ritual for the transfiguration of the deceased into a divine guardian of sacred wisdom

By the light of the celestial stars above,
I invoke their blessings, their guidance I seek to have.
With reverence and awe, I call upon their might,
To illuminate my path, and guide me through the night.

Oh, stars of the heavens, shining bright and clear,
Bestow upon me your wisdom, draw me near.
As I gaze upon your brilliance, your cosmic dance,
Infuse me with your essence, grant me a celestial trance.

Each star a beacon, a guide in the vast expanse,
I beseech you to lead me, to show me the chance.
To navigate the challenges, to find my way,
Through the ebb and flow, by night and by day.

Blessed stars above, with your celestial glow,
Your ancient wisdom, may it truly bestow.
Guide me in my journey, with your celestial sight,
Illuminate my path, fill my heart with your light.

Oh, celestial stars, with your celestial gaze,
Grant me clarity and insight, as I walk life's maze.
May your blessings descend upon me, like stardust from above,
Empowering me with wisdom, with grace and with love.

I honor you, celestial stars, in this sacred rite,
Your presence fills me with wonder, your beauty ignites.
I thank you for your guidance, for your celestial embrace,
As I walk this earthly journey, upheld by your grace.

So mote it be, as I speak this incantation true,
I invite the blessings of the celestial stars into view.
Guide me, protect me, and show me the way,
In your celestial guidance, I forever shall stay.

7. Spell for the reunion of the deceased's soul with their spiritual ancestors

In the depths of the sacred night, where the veil between worlds grows thin and the echoes of ancestral whispers resonate, we shall embark upon a spell for the reunion of the deceased's soul with their spiritual ancestors. With profound reverence and unwavering intent, let us immerse ourselves in the ancient ritual as it might have been performed:

Preparation:

Choose a secluded and consecrated space, cloaked in darkness and adorned with symbols of lineage and spiritual connection. Ignite candles and aromatic incense, their flickering flames and fragrant smoke serving as beacons to guide the departed soul back to their ancestral realm.

Invocation:

Stand at the threshold of the sacred space, facing the gateway that separates the realm of the living from the realm of the departed. Light a white candle, symbolizing purity and spiritual illumination. In a hushed and solemn tone, recite an invocation that resonates with the longing to reunite the departed soul with their spiritual ancestors. Let your words carry the weight of heartfelt intention and reverberate through the unseen realms.

Offering:

Prepare a sacred offering, carefully chosen to honor and appease the spirits of the departed ancestors. It may consist of favorite foods, libations, or symbolic items that held significance to their earthly existence. Arrange the offering upon a beautifully crafted altar, adorned with images and tokens representing the ancestral lineage.

Recitation of Names:

Speak the names of the deceased's ancestors, tracing the lineage back through the ages. With each name uttered, visualize a thread of ethereal energy extending from the departed soul to their spiritual forebears, forming a luminous web of interconnectedness. Invoke the power of the names, calling upon the ancestral spirits to lend their guidance and support.

Sacred Chant:

Enter into a meditative state and begin to chant a sacred melody, resonating with the frequency of the spirit world. Let the rhythm of the chant echo through the chamber, creating a harmonious bridge that traverses the realms. Envision the sound waves carrying the departed soul's essence, drawing it closer to the waiting embrace of the spiritual ancestors.

"O spirits of the ancient ones, hear my call,
From realms beyond, I beseech you all.
By the sacred bond of blood and kin,
I summon thee to gather herein.

In this sacred space, veiled from mortal sight,
I seek reunion, in the realm of eternal light.
Grant passage to the departed soul,
That it may find solace and become whole.

By the power of the ancient incantations,
I invoke the spirits' intercessions.
May the ancestral guides, wise and true,
Guide the departed one and help them through.

Oh, venerable ancestors of wisdom and grace,
Bestow your blessings upon this sacred place.
Open the gates of the divine realm,
Let the departed soul at last be overwhelmed.

By the threads of fate and cosmic design,
Bind the departed with ancestors' line.
Let the soul be embraced in loving embrace,
And find its rightful abode in this sacred space.

In the realm of spirits, where time is still,
Let the reunion occur as is the divine will.
May the departed soul find peace and rest,
In the company of those they loved best.

With reverence and gratitude, I humbly implore,
Let this spell fulfill its purpose and more.
Guide the soul, dear ancestors, I plea,
To the realms of eternity, so mote it be."

Guiding Light:

Hold a lantern or torch aloft, its gentle glow symbolizing the guiding light that leads the departed soul on its journey. Walk slowly and deliberately around the sacred space, illuminating the path that connects the realms. As you move, recite words of guidance and protection, invoking the assistance of benevolent spirits to ensure a safe passage for the soul.

Communion:

Create a moment of stillness and silence within the chamber, allowing the energy of the departed soul and the ancestral spirits to intertwine. Open your senses and be receptive to any signs, sensations, or messages that may manifest from the spiritual realm. Engage in silent communion, offering prayers and gratitude for the presence of the departed soul and the wisdom of the ancestors.

Release and Farewell:

With profound gratitude and a heart filled with reverence, bid farewell to the departed soul and the ancestral spirits. Express gratitude for their presence and the blessings bestowed upon the ritual. Slowly extinguish the candles, allowing the darkness to reclaim the sacred space and signaling the conclusion of the spell.

Integration and Reflection:

Take time to reflect upon the profound significance of the spell and its impact on the departed soul's journey. Engage in introspection, contemplating the potential reconnection with ancestral wisdom and the enduring bond between generations. Consider dissenting opinions and alternate perspectives, nurturing a balanced and objective understanding of the spell's purpose and implications.

Remember, seeker of ancestral reunion, this spell is a sacred and intimate ritual that transcends the boundaries of time and mortality. Approach it with utmost respect, sincerity, and a deep reverence for the spiritual interconnectedness between the living and the departed. May the reunion of the deceased's soul with their spiritual ancestors bring solace, guidance, and a profound sense of belonging to both realms.

8. Spell for the liberation of the deceased's soul from the burdens of past lives

By the power of the ancient ones and the eternal flame,
I call upon the spirits to hear my sacred name.
In this realm of existence, where past lives intertwine,
I seek to free the departed soul, no longer confined.

From the depths of time, let the burdens rise,
Unleashing their hold, releasing ties.
With this sacred spell, I command and decree,
Liberate the soul, set it forever free.

With each spoken word, let the past unwind,
Unburdening the soul, leaving the weight behind.
I call upon the forces of light and grace,
To guide the soul to a higher, peaceful place.

Break the chains of karmic cycles past,
Release the burdens that forever last.
Grant the departed soul the freedom to soar,
Into the realm of divine love and more.

May the energy of forgiveness and release,
Bring healing and serenity, bringing inner peace.
Untangle the threads of past lives gone,
In this sacred moment, let their journey be won.

By the power of the divine and cosmic flow,
I release the soul from the shadows that grow.
With love and compassion, this spell is cast,
Setting the deceased soul free at last.

Note: This spell is performed with the intention of liberating the deceased's soul from the burdens of past lives. It is important to approach this spell with respect and reverence, recognizing the complexity and individuality of each soul's journey. The spell calls upon the assistance of higher forces and divine energies to facilitate the process of release and liberation. It is essential to perform this spell with pure intentions and to honor the free will and spiritual growth of the departed soul.

9. Invocation of the god Anubis for guidance and assistance in the afterlife

In the ancient Egyptian belief system, Anubis, the jackal-headed god, held a significant role as the guardian and guide of the afterlife. Here is an invocation that might have been used to call upon Anubis for guidance and assistance:

"Hail, Anubis, mighty god of the divine realm,
With reverence and awe, I call upon thee at this helm.
Oh, Opener of the Ways, Guardian of the Gate,
I seek your presence, your wisdom, and your fate.

Anubis, hear my plea, as I stand before your shrine,
With heart filled with reverence, my devotion I align.
Guide me through the darkness, the trials I may face,
In this sacred journey, bestow upon me your grace.

Bearer of justice, scales in your steady hand,
Help me navigate the Duat, the mystic land.
As I embark on this transformative path,
Grant me strength, protection from the aftermath.

With your keen eyes, see beyond the mortal veil,
Unveil the secrets hidden, let truth prevail.
In the realm of shadows, where spirits roam,
Lead me safely to my destined home.

Anubis, protector of souls, hear my plea,
Guide me through the trials that lie before me.
Grant me your wisdom, your guidance, your might,
As I traverse the realms in eternal night.

In the name of Ma'at, the cosmic balance divine,
I invoke your presence, Anubis, god sublime.
With utmost respect and devotion I implore,
Assist me in this journey, forevermore.

Anubis, I offer my devotion, my loyalty,
May my actions align with your divine decree.
Guide me through the realms, by your divine hand,

As I walk the path to the eternal sand.

Hail, Anubis, guardian of the afterlife's gate,
Accept my heartfelt plea, my reverence innate.
In your name, I embark on this sacred quest,
With your presence, Anubis, I am blessed.

So be it."

10. Ritual of anointing with sacred amulets for spiritual fortification and warding off evil

In the ancient Egyptian tradition, rituals involving the anointing with sacred amulets were performed for spiritual fortification and protection against evil forces. Here is a description of the ritual as it might have been practiced:

Preparation:

Gather the necessary materials for the ritual, including sacred amulets, consecrated oils, and a purified space.
Create an altar or sacred space where the ritual will take place.
Ensure that you are in a calm and focused state of mind, ready to engage in the sacred act of anointing.

Invocation:

Begin by invoking the presence of the gods and goddesses associated with protection, such as Isis, Horus, or Bastet.
Offer prayers and words of reverence, expressing your intention to fortify your spiritual being and ward off evil.

Cleansing:

Perform a purification ritual, either through ablutions or the use of sacred water or incense.
Pass the sacred amulets through the purifying smoke or sprinkle them with the consecrated water, cleansing them of any negative energies.

Anointing:

Take one of the sacred amulets in your hands, holding it with reverence and intention.
Dip your finger into the consecrated oil, and with a gentle touch, anoint the amulet, symbolizing the infusion of divine protection and fortification.
As you anoint each amulet, recite sacred words or prayers that affirm their purpose in warding off evil and strengthening your spiritual defenses.

Placement:

Once anointed, place the sacred amulets in specific locations that align with their intended purpose. For example, you may hang them around your neck, place them near doorways, or carry them with you as personal talismans.
Visualize a protective shield forming around you as the amulets radiate their power and energy.

Final Invocation:

Offer gratitude to the gods and goddesses for their presence and assistance in this ritual.
Express your faith and trust in their protection, knowing that the power of the amulets will safeguard your spiritual well-being.
Close the ritual with a final prayer or affirmation, sealing the intentions and energies of the ritual.

Remember, the ritual of anointing with sacred amulets serves as a potent means of spiritual fortification and protection, invoking the power of the divine to ward off evil and ensure your well-being.

11. Spell for the liberation of the deceased's soul from the chains of worldly desires

In the ancient Egyptian tradition, a spell for the liberation of the deceased's soul from the chains of worldly desires was believed to facilitate the soul's journey to the afterlife. Here is a rendition of the spell as it might have been recited:

Invocation:

Oh, great gods and goddesses, hear my plea,
I beseech thee for the liberation of this soul, set it free.
Release it from the chains of earthly attachments,
And guide it towards the eternal realms of celestial rapture.

Acknowledgment of Worldly Desires:
I recognize the allure of worldly pleasures and the attachments that bind,
But now, in this sacred moment, I seek to unbind.
Let the soul be freed from the temptations that ensnare,
And let it transcend the mundane to a realm beyond compare.

Breaking the Chains:

With the power of the divine, I sever the ties that hold,
The desires that keep the soul from its destiny unfold.
I release the grip of material cravings and ego's sway,
And grant the soul the freedom to follow its destined way.

Transformation and Transcendence:

May the soul ascend on wings of divine grace,
Untethered from worldly concerns and desires' embrace.
Let it soar through the ethereal realms with ease,
Towards the eternal embrace of serenity and peace.

Guidance and Protection:

Oh, great Anubis, the guardian of the afterlife's gate,
Guide this liberated soul, its journey illuminate.
Protect it from malevolent forces that seek to hinder,

And usher it towards its divine destiny, so tender.

Conclusion and Blessings:
With reverence and gratitude, I conclude this sacred rite,
Trusting that the soul's liberation is now set alight.
May it find solace and serenity in the realms beyond,
Embraced by the gods and ancestors, forever fond.

Note: The actual spells used during that time may have varied in form and content depending on personal beliefs and preferences, while still capturing the essence of liberating the soul from worldly desires and guiding it towards spiritual transcendence.

12. Incantation to awaken the dormant spiritual powers within the deceased's spirit

In the mystical realm of ancient Egypt, an incantation to awaken the dormant spiritual powers within the deceased's spirit was spoken with reverence and intention. Here is a rendition of the incantation as it might have been recited:

Invocation:

By the sacred names of gods and goddesses,
I call upon the dormant powers within, with humbleness.
Awaken, O spirit of the departed, from slumber deep,
Rise and embrace the ancient wisdom you shall now reap.

Invocation of Divine Energies:

May the divine light of Ra, the sun god, shine upon you,
Infusing your spirit with vitality and renewal true.
May the wisdom of Thoth, the god of knowledge, be your guide,
As you awaken the dormant powers within, with stride.

Stirring of the Spirit:

From the depths of the underworld's veil,
I summon the hidden powers that shall prevail.
Let the dormant energies rise and surge,
Unleashing the spiritual prowess, an eternal urge.

Sacred Words of Awakening:

By the ancient incantations, long held dear,
I invoke the awakening of powers, crystal clear.
Let the spirit's essence be rekindled and restored,
With divine knowledge and wisdom, deeply stored.

Transmutation of the Spirit:

As the phoenix rises from ashes, reborn anew,
So does your spirit awaken, transcending what once grew.
Shed the limitations of mortality's plight,

Embrace the divine essence, shining bright.

Empowerment and Transformation:

May your spirit soar on wings of divine might,
Empowered by the forces of celestial light.
Awakened and attuned to higher realms' grace,
Embrace your true essence, in this sacred space.

Conclusion and Blessings:

With reverence and awe, I seal this sacred rite,
Trusting that the dormant powers within take flight.
May your spirit now awaken, radiant and free,
Guided by divine wisdom for eternity.

13. Ritual for the communion with the spirits of the celestial birds and their wisdom

In the ancient realm of mystical Egypt, a ritual for the communion with the spirits of the celestial birds and their wisdom was performed with reverence and awe. Here is a description of the ritual as it might have been enacted:

Preparation:

Find a secluded and sacred space where you can perform the ritual undisturbed. Ensure it is a place of tranquility and connection with nature.
Create an altar adorned with symbols and images of celestial birds, such as the falcon or the ibis. Place offerings of fragrant incense, flowers, and sacred herbs.
Invocation:
3. Stand tall with arms outstretched, facing the sky. Close your eyes and take deep breaths, centering your mind and body. Feel the energy of the earth beneath your feet and the vastness of the heavens above.

Speak the sacred invocation to the spirits of the celestial birds, calling upon their wisdom and guidance. Use words such as:

"O majestic beings of the celestial realms,
I invoke your presence with reverence and awe.
Descend upon this sacred space, blessed and divine,
Share with me your wisdom, your guidance sublime."

Communion:

5. Light the incense on the altar, allowing the fragrant smoke to rise and fill the air. This serves as a bridge between the earthly realm and the celestial realms.

Open your heart and mind to the presence of the celestial bird spirits. Feel their energy enveloping you, their wings brushing against your spirit.
Enter a meditative state, focusing on your breath and allowing your consciousness to expand. Visualize yourself soaring through the sky, joining the celestial birds in their flight.
Listen with your inner ear, attuning to the whispers of the celestial birds. They may impart messages, symbols, or visions that carry their wisdom and guidance. Be receptive and open to their teachings.
Prayer and Offering:

9. Offer a prayer of gratitude to the celestial bird spirits for their presence and wisdom. Speak words of thanks and honor, acknowledging their sacred role as messengers between the earthly and celestial realms.

Present an offering of gratitude on the altar, such as grains or seeds, symbolizing your appreciation and willingness to cultivate the wisdom received.
Take a moment to silently express your intentions for utilizing the wisdom gained from the communion with the celestial birds. Reflect on how it may enhance your spiritual journey and bring blessings to your life and the lives of others.
Closure:
12. Slowly return your awareness to the physical realm, grounding yourself by connecting with the earth beneath your feet. Offer a final expression of gratitude and farewell to the celestial bird spirits.

Extinguish the incense, symbolizing the completion of the ritual and the closing of the sacred space.

Reflect on the insights and wisdom received during the communion with the celestial birds. Record any significant experiences or messages in a journal for future contemplation.

14. Spell for the transmigration of the deceased's soul into the realm of eternal love and compassion

In the realm of ancient Egypt, a spell for the transmigration of the deceased's soul into the realm of eternal love and compassion was spoken with profound reverence and intention. Here is a rendition of the spell as it might have been chanted:

O benevolent gods and goddesses,
Hear my plea, listen to my voice.
In this sacred hour of transition,
Guide the soul with love's gentle embrace.

By the power of Ma'at's feather,
Let the heart be light, free from burden.
May it soar upon the wings of compassion,
And find solace in the realm of eternal love.

I call upon Osiris, the merciful judge,
To weigh the deeds of the departed.
May the scales tip in favor of purity,
And grant passage to the realm of divine compassion.

Isis, mother of all, hear my words.
Wrap the departed in your loving embrace.
Guide their spirit through the sacred rites,
To the eternal realm of boundless love.

May the gates of Aaru open wide,
Revealing the path to eternal serenity.
As the sun sets upon the earthly life,
May it rise anew in the realm of eternal love.

Let the soul be washed in the waters of Nun,
Cleansed of earthly attachments and desires.
Transmigrate, O soul, into the realm of divine light,
Where love and compassion reign supreme.

As the lotus blooms upon the sacred waters,

So shall the soul bloom in eternal love.
In the embrace of Nut's starry sky,
May the departed find everlasting peace.

With reverence and devotion, I speak this spell,
With faith and trust in the ancient ways.
May the transmigration be swift and smooth,
And the soul find eternal love and compassion.

15. Invocation of the goddess Ma'at for truth and justice in the afterlife

In the solemn realm of ancient Egypt, the invocation of the goddess Ma'at for truth and justice in the afterlife was a sacred rite performed with unwavering devotion. Here is an invocation that seeks the presence and guidance of Ma'at:

O Ma'at, goddess of truth and justice,
Bearer of the cosmic scales of balance,
I call upon you with reverence and awe.
In this realm of transition and judgment,
May your divine presence illuminate the way.

Goddess of order and harmony,
Your feather of truth weighs the hearts,
Discerning the purity within each soul.
Grant us your wisdom and discernment,
That we may navigate the path of righteousness.

Ma'at, your presence brings clarity,
Dispelling the shadows of falsehood.
In this afterlife journey, we seek your guidance,
To navigate the labyrinthine halls of judgment.
Shine your light upon our deeds and intentions.

With your graceful touch, O Ma'at,
Let truth prevail over deceit,
Justice triumph over injustice.
Grant solace to the righteous,
And grant understanding to those who seek it.

Ma'at, your wings span the heavens,
Your presence encompasses all.
We beseech you to guide the deceased,
To ensure a just and righteous fate.
May their hearts be light as your feather,
Their souls worthy of eternal communion.

In the realm of the divine tribunal,
Where the scales of judgment are held,

May your presence permeate the air,
Infusing truth and justice into every verdict.
Grant the deceased a fair and honorable reckoning.

O Ma'at, goddess of the cosmic order,
Your presence reassures the righteous,
And strikes fear into the hearts of the unjust.
Be the beacon of truth in the afterlife,
And ensure that justice prevails for all.

As I invoke your name, O Ma'at,
May your essence be woven into the fabric of eternity.
Guide the deceased with your unwavering scales,
That their souls may find everlasting peace.
In your name, O Ma'at, I seek truth and justice.

Please note that the actual rituals and invocations may have varied among different individuals and religious practices. Adaptations can be made to align with personal beliefs and spiritual traditions while honoring the essence of seeking truth and justice through the presence of the goddess Ma'at.

16. Ritual of purification through the sacred prayers of the eternal priesthood

In the sacred annals of ancient Egypt, the ritual of purification through the sacred prayers of the eternal priesthood held profound significance. Engage in the following ritual to experience purification and spiritual renewal through the power of prayer:

Preparation:

Find a serene and undisturbed space where you can devote yourself to the ritual.
Create an atmosphere of reverence by lighting incense or candles.
Assume a comfortable posture, either sitting or standing, with your spine erect and your body relaxed.
Invocation:

Begin by closing your eyes and taking deep, intentional breaths, allowing your mind to settle and your body to relax.
Call upon the divine presence and guidance of the eternal priesthood, who have preserved the sacred knowledge and performed these rituals throughout the ages.
Recite an invocation, such as:
"O revered priesthood, custodians of ancient wisdom,
I humbly seek your presence and guidance.
Grant me purification through your sacred prayers,
And awaken my spirit to divine communion."

Prayers of Cleansing:

With an open heart and focused mind, offer prayers of purification and cleansing.
Invoke the names of revered deities and seek their blessings, such as:
"Oh Ra, radiant sun god, purify my body, mind, and spirit.
Oh Isis, divine mother, cleanse me of impurities and restore my inner harmony.
Oh Thoth, god of wisdom, grant me clarity and understanding."
Self-Reflection and Repentance:

Engage in introspection and self-reflection, acknowledging any actions or thoughts that have caused disharmony or veered from the path of righteousness.
Express sincere repentance for these transgressions, seeking forgiveness and the strength to align with higher virtues.

Intercession:

Offer prayers for loved ones, the deceased, and all beings in need of purification and divine guidance.
Extend your intentions beyond yourself, showing compassion and invoking blessings for the collective well-being.
Sacred Affirmations:

Recite affirmations that reinforce your commitment to a virtuous life, spiritual growth, and alignment with divine principles.
Use affirmations like:
"I am a vessel of divine light, purified and ready to receive the sacred blessings.
I walk the path of truth, justice, and compassion.
May the sacred prayers of the eternal priesthood guide my every step."

Gratitude and Benediction:

Express gratitude to the eternal priesthood, the divine deities, and the universal forces for their presence and support.
Conclude the ritual with a benediction, such as:
"May the purification gained through these sacred prayers
Illuminate my path, uplift my spirit, and bring me closer to divine communion.
As I emerge from this ritual, may I radiate purity and become a beacon of love and light."

Take a moment to sit in silence, allowing the energy and blessings of the ritual to integrate within you. When you feel ready, gently open your eyes and proceed with a sense of renewed purpose and spiritual fortitude.

17. Spell for the transformation of the deceased into a vessel of divine healing and restoration

In the ethereal realm of ancient enchantments, a spell unfolds to facilitate the transformation of the departed into a vessel of divine healing and restoration. Through the invocation of sacred words and profound intentions, one may tap into the realms of healing and become a conduit for divine energies. Embark upon this mystical journey to embrace the spell for the transformation of the deceased into a vessel of divine healing and restoration:

Preliminary Preparations:

Seek solace within a tranquil space, consecrated and free from worldly distractions. Illuminate the surroundings with the gentle glow of candles, and infuse the air with the fragrance of purifying incense.
Assume a position that resonates with your inner harmony, allowing your body and mind to relax into a state of receptivity.
Invocation of Divine Forces:

Close your eyes and focus your consciousness on the sacred energies that surround you.
Call forth the celestial guardians of healing and restoration, beseeching their presence and divine guidance.

Speak forth an invocation, allowing the words to flow with sincerity and reverence:
"Oh, benevolent spirits of healing and restoration,
I summon your divine essence and beseech your transformative power.
Grant me the ability to embody a vessel of divine healing and restoration,
A conduit for profound rejuvenation and boundless compassion."

Sacred Affirmations:

Utter words of affirmation that harmonize your being with the desired transformation, infusing your essence with the divine energies of healing and restoration.
Repeat affirmations with unwavering faith, resonating with the power of the spoken word:

"I am a vessel of divine healing, radiating with compassion and grace.

Through the divine energy within me, I restore balance and harmony.
May my presence and touch bring forth profound healing and restoration."

Visualization:

Envision yourself as a vessel of divine energy, filled with radiant light and boundless compassion.
Visualize a gentle luminosity emanating from your heart, expanding with each breath, permeating every cell of your being.
Allow this healing light to envelop you, infusing your spirit, mind, and body with divine love, wisdom, and restoration.

Incantation:

Chant a sacred incantation, invoking the powers of healing and restoration to be channeled through you.
Let the incantation flow from your lips, carrying the essence of your intentions:
"By the ancient forces of healing and restoration,
I invoke divine transformation and profound rejuvenation.
As I embrace the realm beyond mortal bounds,
May I become a vessel of divine healing and boundless compassion."

Channeling Divine Energies:

Concentrate on channeling the divine healing energies through your being, allowing them to flow unhindered.
Extend your hands outward, palms facing upward, symbolizing your willingness to receive and transmit divine healing energies.
Sense the energy coursing through your hands, connecting you to the sacred realms of healing and restoration.

Intentions and Healing:

Set your intentions to be a vessel of divine healing and restoration, for the benefit of oneself and others.
Direct the healing energy towards specific areas or individuals in need of restoration, be it physical, emotional, or spiritual.
Hold the intentions firmly, envisioning the transformation and rejuvenation of those in need.

Gratitude and Closure:

Express gratitude to the benevolent forces of healing, acknowledging their presence and divine assistance.
Offer heartfelt thanks for the opportunity to become a vessel of divine healing and restoration.

Conclude the spell with a statement of gratitude and closure:

"With deepest gratitude and reverence, I conclude this sacred invocation.
May the divine healing energy continue to flow through me, bringing restoration, solace, and renewal to all in need.
So mote it be."

18. Incantation to invoke the blessings of the celestial moon and its soothing energy

In the realm where the mystic forces converge, an incantation arises to beckon the blessings of the celestial moon and its soothing energy. Through the resonance of sacred words and the power of intention, one can invoke the ethereal presence of the moon, drawing upon its serene and healing essence. Embark upon this enchanting journey as we delve into the incantation to invoke the blessings of the celestial moon and its soothing energy:

Preliminary Preparations:

Retreat to a serene and undisturbed space, where the moon's luminous rays may freely grace your presence.
Arrange your surroundings with objects that reflect the moon's serene energy, such as silver-hued ornaments or reflective surfaces.
Assume a posture that resonates with tranquility, allowing your body and mind to find solace in the stillness.

Invocation of the Moon:

Close your eyes and turn your attention inward, attuning yourself to the unseen rhythms of the cosmos.
Visualize the celestial moon, its radiant form casting a gentle glow upon the Earth, filling the night sky with luminescence.
Speak forth an invocation, allowing the words to flow with reverence and sincerity:
"Oh, celestial moon, enchantress of the night,
I beseech your presence, bathed in silvery light.
With reverence, I invoke your soothing energy,
Bless me with your tranquil grace and divine serenity."
Connection and Affirmations:

Utter affirmations that resonate with your intention to connect with the moon's soothing energy, inviting its blessings into your being.
Repeat these affirmations, allowing their resonance to harmonize with the moon's tranquil essence:
"I am attuned to the celestial moon's radiant energy,
Its gentle light fills my spirit, setting me free.
May its soothing glow envelop my heart and mind,
Bringing peace, harmony, and tranquility entwined."

Embracing Lunar Energy:

Envision the moonlight gently cascading upon you, permeating your entire being with its serene energy.
Absorb this soothing energy into every cell of your body, allowing it to calm and revitalize your spirit.
Breathe in deeply, imagining the moon's tranquil light infusing your lungs, revitalizing your life force with each inhale.

Incantation:

Chant a sacred incantation to invoke the moon's blessings and align yourself with its serene energy.
Let the incantation flow from your lips, carrying the essence of your intentions:
"By the celestial moon's enchanting glow,
I summon its blessings, its tranquil flow.
Moonlight's serenade, I invoke in this hour,
Shower upon me your soothing power."
Alignment and Connection:

Focus your attention on aligning your energies with the moon's tranquil frequency.
Feel a deep connection between your essence and the moon's serene presence, as if you are becoming one with its soothing energy.
Allow this connection to nurture and replenish your spirit, bringing you a sense of calm and inner peace.

Moonlit Intentions:

Set your intentions for the moon's blessings, whether it be emotional healing, spiritual guidance, or a sense of serenity.
Project your heartfelt desires into the moonlit expanse, knowing that its energy will amplify and support your intentions.
Hold these intentions firmly, trusting in the moon's wisdom and its ability to manifest your heartfelt aspirations.

Gratitude and Closure:

Express gratitude to the celestial moon for its blessings and the soothing energy it has bestowed upon you.
Offer heartfelt thanks for the tranquility and serenity that you have received during this sacred invocation.
Conclude the incantation with a statement of gratitude and closure:

"With deepest gratitude, I release this invocation to the cosmic flow.
May the moon's blessings continue to grace my path and bring serenity wherever I go.
So mote it be."
Embrace the soothing energy of the celestial moon, allowing it to nourish your spirit
and bring serenity to your life's journey. As you bask in its gentle glow, may the
moon's blessings envelop you, guiding you towards tranquility and inner harmony.

19. Ritual for the transfiguration of the deceased into a divine guide of sacred mysteries

In the realm where the veil between worlds is thin, a ritual unfolds, dedicated to the transfiguration of the deceased into a divine guide of sacred mysteries. Through the convergence of intention, symbolism, and ancient wisdom, this ritual unveils the transformative journey from mortal essence to ethereal guardian. Embark upon this profound ritual of transfiguration as we delve into its steps and significance:

Preliminary Preparations:

Find a secluded space where the energies of the cosmos and the sacred converge. Create an altar adorned with symbolic artifacts that represent the spiritual realm and the mysteries that lie beyond.
Illuminate the space with candles, casting a soft and flickering glow, reminiscent of the ethereal realms. Arrange aromatic herbs and incense, purifying the atmosphere and invoking a sense of transcendence.
Still your mind, breathing deeply and fully, aligning your intentions with the sacred purpose of the ritual. Embrace a state of reverence and openness to the divine energies that will be invoked.

Invocation of Divine Presence:

Begin the ritual by invoking the presence of the divine, the guides of sacred mysteries. Speak these words with utmost respect and devotion:
"O ancient guardians of sacred wisdom,
Hear my call and grace this sacred space.
I beseech your presence, divine guides,
To witness and bless this transfiguration."
Communion with Ancestral Spirits:

Light a white candle, symbolizing the purity and connection with ancestral spirits. Gaze into its flame, allowing your focus to transcend the physical realm and merge with the ethereal plane.
With sincerity, speak these words to honor the ancestors:
"Ancestral spirits, holders of ancient knowledge,
I invoke your presence in this sacred rite.
Guide the transfiguration of the departed,

Unveiling the mysteries of eternal light."

Transfiguration Ritual:

Place a small mirror on the altar, symbolizing the reflection and transformation of the deceased into a divine guide. Surround it with offerings such as sacred herbs, crystals, or symbolic objects.
Focus your gaze upon the mirror, allowing it to become a gateway between worlds.
With deep intention and unwavering belief, recite this transfiguration spell:
"From mortal form to spirit divine,
I beseech the transformation to shine.
Departed soul, release earthly ties,
Embrace the mysteries that eternal life implies."

Visualization and Energy Transfer:

Envision the departed soul bathed in a radiant light, slowly transcending its mortal limitations. Visualize the divine essence within them awakening, shimmering with the wisdom of the ages.
Extend your hands towards the mirror, offering your energy and intention to facilitate the transfiguration process. Feel the connection between yourself, the departed, and the divine realms strengthening as the energy flows through you.
Channel your intention and energy, allowing the mirror to become a vessel of transformation. Trust in the divine process unfolding, guiding the departed towards their destiny as a guardian of sacred mysteries.

Benediction and Farewell:

Express gratitude to the divine guides and ancestral spirits for their presence and assistance in the transfiguration ritual. Offer words of farewell and gratitude, acknowledging the profound transformation that has taken place.
Conclude the ritual with a final blessing:
"With deepest gratitude and reverence, I bid you farewell,
Departed soul, now a guardian of sacred mysteries.
May your presence guide and inspire seekers of truth,
Forever enshrined in the realm of eternal light."

20. Spell for the reunion of the deceased's soul with their spiritual allies and protectors

In the sacred realms where spirits intertwine, a spell unfolds, weaving the reunion of the deceased's soul with their spiritual allies and protectors. Through the incantation of ancient words and the invocation of divine forces, this spell bridges the gap between realms, calling forth the aid and guidance of loyal guardians. Embark upon this journey of reunion as we delve into the words and intentions that unlock the gates of connection:

Silence descends as the spirit yearns for kin,
In the realm beyond, where allies dwell within.
By the power of ancient forces and sacred decree,
I call upon the guardians, attentive may they be.

Spirits of old, benevolent and true,
Hear my plea, as I reach out to you.
With reverence and respect, I summon your might,
Unite us once more, in this ethereal flight.

Guide the departed soul through the astral expanse,
Bring forth the allies, who offer their advance.
Together we journey, in harmony and grace,
Embracing the wisdom, and blessings we embrace.

Protectors of old, from realms far and near,
Descend upon this sacred space, appear.
Shield and guide, with your unwavering might,
Lead the soul to safety, in this mystical flight.

Let the barriers dissolve, the veils drawn away,
Reveal the hidden paths, where spirits sway.
In the sacred union of kin and ally,
Empower the soul, let the reunion amplify.

By the cosmic currents and celestial light,
I beckon the spirits, with all my might.
May their presence be felt, their guidance be known,
As the soul reunites, no longer alone.

With gratitude and reverence, I honor your aid,
For the reunion of spirits, for the bond remade.
Together we stand, united in purpose and quest,
Blessed be this reunion, in the realms that manifest.

As the words ripple through the dimensions,
May the reunion unfold with divine intentions.
Let the departed's soul find solace and reprieve,
In the embrace of allies, who never leave.

With the utterance of this spell, may the reunion be sealed,
May the departed find solace and protection, their wounds healed.
In the company of allies, the soul finds its home,
Forever connected, wherever they may roam.

As the echoes of the incantation fade away,
Know that the reunion is set in motion, come what may.
Trust in the spirits, their guidance sincere,
For the departed's soul is blessed and held dear.

In this spell of reunion, the departed's soul finds its way,
Embraced by allies, protected throughout the astral sway.
May the bond grow strong, eternal and deep,
As spirits and soul reunite, their destinies they shall keep.

21. Invocation of the god Osiris for resurrection and eternal life in the afterlife

In the sacred chambers of the beyond, where the mysteries of life and death intertwine, we invoke the mighty god Osiris, the embodiment of resurrection and eternal life. Through this invocation, we seek his benevolent presence and guidance, beseeching him to bestow his blessings upon the departed soul as it journeys through the realms of the afterlife. Let the ancient words resound and the invocation unfold:

Oh Osiris, mighty ruler of the underworld,
Lord of resurrection and eternal life,
We beseech your divine presence in this sacred rite,
As we embark upon the journey of the departed's soul.

With reverence and devotion, we call upon you,
Bearer of the sacred crook and flail,
Protector of the just and the righteous,
Guide the departed soul with your benevolent gaze.

Oh Osiris, whose wisdom surpasses all bounds,
You who triumphed over death and emerged anew,
We implore you to extend your hand of grace,
To uplift the departed and grant them eternal solace.

From the depths of the Duat, the realm of shadows,
Where life and death intertwine in eternal dance,
Reach out to the departed's soul, O mighty Osiris,
Unveil the path of resurrection and eternal life.

In your divine embrace, let the departed find peace,
Transformed and renewed, free from earthly strife,
Grant them passage through the realms of judgment,
To emerge in the realm of eternal love and light.

Oh Osiris, judge of hearts and weigher of souls,
We invoke your wisdom and impartiality,
May the departed's heart be found pure and just,
In the scales of Ma'at, let their spirit find favor.

Embrace them, O Osiris, in your eternal kingdom,
Where the blessed find everlasting bliss,
Grant them a place among the justified,
To dwell in eternal serenity and tranquility.

As we utter these ancient words and offer our devotion,
We beseech you, Osiris, to hear our plea,
Guide the departed's soul with your unwavering hand,
Lead them to the realm of resurrection and eternal life.

With hearts open and reverence profound,
We offer this invocation, bound by sacred sound,
May the departed find solace and renewal,
In the realm of Osiris, where life is eternal.

Oh Osiris, hear our invocation and heed our call,
Bestow your blessings upon the departed soul,
Grant them resurrection, eternal life, and peace,
In your divine presence, may their spirit find release.

As the words of invocation echo through the sacred space,
May Osiris, the god of resurrection, embrace the departed's grace,
Granting them eternal life, beyond the realm of strife,
Forever in the embrace of Osiris, the god of eternal life.

22. Ritual of anointing with sacred symbols for spiritual empowerment and enlightenment

In the sacred realm where mortal and divine converge, we embark upon a ritual of anointing, a ritual that empowers and enlightens the spirit. Through the sacred symbols and their divine essence, we seek to awaken the innermost potential and kindle the flame of spiritual enlightenment. Let us commence this ritual of anointing with reverence and intention:

Gather the sacred symbols that hold profound significance,
Symbols of ancient wisdom and divine guidance,
Symbols that bridge the realms of mortal and divine,
Their power emanating through time, space, and beyond.

Prepare the sanctified oils, infused with celestial energy,
Each drop a reservoir of divine essence and grace,
Charged with the vibrations of enlightenment and empowerment,
A potent elixir to anoint the seeker's spirit.

In a tranquil and consecrated space, where spirits may dwell,
Cleanse the space of impurities and worldly distractions,
Create an altar adorned with sacred symbols and offerings,
A sanctuary for the divine and a vessel for transformation.

Stand before the altar, with heart and mind focused,
Breathe deeply, grounding yourself in the present moment,
Invoke the divine forces that resonate within the symbols,
Inviting their presence and blessings to fill the space.

Take the sacred oil in your hands, feeling its energy,
Dip your fingertips into the elixir of spiritual empowerment,
Begin the anointing, tracing sacred symbols upon your body,
With each stroke, feel the divine energy igniting within.

Anoint your forehead, the seat of higher consciousness,
Symbolizing the awakening of inner wisdom and enlightenment,
Anoint your heart, the center of divine love and compassion,
Symbolizing the expansion of spiritual connection and empathy.

Anoint your hands, the instruments of divine action,
Symbolizing the empowerment to manifest sacred purpose,
Anoint your feet, the pathfinders on the journey of the soul,
Symbolizing the alignment with divine guidance and direction.

As the sacred symbols merge with your being,
Feel their energy infusing every cell and fiber of your being,
Igniting the dormant spark of divine potential within,
Empowering your spirit, enlightening your path.

With gratitude and reverence, conclude the ritual,
Offer thanks to the divine forces that have blessed you,
Carry the sacred symbols within your heart and soul,
Guiding your steps on the sacred path of spiritual empowerment.

As the anointing ritual concludes, may the seeker be embraced by the power and
wisdom of the sacred symbols, empowered to walk the path of enlightenment and
spiritual growth. May the divine essence within be awakened, illuminating the journey
towards self-realization and divine connection.

23. Spell for the liberation of the deceased's soul from the limitations of earthly existence

In the realm betwixt the mortal and the divine, where the ephemeral meets eternity, we embark upon a solemn spell of liberation, a spell to free the departed soul from the shackles of earthly existence. With reverence and intent, we call upon the cosmic forces to guide us in this profound endeavor. Let the words be spoken and the energies set in motion:

By the celestial symphony that resonates through the cosmos,
By the ancient rhythms of creation and dissolution,
By the sacred breath that animates all existence,
I beseech the forces of liberation to heed my call.

In the name of the eternal essence that transcends form,
In the name of the boundless spirit that knows no boundaries,
In the name of the departed soul longing for release,
I invoke the powers of liberation to bestow their grace.

From the depths of earthly attachments and desires,
From the entanglements that bind the spirit to mortality,
From the illusions that veil the truth of divine existence,
I summon the winds of liberation to blow away these veils.

With words of power and intent, let the spell be cast,
Let the veils be lifted, and the spirit be set free,
Unburdened by the limitations of earthly existence,
Transcending the boundaries of time and space.

By the sacred flame that burns eternal,
By the cosmic river that flows beyond comprehension,
By the wisdom of the ancients and the gods of old,
I call upon the forces of liberation to release the departed soul.

May the chains of mortality be broken,
May the spirit soar on wings of divine light,
May the limitations of earthly existence be dissolved,
As the soul embraces its true essence, unencumbered and free.

With reverence and gratitude, I release this spell,
Knowing that the cosmic forces have heard my plea,
May the departed soul find solace and liberation,
Transcending the limitations of earthly existence for eternity.

As the words of the spell fade into the cosmic winds, may the departed soul be liberated from the chains of earthly existence, soaring towards the realms of transcendence and eternal freedom. May the spirit find its true essence and embrace the boundless possibilities of the divine.

24. Incantation to awaken the dormant spiritual awareness within the deceased's spirit

In the realm betwixt the veils of existence, where the ethereal and the corporeal intertwine, we gather to invoke the awakening of dormant spiritual awareness within the departed soul. With reverence and purpose, we call upon the celestial forces to guide us in this sacred endeavor. Let the words be spoken and the energies enkindled:

By the cosmic harmonies that resonate through the celestial spheres,
By the ancient wisdom that echoes through the fabric of time,
By the divine spark that lies dormant within the departed soul,
I beseech the forces of awakening to heed my invocation.

In the name of the eternal spirit that transcends mortal boundaries,
In the name of the ancient wisdom that illuminates the path,
In the name of the departed soul seeking enlightenment,
I invoke the powers of awakening to bestow their grace.

From the depths of slumber and veiled consciousness,
From the shadows that cloak the inner knowing,
From the realms beyond mortal perception,
I summon the forces of awakening to stir the spirit.

With words of power and resonance, let the incantation resound,
Let the dormant awareness within the spirit be stirred,
Breaking through the layers of forgetfulness and illusion,
Igniting the divine flame of consciousness once more.

By the sacred light that illuminates the path,
By the celestial guideposts that lead to enlightenment,
By the wisdom of the ages and the gods of old,
I call upon the forces of awakening to infuse the departed soul.

May the veils of ignorance be lifted,
May the spirit awaken to its true essence,
May the dormant awareness be ignited,
As the soul embarks on a journey of self-discovery.

With reverence and gratitude, I release this incantation,
Knowing that the cosmic forces have heard my plea,
May the departed soul awaken to its divine purpose,
Embracing the expansive realms of spiritual awareness.

As the echoes of the incantation fade into the cosmic ether, may the dormant spiritual awareness within the departed soul be stirred. May the veils of ignorance and forgetfulness be lifted, and may the spirit embark on a journey of self-discovery and enlightenment. May the divine flame of consciousness be reignited, illuminating the path to spiritual awakening and understanding.

25. Ritual for the communion with the spirits of the celestial sun and its life-giving energy

In the sacred embrace of the celestial sun, where its radiant beams bestow life and illumination upon all existence, we gather to commune with the spirits that dwell within its fiery realm. Through this ritual, we seek to establish a profound connection with the life-giving energy of the sun and the guiding spirits that reside therein. Let the ritual unfold and the energies converge:

In a place bathed in the golden light of day,
Where the sun's rays grace the sacred ground,
We gather with reverence, seeking communion,
With the spirits of the celestial sun, profound and profound.

With hearts open and spirits attuned,
We stand in awe of the sun's radiant glow,
Its life-giving energy, its boundless power,
That nourishes all beings, high and low.

In this sacred space, we offer our praise,
To the sun, the celestial orb, divine and bright,
We honor its majesty, its enduring presence,
And seek to merge with its essence, pure and light.

With arms outstretched and faces upturned,
We bask in the warmth of its benevolent rays,
Feeling the energy infuse our very being,
Awakening within us a transcendent gaze.

In this communion with the celestial sun,
We embrace the spirits that dwell within,
Guiding us with wisdom, love, and grace,
As we traverse life's journey, through thick and thin.

Oh, spirits of the sun, hear our call,
As we seek your guidance and blessed embrace,
Infuse us with your radiant energy and vitality,
Illuminate our path with your celestial grace.

May the sun's brilliance fill our souls,

Empowering us with life's abundant flow,
May its light awaken our inner essence,
Igniting the divine spark within, aglow.

With hearts filled with gratitude and awe,
We conclude this ritual of communion and praise,
Carrying the sun's energy within our spirits,
Guided by its light, through all our days.

As the ritual comes to a close, may the communion with the spirits of the celestial sun leave an indelible mark upon our souls. May we carry within us the radiant energy and wisdom bestowed upon us, guided by the sun's light throughout our earthly sojourn. May the spirits of the sun continue to inspire and uplift us, nurturing our spirits with their boundless love and guidance.

26. Spell for the transmigration of the deceased's soul into the realm of eternal harmony and balance

In the realm of eternal harmony and balance, where the cosmic forces dance in perfect synchrony, we invoke the power of divine transformation to guide the transmigration of the deceased's soul. Through this spell, we seek to align the soul with the harmonious energies of the universe and facilitate its journey into the realm of everlasting equilibrium. Let the incantation resonate and the energies harmonize:

By the celestial symphony of cosmic spheres,
By the rhythmic dance of stars and planets bright,
I call upon the forces of divine harmony,
To guide the transmigration of the departed's soul tonight.

From the realm of earthly existence,
To the realm of everlasting balance and peace,
May the soul be free from turmoil and discord,
In this sacred transition, may it find release.

Oh, cosmic forces, in your majestic grace,
Align the soul with the harmonious flow,
Guide its journey through the astral realms,
To the realm where eternal balance does bestow.

May the soul shed the burdens of earthly strife,
As it traverses the realms of boundless space,
May it resonate with the cosmic frequencies,
Embracing serenity, harmony, and grace.

Let the celestial energies envelop the soul,
Elevating it to realms of tranquility untold,
Where equilibrium reigns supreme,
And harmony's symphony unfolds.

By the power of this sacred spell,
Let the transmigration of the soul commence,
Into the realm of eternal harmony and balance,
Where peace and serenity shall never hence.

As the spell is cast and the energies set in motion, may the soul of the departed embark upon its transmigration into the realm of eternal harmony and balance. May it find solace and serenity in the embrace of cosmic forces, resonating with the harmonious rhythms of the universe. May the journey be one of enlightenment and profound equilibrium, guiding the soul towards its ultimate destination of everlasting peace.

27. Invocation of the goddess Hathor for beauty and joy in the afterlife

In the realm of the afterlife, where beauty and joy transcend earthly limitations, we invoke the divine presence of the goddess Hathor. With reverence and awe, we call upon her to bestow upon the deceased's soul the blessings of eternal beauty and boundless joy. Let the invocation resonate and the energies of Hathor manifest:

Oh, Hathor, radiant goddess of beauty and joy,
With awe and reverence, we beseech your divine presence,
In the realms beyond earthly existence,
Where the soul seeks eternal splendor and blissful essence.

Goddess of love and mirth, with a golden crown,
Bearer of the sistrum, the symbol of your grace,
We invoke your power, O Hathor, to bestow
Beauty and joy upon the soul in this sacred space.

Oh, Hathor, with your enchanting dance and melodic voice,
Illuminate the path of the departed with your divine light,
Let beauty blossom in every corner of the afterlife,
And joy resound through the eternal night.

Grant the deceased's soul everlasting youth,
A visage adorned with ethereal radiance and grace,
Let the spirit be immersed in blissful delight,
As it dwells in your celestial embrace.

May the soul be adorned with your heavenly gifts,
Bathed in the elixir of eternal beauty and charm,
Let every moment in the afterlife be filled with joy,
As your divine essence shields it from all harm.

Hathor, mighty goddess, we call upon your name,
Guide the soul to the realm of perpetual delight,
Where beauty flourishes in every form,
And joy reverberates with every sight.

As the invocation resonates and the blessings of Hathor unfold, may the deceased's soul be adorned with eternal beauty and boundless joy. May Hathor's presence illuminate the afterlife, infusing it with enchantment and delight. May the soul experience the eternal bliss and radiate the divine splendor bestowed upon it by the goddess of beauty and mirth.

28. Ritual of purification through the sacred gestures of the eternal dance

In the realm of sacred rituals, where the eternal dance holds transformative power, we embark upon the ritual of purification through the sacred gestures. With reverence and intention, we engage in this dance to cleanse the spirit and awaken its divine essence. Let the rhythm guide us as we perform the ritual of purification through the eternal dance:

Preparation:

Find a serene and consecrated space, where the energies of the dance can flow freely. Clear the space of any distractions or obstacles that may hinder the movement. Create an ambiance of reverence, using candles, incense, or sacred objects. Centering:

Stand tall and rooted, connecting with the earth beneath your feet. Breathe deeply, allowing the breath to expand and fill your entire being. Visualize a radiant light surrounding you, purifying and energizing your spirit.

Setting Intentions:

Set your intention for the dance ritual. It may be a desire for inner purification or release from negativity. Focus on the specific aspects of your being or experiences that you wish to cleanse and purify. Consciously affirm your intention, infusing it with clarity and determination.

Dance of Release:

Begin the dance, allowing your body to move freely in response to the rhythm and energy within. With each movement, visualize and feel the release of stagnant energies, blockages, and impurities. Express yourself fully, using gestures and motions that embody the liberation and purification of your spirit. Dance of Renewal:

As the dance unfolds, shift your focus to inviting in revitalizing and transformative energies.

Let your movements become more fluid, graceful, and uplifting, symbolizing the renewal of your spirit.
Visualize the cleansing and purifying energy flowing through you, rejuvenating and restoring your essence.

Dance of Integration:

Gradually slow down the dance, allowing your movements to become more gentle and mindful.
Bring your attention to your breath, syncing it with the rhythm of the dance, and creating a sense of unity.
Feel the harmonious integration of purified energies within your being, as you embrace a state of balance and wholeness.

Closing:

As the dance concludes, stand still and observe the sensations, emotions, and insights that arise within you.
Express gratitude for the purification and renewal experienced through the sacred dance.
Take a few deep breaths, grounding yourself in the present moment, and allowing the energy to settle within you.
As the dance draws to a close, may the sacred gestures of the eternal dance purify your spirit, liberate your essence, and awaken the divine within you. May the rhythm guide you towards inner clarity and renewal, as you embrace the transformative power of this ritual of purification through the sacred dance.

29. \Spell for the transformation of the deceased into a vessel of divine wisdom and discernment

In the realm of ancient mysticism, where the veil between worlds is thin, we invoke the spell for the transformation of the deceased into a vessel of divine wisdom and discernment. Through this sacred incantation, we call upon the cosmic forces to infuse the departed soul with profound insight and discerning knowledge. Let the words resonate as we weave the spell for the transformation:

By the ancient wisdom that flows through the cosmic streams,
By the celestial knowledge that transcends mortal dreams,
I invoke the powers of the divine and the unseen,
To transform this departed soul, now and forever keen.

From the depths of the primordial well of knowing,
Let the currents of wisdom be forever flowing,
Through the spirit of the departed, now set free,
Grant them divine wisdom and discernment eternally.

May their essence be infused with enlightened thoughts,
As they transcend the limitations that earthly life wroughts,
Grant them the clarity to see beyond illusion's veil,
To discern truth from falsehood, without fail.

Empower their vessel with ancient secrets and lore,
So that wisdom's light may radiate evermore,
Grant them the gift of discernment, keen and bright,
To navigate the realms of knowledge with insight.

By the sacred symbols and cosmic signs align,
Let the departed soul become a vessel divine,
Filled with the wisdom of ages, both seen and unseen,
Guided by the hand of knowledge, forever serene.

As this spell is cast, so mote it be,
With reverence and respect, I set the spirit free,
May divine wisdom dwell within their sacred vessel,
Guiding them on the path of understanding, subtle and subtle.

In the realm of the afterlife, where mysteries unfold,
May this departed soul's wisdom be untold,
Transformed into a vessel of discernment, pure and true,
Forever connected to the cosmic wisdom imbued.

So it is spoken, so it is done,
As the divine powers align and become one,
May the deceased embrace their newfound role,
A vessel of divine wisdom, to enlighten the soul.

As we utter these words, may the transformation be complete,
And the deceased soul become a beacon of wisdom's seat,
May their journey through eternity be marked by insight,
And their spirit forever radiate divine wisdom's light.

Let the spell weave its magic, let the transformation be,
As the deceased becomes a vessel of wisdom, for all to see,
In the realm of the afterlife, let them shine,
A guardian of knowledge, an embodiment of the divine.

As the spell settles and the words dissipate,
May the vessel of wisdom rise, resolute and great,
And may the departed soul embrace their sacred role,
A vessel of divine wisdom, eternally whole.

In the realm of the divine, where wisdom prevails,
May this spell's transformation forever unveil,
A vessel of discernment, the departed shall be,
Guided by divine wisdom for all eternity.

So it is, and so it shall be, for the transformation is complete,
As the vessel of divine wisdom takes its seat,
In the realm of the departed, where knowledge abounds,
The deceased soul becomes a vessel profound.

Let the spell's magic empower and guide,
As the deceased embraces wisdom's tide,
Transformed into a vessel of divine insight,
Forever connected to the cosmic wisdom's light.

May the departed find solace in this sacred transformation,

And may their journey be filled with divine revelation,
As they embody the vessel of wisdom's grace,
Guided by divine discernment, in every place.

Thus, the spell is cast, the transformation is begun,
And the deceased becomes a vessel of wisdom, one by one,
May their spirit soar with divine wisdom's wings,
And forever be hailed as a sage among other things.

In the realm of eternal wisdom, where mysteries reside,
May the departed soul's vessel forever abide,
A conduit of divine insight and discernment's flame,
Guiding others through knowledge, in wisdom's name.

As the incantation fades and the spell takes hold,
May the deceased's spirit be forever bold,
Transformed into a vessel of divine wisdom and sight,
Guided by celestial forces, forever shining bright.

So mote it be, in the realms of divine embrace,
May the deceased find solace in wisdom's grace,
Transformed into a vessel of discernment's might,
Forever embodying divine wisdom's light.

30. Incantation to invoke the blessings of the celestial fire and its transformative power

In the realm of ancient mysticism, where the cosmic forces intertwine, we invoke the incantation to invoke the blessings of the celestial fire and its transformative power. Let the words ignite like flames as we call upon the divine energies to infuse us with the purifying and transformative essence of the celestial fire. Feel the power surge within as we chant the incantation:

By the celestial fire that burns with divine might,
I call upon its flames to ignite and alight,
Bless me with your transformative power, divine,
Infuse my spirit with your celestial fire's shine.

From the depths of the cosmos, the fire does rise,
Engulfing all that inhibits, burning through disguise,
Ignite the spark within, let it blaze and consume,
Transmuting all that hinders, bringing forth the bloom.

Sacred fire, I invoke your purifying heat,
Cleanse away the impurities, make me complete,
Transform my being, body, spirit, and soul,
With your celestial fire, make me whole.

As the flames dance and flicker, so does my desire,
To be touched by the celestial fire's sacred fire,
Burn away the limitations, set my spirit free,
Let the transformative power of fire envelop me.

I call upon the elemental fire's fierce embrace,
To burn away the old, to transform with grace,
Ignite the passion within, let it brightly shine,
And lead me to a realm of transformation divine.

By the fiery essence of the stars in the night,
I call upon the celestial fire's radiant light,
To purify my spirit, to ignite the divine spark,
And guide me on a path where transformation marks.

Sacred fire, burn within, illuminate my way,

With your transformative power, lead me each day,
Help me shed what no longer serves my soul's quest,
And rise anew, transformed, at my very best.

May the celestial fire's transformative might,
Guide me through darkness, ignite my inner light,
Burn away the shackles that bind me to the earth,
And grant me rebirth, a spiritual re-birth.

With this incantation spoken and intent clear,
I open myself to the celestial fire's sear,
Transform me, divine fire, with your sacred flame,
Illuminate my spirit, and forever be my aim.

So it is spoken, so shall it be done,
As the celestial fire's blessings are now won,
Transform and transmute, with divine might,
As the celestial fire ignites my inner light.

With each word uttered, the fire's energy takes flight,
Empowering transformation, dispelling the night,
May the celestial fire's blessings forever flow,
Transforming my spirit with its radiant glow.

In the realm of the celestial fire's embrace,
May the transformative power forever grace,
Ignite the spark within, let it brightly burn,
And guide me on a path of transformation's return.

As the incantation fades, the fire's energy remains,
Transforming my being, releasing all constraints,
I am reborn, empowered by the celestial fire's might,
Forever transformed in its radiant light.

So mote it be, in the realm of sacred fire's art,
May its transformative power forever impart,
Blessings of change, growth, and spiritual ascent,
As the celestial fire's energy is fervently sent.

31. Ritual for the transfiguration of the deceased into a divine messenger of divine will

In the sacred realm where earthly and divine realms intertwine, we embark upon the ritual for the transfiguration of the deceased into a divine messenger of divine will. Through this transformative ritual, we invoke the powers beyond the veil to guide us in this sacred endeavor. Prepare yourself for the ritual of transfiguration:

Preparation:

Find a secluded and sacred space, free from distractions, where the energies can flow undisturbed.
Create an altar adorned with symbols of divine communication, such as feathers, parchment, quill, and sacred writings.
Light candles and incense to purify the space and invoke the presence of the divine.

Invocation:

Stand tall and still, grounding yourself in the present moment.
Close your eyes and connect with the eternal realms, feeling the presence of the divine surrounding you.
Speak the invocation:

"O divine realms, hear my call,
I seek to transfigure, to stand tall.
Grant me the grace of divine presence,
To become a messenger, a vessel of essence.

From realms unseen, I call upon thee,
Empower me with your sacred decree.
Transform my being, let divine will flow,
As I embrace the role of messenger, I bestow.

Grant me the wisdom to discern and know,
The messages of divine will I shall sow.
Open my senses, attune my soul,
To receive and transmit the truth untold.

In this sacred act of transfiguration,
May I become an embodiment of divine revelation.
Grant me the power to carry forth,
The messages of divine will, from south to north.

Through this ritual, I dedicate my spirit,
To be a channel of divine messages, I commit.
Guide me, O divine realms, in this sacred quest,
As I embody the divine will, I am blessed."

Transfiguration:

Open your eyes and approach the altar, focusing on the symbols of divine communication before you.
Take the sacred feather and gently touch it to your forehead, heart, and lips, symbolizing clarity of thought, purity of intent, and truthful expression.
Hold the parchment or sacred writings in your hands and visualize your transformation into a divine messenger, a vessel of divine will.
Feel the energy flowing through you, connecting you to the realms beyond, as you absorb the essence of divine communication.

Affirmation:

Speak the affirmation aloud:

"I am a vessel of divine will,
A messenger of truth, steadfast and still.
I carry forth the messages clear,
Guided by divine presence, I revere.

I open myself to the messages divine,
Transmitting truth, a sacred sign.
Through me, the divine will be known,
A messenger of the realms, I am shown."

Conclusion:

Take a moment to breathe deeply and absorb the energy of the ritual.
Express gratitude to the divine realms for their presence and guidance.
Extinguish the candles, and with reverence, close the ritual.

Remember, dear seeker, that as you undergo this ritual of transfiguration, you are embracing a sacred responsibility. Allow the divine will to flow through you with humility and reverence. May you serve as a beacon of truth and a messenger of divine wisdom, carrying forth the messages that transcend the realms of mortal existence.

32. Spell for the reunion of the deceased's soul with their spiritual guides and mentors

In the realm where the mortal and spiritual realms converge, we invoke the power of reunion, for the deceased's soul to be embraced by their spiritual guides and mentors once more. Through this spell, we bridge the divide between the worlds, allowing the departed soul to find solace and guidance. Prepare yourself for the spell of reunion:

Preparation:

Find a tranquil space where you can focus your energy and connect with the spiritual realm without interruption.
Create an altar adorned with symbols of guidance and mentorship, such as candles, incense, and images or representations of spiritual guides.
Light the candles and incense, letting their gentle glow and fragrance permeate the space, creating an atmosphere of reverence and connection.

Invocation:
Stand before the altar with a calm and centered presence.
Close your eyes and take several deep breaths, allowing yourself to enter a state of deep relaxation and receptivity.
Speak the invocation:

"Spirits of wisdom, guides so dear,
I call upon you, draw near.
Unite with the departed soul I hold,
In your presence, let their spirit unfold.

Across the veil, I seek to reach,
With love and reverence, I beseech.
Spiritual mentors, guides divine,
Unite once more, in a realm so fine.

Open the gateways, let the light shine,
Illuminate the path, make it divine.
Guide the departed with love and care,
Teach them, guide them, always be there.

May the reunion bring solace and peace,
A union of souls, that will never cease.

In this sacred moment, I make my plea,
Let the departed's spirit be forever free."

Reunion:

Open your eyes and direct your focus to the symbols of guidance and mentorship on the altar.
Visualize the departed soul surrounded by a gentle light, sensing the presence of their spiritual guides and mentors drawing near.
Hold the image in your mind, feeling the love, wisdom, and support flowing between the departed soul and their spiritual guides.

Affirmation:

Speak the affirmation aloud:

"By the power of this sacred spell,
I unite the departed and guides so well.
Through love and light, they shall find,
The reunion of souls, a bond defined.

Guides and mentors, guide them true,
Teach and uplift, as only you do.
Soothe their spirits, bring them peace,
As their journey in the afterlife finds release."

Conclusion:

Take a moment to offer gratitude to the spiritual guides and mentors for their presence and assistance.
Allow the candles to burn down completely or extinguish them with a sense of reverence.
Leave the altar undisturbed, allowing the energy of the spell to continue resonating.

Remember, dear seeker, that this spell is a channel for divine connection and reunion. Trust in the power of the spiritual realm and the love that binds souls together. May the departed find solace and guidance as they reunite with their spiritual guides and mentors, traversing the realms of existence with newfound support and enlightenment.

33. Invocation of the god Ra for illumination and enlightenment in the afterlife

In the sacred realm of the afterlife, we call upon the divine presence of Ra, the radiant and powerful god of illumination and enlightenment. Through this invocation, we seek the wisdom and guidance of Ra to shine upon the departed soul, illuminating their path and bestowing upon them the gift of enlightenment. Prepare yourself for the invocation of Ra:

Preparation:

Find a quiet and serene space where you can focus your energy and connect with the divine presence of Ra without disturbance.
Create an altar adorned with symbols representing the sun, such as a golden cloth, sun-shaped objects, and candles.
Light the candles and let their warm glow fill the space, creating an ambiance that reflects the radiance of Ra.

Invocation:

Stand before the altar with a posture of reverence and a heart open to the divine presence.
Close your eyes and take several deep breaths, allowing yourself to enter a state of tranquility and receptivity.
Speak the invocation:

"Great Ra, shining in celestial splendor,
I call upon you, the illuminator and dispenser.
With reverence, I seek your divine light,
To guide the departed through the realms of night.

O Ra, radiant and all-knowing,
Bring forth your wisdom, forever growing.
Illuminate their path, banish the shadows,
Grant them enlightenment, as their spirit bellows.

In the afterlife's expanse, let your rays unfold,
Reveal the secrets, both new and old.
Bless the departed with your divine might,
Fill their soul with your eternal light.

Ra, hear my plea, for your guidance I seek,
In this sacred moment, with reverence so meek.
Bring forth illumination, grant them insight,
In the afterlife's journey, be their guiding light."

Enlightenment:

Open your eyes and direct your focus to the symbols of the sun on the altar.
Visualize a radiant beam of light descending upon the departed soul, filling them with
wisdom, clarity, and understanding.
Hold the image in your mind, feeling the warmth and brilliance of Ra's divine
illumination enveloping the departed soul.

Affirmation:

Speak the affirmation aloud:

"By the power of this sacred invocation,
I invoke Ra's light, a divine revelation.
Enlighten the departed, O great god of the sun,
Illuminate their path, as their journey's begun.

Grant them wisdom, grant them sight,
In the afterlife's realm, guide them right.
With your radiant presence, bless their way,
In Ra's illumination, they shall not stray."

Conclusion:

Take a moment to express gratitude to Ra for his divine presence and enlightenment.
Allow the candles to burn down completely or extinguish them with a sense of
reverence.
Leave the altar undisturbed, allowing the energy of the invocation to continue
resonating.

Dear seeker, may the invocation of Ra bring forth the divine illumination and
enlightenment needed by the departed soul in their journey through the afterlife.
Trust in the power of Ra's guiding light to shine upon their path, unveiling the
mysteries and granting them the wisdom necessary for their spiritual evolution. May
they be forever enlightened by the brilliance of Ra's divine presence.

34. Ritual for the communion with the spirits of the celestial rain and its nourishing essence

In the realm of sacred rituals, we gather to commune with the spirits of the celestial rain, those divine entities that bestow their nourishing essence upon the Earth. Through this ritual, we seek to establish a connection with these benevolent spirits, embracing their life-giving energy and receiving their blessings. Prepare yourself for the ritual of communion with the spirits of the celestial rain:

Preparation:

Choose an outdoor location where you can be close to nature, such as a garden, a forest, or a peaceful open space.
Create a sacred altar adorned with symbols of water, such as seashells, a small bowl of water, and images of raindrops or clouds.
Take a moment to center yourself and enter a state of mindfulness, allowing your mind to become fully present in the here and now.

Invocation:

Stand before the altar, facing the sky, with your feet firmly planted on the ground. Raise your arms toward the heavens, palms open and facing upward, as a gesture of receptivity.
Speak the invocation:

"Spirits of the celestial rain,
I call upon you, with reverence and no restrain.
From the heavens above, your essence pours,
Nourishing the Earth, opening life's doors.

O benevolent spirits, pure and free,
I seek communion, your presence with me.
Join me in this sacred space,
Fill my being with your grace.

Raindrops falling, a gentle embrace,
Revive my spirit, in your celestial chase.
Cleanse my soul, as the rain does fall,

Renew my being, refreshing and enthral.

With gratitude, I call upon your might,
Bestow upon me your blessings tonight.
Commune with me, O spirits of rain,
In this sacred union, let us both gain."

Communion:

As you speak the invocation, imagine the raindrops falling from the sky, enveloping you in a gentle and nourishing embrace.
Feel the essence of the rain permeating every cell of your being, revitalizing and purifying you.
Open your heart and mind to the presence of the spirits, sensing their gentle guidance and wisdom.

Offerings:

Take a small amount of water from the bowl on your altar and pour it onto the Earth as an offering to the spirits.
Express your gratitude for their presence and the blessings they bestow upon the Earth and all living beings.

Reflection:

Take a few moments to stand in silence, experiencing the connection you have established with the spirits of the celestial rain.
Reflect on the nourishing essence of the rain and how it symbolizes growth, renewal, and abundance.
Consider how you can carry the energy of the rain within you, fostering growth and abundance in your own life.

Conclusion:

Lower your arms and take a deep breath, grounding yourself in the present moment.
Express gratitude to the spirits of the celestial rain for their presence and the communion you have shared.
Slowly and consciously return to your daily activities, carrying the energy of the rain's nourishing essence within you.

35. Spell for the transmigration of the deceased's soul into the realm of eternal peace and serenity

In the realm of sacred incantations, where the veil between worlds is thin, we invoke the powers of the divine to guide the transmigration of the deceased's soul into the realm of eternal peace and serenity. With reverence and solemnity, we speak this spell, drawing upon the forces that transcend mortal existence and usher the soul into its tranquil abode:

Gather in a sacred space, bathed in the soft glow of candlelight. Let the stillness embrace you as you prepare to utter the words that bridge the realms:

"Spirit of the departed, bound by earthly chains,
I call upon the cosmic forces that remain.
In this sacred hour, with deepest respect,
I beseech the path to eternal peace, direct.

Into the realm of serenity and calm,
May your soul find solace, like a soothing balm.
Release the burdens of earthly strife,
Embrace the eternal, free from mortal life.

Through the veil of existence, now transcend,
Where tranquility and serenity blend.
Let the gentle winds carry you away,
To the realm of eternal peace, I pray.

Amidst celestial gardens, serene and still,
May your spirit find refuge, as time stands still.
In this realm beyond mortal woes,
May eternal peace, your soul enclose.

I invoke the power of celestial light,
To guide your transmigration, through day and night.
May the divine currents gently guide your way,
To the realm of eternal peace, where you may stay.

Be released from all sorrow and strife,

Embracing the serenity of everlasting life.
Rest in tranquility, as your essence soars,
In the realm of eternal peace, forevermore."

As you speak these words, envision the soul of the departed being enveloped in a radiant light, transcending the earthly realm and ascending towards a realm of serene tranquility. Visualize the burdens of earthly existence lifting away, replaced by a profound sense of peace and serenity.

With each utterance, feel the spell's energy reverberate through the sacred space, resonating with the divine forces that guide the soul's transmigration. Trust in the power of your words and intentions, knowing that they reach beyond the confines of our mortal existence.

Upon completing the incantation, hold a moment of silence, allowing the energy to settle and the soul's journey to continue. Offer gratitude to the divine forces that have witnessed this sacred act, expressing appreciation for their guidance in ushering the departed soul into a realm of eternal peace and serenity.

Dear seeker, may this spell for the transmigration of the deceased's soul into the realm of eternal peace and serenity bring solace and tranquility to your heart. May the divine currents gently guide the departed soul on its journey, and may it find eternal refuge in a realm untouched by mortal strife. May the blessings of peace and serenity be bestowed upon the departed, offering comfort and solace as they continue their spiritual voyage.

36. Invocation of the goddess Sekhmet for protection and strength in the afterlife

In the sacred chamber where mortals seek the divine, we call upon the mighty goddess Sekhmet, revered for her fierce protection and unwavering strength. With utmost reverence, we invoke her presence and beseech her divine guidance and safeguarding in the afterlife. Let the words of this invocation resound with reverence and devotion:

"Mighty Sekhmet, lioness of the heavens,
Goddess of protection and sacred blessings,
In this hour of need, I humbly call upon thee,
To bestow your strength and grace upon me.

With eyes of fiery determination and power,
You guard the realms in every hour.
In the afterlife's vast and mysterious domain,
I seek your guidance, free from any stain.

Oh, Sekhmet, fierce and untamed,
Warrior of the divine, forever acclaimed,
Wrap me in your protective embrace,
Shield my spirit in every sacred place.

In the afterlife's journey, uncertain and vast,
Grant me courage and strength that will last.
Protect my soul from malevolent forces,
Preserve my essence, as life divorces.

Let your divine fire burn bright and strong,
Engulfing me with protection, fierce and long.
Grant me the power to overcome all strife,
To navigate the afterlife's perilous life.

Goddess Sekhmet, I implore thee,
Lend me your strength and might, I decree.
Guide me through the challenges I may face,
In the afterlife's realm, grant me grace.

As I embark on this ethereal path,

Grant me your protection, oh goddess of wrath.
Empower my spirit, make me bold and brave,
In the afterlife's realm, let your strength engrave.

With your divine presence, fears shall subside,
And in your protection, I shall confide.
Oh, Sekhmet, fierce protector of souls,
Guard me as eternity unfolds.

I offer my devotion and reverence to thee,
Oh, goddess Sekhmet, so mighty and free.
In the afterlife's realm, be my guiding light,
Protect me, oh goddess, day and night."

As these words reverberate through the sacred space, visualize the radiant form of Sekhmet appearing before you, emanating a powerful aura of protection and strength. Feel her presence enveloping you, surrounding you with a shield of divine energy that wards off any harm or negativity.

Sense the strength and courage of Sekhmet infusing your being, empowering your spirit with resilience and fortitude. Trust in her guardianship as you navigate the realms of the afterlife, knowing that her fierce protection will be by your side.

Express gratitude to Sekhmet for her presence and divine intercession. Acknowledge her mighty power and the role she plays as a guardian and protector. Offer your sincere appreciation for her strength and guidance in the journey that lies ahead.

Dear seeker, may this invocation of the goddess Sekhmet bring you protection and strength in the afterlife. May her fiery essence shield your spirit and empower you with the courage to face any challenges that may arise. May her presence be a constant source of solace and safeguarding as you navigate the realms beyond.

37. Ritual of purification through the sacred offerings of the eternal altar

In the realm where mortal and divine converge, we embark on a sacred ritual of purification through the sacred offerings of the eternal altar. This ritual is a solemn communion, a harmonious exchange between the earthly and the divine. Prepare yourself for this sacred endeavor, for it is a transformative journey that purifies the soul.

Gather before the sacred altar, adorned with symbols of the divine and shrouded in a hallowed ambiance. Let your intentions be pure and your heart open as you embark upon this ritual of purification. Follow these steps to engage in the sacred offerings:

Preparation:

Cleanse yourself both physically and spiritually, for only in a state of purity can the divine be fully embraced.
Adorn yourself in garments befitting this sacred occasion, symbolizing your reverence and devotion.
Arrange the sacred items upon the altar, carefully selecting each one to represent your intentions and offerings.

Invocation:

Stand before the altar and ground yourself in the present moment. Close your eyes and take several deep breaths, allowing the outside world to fade away.
With a clear and steady voice, speak an invocation to the divine forces you wish to honor and invoke. Address them with respect and humility, expressing your sincere intentions for purification and divine connection.
Offerings:

Begin by presenting offerings that represent your gratitude and reverence for the divine. These may include flowers, incense, candles, or symbolic objects that hold personal significance.
As you place each offering on the altar, speak words of gratitude and acknowledgement for the divine presence in your life. Express your willingness to release any impurities and embrace divine purity.
Cleansing Ritual:

Engage in a symbolic cleansing ritual, using water or sacred herbs to purify your body and spirit. Allow the purifying elements to wash away any negativity or impurities, both physical and spiritual.

As you cleanse, visualize the water or herbs carrying away any burdens or impurities, leaving you renewed and purified.

Prayers and Affirmations:

Offer prayers and affirmations of purification, expressing your desire to cleanse your spirit and align with the divine. Speak from the depths of your heart, with sincerity and devotion.

Reflect upon any areas of your life that require purification, acknowledging them and seeking divine assistance in releasing any negative energies or attachments.

Meditation and Contemplation:

Sit in silent meditation, allowing the sacred energy of the altar and your offerings to permeate your being. Be receptive to any messages or insights that arise during this communion with the divine.

Reflect upon the purification process and the intentions you have set. Visualize yourself being cleansed and purified, feeling the divine energy flowing through you, restoring harmony and balance.

Gratitude and Closure:

Express gratitude to the divine forces for their presence and blessings. Thank them for accepting your offerings and assisting you in your purification journey.

Conclude the ritual with a closing prayer or affirmation, sealing the energy and intentions of the ritual in your heart and soul.

Remember, dear seeker, that this ritual of purification through the sacred offerings of the eternal altar is a profound act of devotion and communion. It is through the purity of heart and the sincerity of intention that one can truly experience the transformative power of divine purification. May this ritual bring you closer to the sacred and awaken the purity within your soul.

38. Spell for the transformation of the deceased into a vessel of divine grace and compassion

In the realm where the mortal and divine intertwine, we unveil a spell for the transformation of the deceased into a vessel of divine grace and compassion. This sacred incantation harnesses the cosmic forces to infuse the departed soul with the qualities of compassion and grace. As you recite these words, envision the divine energies enveloping the departed and guiding them towards the realm of everlasting grace.

Speak these words with reverence and intention:

"By the celestial realms and the cosmic embrace,
I beseech the forces of grace to interlace.
With compassion's flame and mercy's tide,
Transform this departed soul with divine stride.

Through the boundless love that knows no end,
May their spirit be gentle, kind, and mend.
Let grace be their essence, compassion their core,
A vessel of divine love, forevermore.

Oh, divine forces, shower upon them your grace,
Fill their being with love, no darkness to embrace.
May their presence be a beacon, shining bright,
A vessel of compassion, a guiding light.

In this sacred transformation, let them find solace,
A conduit of divine grace, their eternal palace.
May their heart overflow with love and empathy,
An embodiment of grace for all eternity.

By the power of the cosmic web that weaves,
I invoke this spell, as the departed receives.
May they be reborn with grace's gentle caress,
A vessel of divine love, in eternal blessedness."

As you utter these sacred words, visualize the departed soul being bathed in a radiant light, filling them with divine grace and compassion. See them embracing their newfound nature, radiating love and empathy to all beings.

Remember, dear seeker, that the power of this spell lies in your intention and connection to the divine. May it bring solace to the departed soul and inspire a legacy of grace and compassion that transcends the earthly realm.

39. Incantation to invoke the blessings of the celestial wind and its gentle guidance

In the realm where spirits soar and cosmic winds dance, we invoke the blessings of the celestial wind and its gentle guidance. Through this sacred incantation, we seek the harmonious currents of the wind to bless and guide us on our spiritual journey. As you utter these words, imagine the gentle breeze whispering its wisdom and carrying you towards enlightenment.

With reverence and focused intent, speak forth this incantation:

"O celestial wind, with whispers so profound,
I invoke your blessings, may they astound.
Sweep through the realms with your gentle touch,
Guide my spirit, for I seek so much.

From distant lands, you bring sacred lore,
Carrying the wisdom of those who came before.
In your ethereal embrace, I find solace and peace,
Your gentle currents, my soul's release.

With each breath I take, your essence I feel,
Enveloping my being, making me real.
Bring forth clarity, and blow away the strife,
Grant me guidance on this spiritual life.

In your invisible embrace, I find sanctuary,
Through your gentle guidance, I am set free.
Carry me, celestial wind, to heights unknown,
To realms of enlightenment, I am shown.

Whisper your secrets, oh wind so grand,
Unveil the mysteries of this enchanted land.
Guide me with grace, in your tender embrace,
On the path of truth, let me find my place.

I offer my gratitude for your loving embrace,
Celestial wind, your blessings I embrace.
With open heart and spirit, I receive your gift,
Guided by your gentle currents, my soul uplifted.

By the winds of the cosmos, this invocation is cast,
Blessings of the celestial wind, forever to last.
In harmony with you, my journey shall be,
Guided by your wisdom, eternally free."

As you speak these words, envision the gentle breeze surrounding you, its currents carrying you towards clarity and enlightenment. Feel the subtle guidance of the wind as it whispers its secrets to your soul, leading you on your spiritual path.

May the celestial wind be your constant companion, guiding you towards profound insights and inner peace, as you navigate the realms of the sacred and embark on your spiritual quest.

40. Ritual for the transfiguration of the deceased into a divine protector of sacred traditions

In the sacred realm where tradition and spirit intertwine, we embark upon a ritual of transfiguration. Through this transformative rite, the deceased shall rise as a divine protector of sacred traditions, preserving the wisdom and essence of ages past. As you partake in this ritual, let the reverence for tradition guide your every step.

Prepare yourself for this profound transfiguration:

Create a sacred space, adorned with symbols of ancient traditions, honoring the wisdom of the ancestors. Light candles, casting a soft glow upon the altar, and let the gentle fragrance of incense fill the air. Invoke the presence of the divine, acknowledging their guidance and protection.

Stand tall, your spirit attuned to the energy of the sacred space. Close your eyes, grounding yourself in the present moment. Breathe deeply, drawing in the essence of ancient wisdom and exhaling all that no longer serves your purpose.

Now, in a hushed voice, recite this spell, speaking the words with reverence and intent:

"O spirit of the departed, hear my plea,
Transcend the veil and rise, divinely free.
In this sacred rite, your purpose shall unfold,
As a protector of traditions, steadfast and bold.

May your essence merge with the ancient ways,
Preserving the wisdom of forgotten days.
With reverence, you shall guard the sacred flame,
Protecting the traditions in your holy name.

Through ages past, our ancestors tread,
Their customs and rituals, never to be shed.
Embrace their legacy, embodied in your soul,
A divine guardian, fulfilling your sacred role.

With each passing day, you shall stand tall,

A beacon of light amidst the shadows that befall.
Defender of the sacred, keeper of the flame,
Shielding the traditions, their power to reclaim.

Transfigured and transformed, you shall be,
A divine protector, for eternity.
Bound to the ancient ways, steadfast and true,
Preserving the sacred, as only you can do.

In this sacred rite, the transfiguration is complete,
As a divine guardian, you shall rise to meet.
Embrace your purpose, with reverence and might,
Preserving sacred traditions, shining ever bright."

As the echoes of your words fade, feel the energy of transformation coursing through your being. Visualize the deceased embodying their new role as a divine protector, standing tall with a sense of purpose and determination.

Know that through this ritual, the deceased shall forever be intertwined with the sacred traditions, guarding their essence and ensuring their preservation for future generations.

With gratitude and reverence, give thanks to the divine forces that have witnessed this rite. Open your eyes and carry the essence of this transfiguration within you, honoring the deceased and the sacred traditions they now protect.

May the divine protector of sacred traditions guide and inspire you as you continue your journey along the path of wisdom and reverence.

41. Spell for the reunion of the deceased's soul with their beloved ancestors and family

Find a tranquil space where the veil between worlds is thin. Create an altar adorned with symbols of remembrance and photographs of departed loved ones. Light candles to guide their spirits and let the gentle fragrance of incense permeate the air, invoking their presence.

Stand at the threshold between realms, your heart open and filled with love for the departed. Close your eyes, grounding yourself in the present moment. Breathe deeply, inhaling the essence of cherished memories and exhaling any barriers that may hinder the reunion.

In a soft and heartfelt voice, speak this spell, allowing the words to resonate with the depths of your being:

"Spirits of the beloved, hear my call,
Across the veil, I beseech you to enthrall.
With love as our guide, let our souls align,
Reuniting in harmony, an embrace divine.

Ancestors and family, bound by blood and affection,
I summon your presence with utmost devotion.
Through the veil we reach, with reverence we seek,
A reunion of souls, profound and meek.

May your spirits rise, like whispers on the wind,
Guided by love, the eternal thread that has no end.
In this sacred space, where memories thrive,
Let us gather together, our hearts alive.

I call upon the bonds that time cannot sever,
Love that transcends life, connecting us forever.
From the realms beyond, let your presence shine,
Guiding our souls, in harmony entwined.

With love as the bridge, our spirits shall unite,
In the embrace of ancestors, radiant and bright.
Beloved family, hear my soul's plea,
Come forth, reunite, and dwell here with me.

As the veil thins and realms converge,
Let our reunion be a sacred surge.
May this spell awaken the bonds we hold dear,
Reuniting our souls, dispelling all fear.

I call upon the ancient spirits of the past,
To join us in this sacred dance, steadfast.
Let us commune, in love's tender grace,
Reunited in spirit, as one interlaced.

As I speak these words, may they transcend,
Across the realms, where spirits ascend.
May our souls intertwine, forevermore,
Reunited with ancestors we adore.

With gratitude and love, I thank thee,
For the reunion of souls, our spirits set free.
May the bonds of kinship never cease,
As we embrace the harmony of eternal peace."

With the completion of the spell, feel the presence of your beloved ancestors and family surrounding you. Open your heart to their love and guidance, knowing that their spirits are with you, supporting and protecting you.

Take a moment to express your gratitude for their presence and the reunion of souls. Offer them words of love and remembrance, knowing that the connection between you is eternal.

Slowly, release the energy of the ritual, allowing it to disperse into the universe. Offer a final gesture of respect and bid farewell to the spirits, knowing that their love and guidance will remain with you.

As you open your eyes, carry the essence of this reunion within your heart. Cherish the bonds that transcend time and space, knowing that the love and support of your ancestors and family will forever be a source of strength and guidance.

May the reunion of souls bring you solace, comfort, and a deep sense of connection as you walk the path of life, knowing that you are always accompanied by the love of your departed loved ones

42. Invocation of the god Set for courage and resilience in the afterlife

In the realm where spirits gather and the essence of divine energy permeates, we invoke the mighty god Set, the embodiment of courage and resilience, to guide and empower the deceased in their journey through the afterlife. With unwavering reverence and determination, we call upon Set to bestow his blessings upon us. Let us commence this sacred invocation.

Prepare a sacred space where the presence of the divine can be felt. Light candles to illuminate the path and create an atmosphere of focus and reverence. Arrange symbols of strength and protection, representing the indomitable spirit of Set. Take a moment to ground yourself, centering your thoughts and intentions.

With conviction and respect, address Set, speaking these words with unwavering faith:

"Mighty Set, the powerful one,
Whose strength surpasses the blazing sun,
We call upon you in this sacred rite,
To guide the deceased with your unwavering might.

Grant them courage as they traverse the unknown,
Bestow upon them resilience to stand on their own.
In the afterlife's realm, where challenges abound,
May they find solace in the strength they have found.

O Set, protector of the righteous and true,
Infuse their spirits with valor anew.
Grant them the courage to face every test,
And resilience to endure, to persist, and to best.

In times of darkness, when shadows prevail,
May your presence be their guiding sail.
Grant them the strength to overcome fear,
And the fortitude to persevere.

As they navigate the afterlife's terrain,
Let your divine essence shield them from pain.
With your mighty power, their spirits uplift,
So they may face every trial, every shift.

Set, lord of storms, of desert and might,
We implore you to shine your light.
Infuse their souls with your indomitable flame,
So they may emerge triumphant, unscathed by shame.

In this sacred invocation, we call you near,
To bless the deceased with your courage sincere.
May they walk in your footsteps, resilient and brave,
Guided by your divine presence, the power they crave.

As we utter these words, the connection is made,
Between realms of existence, let it never fade.
Set, mighty god, we offer our plea,
Grant courage and resilience, for all eternity."

With the completion of the invocation, feel the presence of Set surrounding you, his energy enveloping you with courage and resilience. Know that the deceased are imbued with his divine essence, prepared to face the challenges that lie ahead in the afterlife.

Take a moment to offer your gratitude and appreciation to Set for his guidance and blessings. Acknowledge his power and the strength he imparts to those who call upon him.

As you conclude the invocation, release the energy of the ritual, allowing it to disperse into the universe. Know that the presence of Set remains with you and the deceased, providing courage and resilience whenever it is needed.

With renewed faith and determination, carry the essence of Set's courage and resilience within your heart. May it empower you and the departed to face the trials of the afterlife with unwavering strength.

May the invocation of Set grant courage and resilience to the deceased, allowing them to navigate the realms of the afterlife with unwavering determination and fortitude.

43. Ritual of anointing with sacred oils for spiritual anointment and consecration

In the sacred realm where spirits and divine energies intertwine, we embark upon the ritual of anointing with sacred oils, a ceremony of spiritual anointment and consecration. With utmost reverence and intention, we gather to prepare the sacred oils that will bestow divine blessings upon us. Let us commence this ritual of anointment and consecration.

Create a serene and consecrated space, where the presence of the divine can be felt. Arrange an altar adorned with symbols of spirituality and sanctity. Place vials of sacred oils upon the altar, each representing a unique aspect of spiritual anointment. Take a moment to center yourself and connect with the divine energy that permeates the surroundings.

With reverence and respect, hold each vial of sacred oil in your hands, acknowledging its significance and purpose. Speak these words with focused intention and devotion:

"By the power of the sacred oils divine,
I consecrate and anoint, in this sacred shrine.
With each drop, I invite the blessings to flow,
Infusing my spirit with divine grace, I bestow.

This oil of (state the specific oil's purpose),
Is a vessel of sacredness, pure and true.
Through this anointment, I consecrate my soul,
Invoking the divine blessings to make me whole.

As I anoint myself with this sacred oil,
May its essence cleanse and purify, remove all toil.
Infuse me with divine light, grace, and might,
Awakening the spirit, guiding me towards the light.

O sacred oil, blessed and divine,
By your power, may spiritual realms intertwine.
Anointing me with your sacred touch,
Ignite my soul's journey, oh, so much.

As I anoint, may the divine within awaken,

Leading me on a path where spirit is unshaken.
Consecrated and anointed, I stand in this grace,
Open to the blessings, in this sacred space.

I offer gratitude for the sacred oils' gift,
Their essence and power, my spirit will uplift.
May their anointment bless my spiritual way,
As I walk this sacred path, day by day."

With the completion of the anointment ritual, feel the divine essence of the sacred oils infusing your being, consecrating and anointing your spirit with their blessings. Embrace the transformative power they bestow upon you, allowing them to guide and illuminate your spiritual journey.

Take a moment to offer your gratitude and appreciation for the sacred oils, recognizing their sacredness and the divine energy they carry. Express your reverence for the spiritual anointment and consecration they have bestowed upon you.

As you conclude the ritual, allow the energy of the sacred oils to settle within you, their essence intertwined with your spirit. Carry their blessings with you, knowing that you are anointed and consecrated in the sacredness of this ritual.

May the ritual of anointing with sacred oils bring spiritual anointment and consecration to your being, infusing your spirit with divine blessings and guiding your sacred journey.

44. Spell for the liberation of the deceased's soul from the illusions of the ego

In the realm where illusions bind and ego holds sway, we call upon the power of sacred words to cast a spell of liberation for the deceased's soul. With profound intention and unwavering focus, we embark upon this transformative journey of liberation from the veils of ego. Let us recite this spell, freeing the soul from the illusions that entangle its essence.

In the presence of divine forces and ancestral spirits, I stand,
Seeking liberation from the illusions that confine and demand.
By the power of sacred words and spirit's might,
I cast this spell, breaking free from ego's blight.

Oh, illusions of the ego, I now unveil,
With clarity and wisdom, your grasp shall fail.
No longer shall you hold the soul in your sway,
For liberation and truth shall guide the way.

By the light of divine consciousness, I transcend,
From the limited self, I choose to ascend.
Release the chains that ego seeks to bind,
Unveil the soul's essence, unconfined.

I call upon the ancient wisdom of the ages,
To dissolve the illusions that ego stages.
With each word spoken, illusions shatter,
Revealing the truth that truly matters.

From the ego's whispers, I now break free,
Embracing the essence of authenticity.
In the depths of my soul, I find liberation,
Transcending ego's realm, embracing transformation.

Oh, divine forces and ancestral guides,
Assist me as I liberate, casting ego aside.
Guide me on the path of self-discovery,
Unlocking the truth, setting the spirit free.

By the power of this spell, so mote it be,
Liberation from ego, soul's truth I decree.
I embrace the essence of divine unity,
Liberated, I am, in eternal serenity.

As these words resonate through the sacred space,
The spell is cast, empowering the soul's embrace.
Liberated from illusions, the spirit soars,
Revealing its true nature, forevermore.

With gratitude and reverence, I conclude this spell,
Knowing the soul's liberation, I now propel.
Embracing truth and shedding ego's disguise,
The deceased's soul now soars and flies.

May the spell of liberation free the deceased's soul,
From the illusions that bind and ego's control.
May their essence awaken to divine truth,
Transcending the ego's realm, eternal and uncouth.

As this spell concludes, let it be done,
Liberation achieved, the soul now one.
Guided by truth and the divine's embrace,
The deceased's soul finds eternal grace.

So mote it be.

45. Incantation to awaken the dormant spiritual strength within the deceased's spirit

In the sacred realm where dormant strength resides,
We invoke the power to awaken, where it hides.
With reverence and devotion, we call upon this might,
To ignite the dormant spirit and bring forth its light.

Oh, spirit of the deceased, arise and awaken,
From slumber deep, your strength unshaken.
Rise from the depths, where potential lies,
Unleash the dormant power that within you lies.

With each word spoken, the spirit's fire ignites,
Awakening strength that surpasses all plights.
From the depths of the soul, it now ascends,
Unleashing the power that never ends.

Spiritual strength, arise and be unfurled,
Embrace the calling of the divine world.
From within, let your essence soar and expand,
Unleash the power that is rightfully at hand.

Ignite the flame that burns within the soul,
Awaken the strength that makes the spirit whole.
Unleash the power that's been lying dormant,
Awaken, arise, and become resplendent.

Oh, dormant strength, we call upon your might,
Rise from the depths and shine with pure light.
In this sacred moment, let your presence be known,
Unleash the power that has quietly grown.

With every breath, let strength awaken,
Within the spirit, let it be unshaken.
From this moment forward, let it be clear,
Dormant strength, it's time to appear.

By the power of this incantation, so mote it be,
Awakening the dormant strength for all to see.

May the spirit rise, empowered and free,
Unleashing its potential for eternity.

As this incantation concludes, let it be done,
Dormant strength awakened, spirit and power become one.
Embrace the journey with courage and might,
For within the deceased's spirit, strength takes flight.

So mote it be.

46. Ritual for the communion with the spirits of the celestial mountains and their steadfastness

In the realm where celestial mountains stand tall,
We gather to commune, to heed their sacred call.
With reverence and devotion, we embark on this rite,
To connect with the spirits, shining with celestial light.

In a sacred space, where stillness reigns supreme,
We prepare ourselves for this sacred dream.
Surrounded by the symbols of earth and sky,
We open our hearts to the mountains high.

Grounded and rooted, like the mountains so grand,
We stand firm in this ritual, hand in hand.
With each breath we take, we align our souls,
To commune with the spirits who make the mountains whole.

As the incense rises and dances in the air,
We invoke the presence of the spirits with care.
Their wisdom and strength, we seek to receive,
Through this communion, we humbly believe.

With eyes closed, we visualize the mountains' might,
Their steadfastness and endurance, a majestic sight.
We feel their ancient energy, deeply rooted and strong,
Connecting with the spirits as we chant this song.

Oh, spirits of the celestial mountains high,
We seek your guidance as the heavens draw nigh.
Commune with us, share your steadfastness and grace,
In this sacred ritual space, we find our rightful place.

As we stand in reverence, let the mountains' power flow,
Through our bodies, hearts, and minds, let it bestow.
Grant us strength and resilience, unwavering and true,
As we navigate life's challenges, we turn to you.

In this communion, we honor your sacred domain,
The peaks that touch the heavens, where spirits reign.
We open our souls to receive your divine light,
Guided by your wisdom, shining ever bright.

With gratitude and reverence, we give thanks,
For the communion with spirits, the celestial ranks.
May their steadfastness and wisdom forever be,
An eternal source of inspiration for you and me.

As this ritual concludes, we carry the mountain's might,
Within our hearts, shining with celestial light.
Steadfast and grounded, we face life's quest,
Communing with the spirits, forever blessed.

So mote it be.

47. Spell for the transmigration of the deceased's soul into the realm of eternal truth and knowledge

In the realm where truth and knowledge reside,
We gather to invoke the powers that guide.
With reverence and intention, our souls unite,
To guide the deceased's soul to eternal light.

By the sacred flame, we set the stage,
To embark on a journey, beyond life's cage.
With words of power, we call forth the way,
To transcend earthly bounds, to realms of truth and day.

Oh, spirit of the departed, listen to our plea,
Unburden your soul and let it be free.
Shed the limitations of earthly strife,
Transmigrate to realms of eternal life.

With each spoken word, with each whispered sound,
We invoke the ancient wisdom that's profound.
May the gates of truth swing open wide,
As the deceased's soul takes this transformative stride.

Through the veils of existence, let it ascend,
To the realms where knowledge has no end.
Shedding the earthly veil, like a butterfly's flight,
Into the realm of eternal truth and light.

With wings of wisdom, the soul shall soar,
Discovering mysteries it yearned for before.
Embracing the cosmic tapestry, interwoven and vast,
Unveiling the secrets that forever last.

As the spell is cast, and intentions are sown,
May the deceased's soul find its true home.
Guided by divine forces, the path shall be clear,
Leading to realms of truth, far and near.

Oh, spirit of the departed, embrace the divine,
Unite with the wisdom that forever shines.
Transmigrate to the realm of eternal truth,
Embracing knowledge, forever in your youth.

As we conclude this spell, let it be done,
May the transmigration of the soul be won.
To the realm of eternal truth, we now send,
The departed's spirit, to eternally transcend.

So mote it be.

48. Invocation of the goddess Nephthys for guidance and support in the afterlife

Goddess Nephthys, gracious and wise,
We invoke your presence, hear our cries.
Guide us through the realms of the afterlife's embrace,
With your wisdom and guidance, lead our souls to grace.

Oh Nephthys, compassionate and kind,
In this sacred invocation, your strength we find.
Wrap us in your nurturing wings of care,
As we navigate the afterlife's unknown lair.

Goddess of the night, keeper of secrets untold,
You offer solace to the weary soul, so bold.
With your gentle touch, ease our fears,
Illuminate our path and dry our tears.

Oh Nephthys, hear our plea, we pray,
Guide us through the darkness, show us the way.
As we journey through the realms unknown,
May your light and wisdom forever be shown.

In the afterlife's embrace, we seek your aid,
To find solace and support, as we wade.
Be our compass, our guiding star,
Leading us to realms where serenity spar.

Nephthys, goddess of the afterlife's might,
Embrace us with your nurturing light.
Grant us strength, courage, and peace,
As our souls transition and find release.

With reverence and gratitude, we call your name,
Nephthys, guide us through the afterlife's terrain.
In your presence, we find solace and trust,
Navigating the realms of the afterlife, we adjust.

Oh, gracious goddess, hear our plea,
Support us in the afterlife's vast sea.

With your guidance, we shall find our way,
In your embrace, forever we'll stay.

Nephthys, goddess of guidance and support,
We honor your presence, forever we'll exhort.
Thank you for your wisdom and loving embrace,
In the afterlife's journey, you provide us grace.

So mote it be.

49. Ritual of purification through the sacred chants of the eternal hymns

Step 1: Preparation

Find a serene and sacred space where you can perform the ritual without disturbance. Create an atmosphere of tranquility and reverence.
Light candles and burn incense to purify the environment and invoke a sacred ambiance.
Sit or stand in a comfortable position, grounding yourself and preparing your mind and body for the ritual ahead.

Step 2: Centering

Close your eyes and take several deep breaths, allowing yourself to become fully present in the moment.
Release any tension or distractions, letting go of the outside world and focusing solely on your inner self.
Imagine a divine light encompassing your being, purifying and cleansing you from within.

Step 3: Invocation

Begin by softly chanting a sacred hymn, invoking the presence of divine energies and spiritual guides.
Call upon the benevolent spirits and deities to witness and bless the ritual of purification.
Open your heart and mind to their guidance and assistance throughout the ritual.

Step 4: Chanting

Select a series of sacred chants or hymns that resonate with the intention of purification.
Chant the hymns with clarity, sincerity, and devotion. Let the vibrations of your voice penetrate deep within, purifying your spirit.
Allow the chants to create a harmonious energy that reverberates throughout your being, washing away impurities and negative energies.

Step 5: Visualization

As you continue chanting, visualize a radiant light descending upon you, enveloping your entire being.
See this light as a purifying force, washing away all impurities, doubts, and fears.
Imagine the light infusing you with divine energy, rejuvenating and restoring your spiritual essence.

Step 6: Release and Surrender

Let go of any attachments or burdens that no longer serve you. Release them into the sacred space, surrendering them to the divine forces.
As you chant, surrender yourself completely to the purification process, trusting in the transformative power of the sacred hymns.
Allow the vibrations of the chants to penetrate deeply within, cleansing your mind, body, and soul.

Step 7: Gratitude

Express gratitude to the divine forces, spiritual guides, and the universe for their presence and support during the ritual.
Acknowledge the purification that has taken place, feeling a sense of renewal and clarity.
Thank the sacred chants for their power to cleanse and uplift your spirit.

Step 8: Closure

Gradually reduce the intensity of the chanting, allowing the energy to settle and your mind to return to a state of calm.
Take a moment to ground yourself, feeling the connection between your physical body and the earth beneath you.
Express a closing prayer or affirmation, sealing the ritual and expressing your intention to carry the purification forward in your life.

Remember, this ritual is a sacred practice of purifying your spirit through the power of sacred chants and hymns. Approach it with reverence, focus, and sincerity, allowing the vibrations and intentions to transform and uplift your being. Embrace the purification process and welcome the renewal and clarity it brings to your spiritual journey.

50. Spell for the transformation of the deceased into a vessel of divine protection and guardianship

By the power of the ancient ones and the sacred forces that guide us, I invoke the divine presence to transform the departed soul into a vessel of divine protection and guardianship. May the spirit of the deceased rise and embrace its sacred purpose. Let the following words be spoken:

Oh, mighty guardians of the realms unseen,
I beseech thee to heed my plea.
Grant this departed soul your divine grace,
Transform them into a guardian of sacred space.

From the realm of mortal life, they have crossed,
Into the realm where divine energies are tossed.
Bestow upon them the strength of ancient lore,
To guard and protect forevermore.

Grant them the wisdom to discern right from wrong,
The courage to confront darkness strong.
In their vessel, let divine light reside,
Guiding and protecting, serving as their guide.

By the power of celestial forces above,
By the spirits of ancestors and gods we love,
I call upon you, sacred and true,
Transform this soul, let their purpose renew.

Let them rise as a guardian, fierce and bold,
A shield against evils, both new and old.
May their presence bring solace and peace,
May their guidance never cease.

With this spell, I weave the threads of protection,
Infusing the departed's essence with divine connection.
By the sacred laws that govern the astral plane,
Let their transformation be complete, devoid of bane.

So mote it be.

In the realm of the departed, let this spell take hold,
Empowering the deceased as a guardian bold.
May they fulfill their sacred role with devotion,
In service to divine protection and guardianship's notion.

Note: This spell is intended as a symbolic representation of transformation and guardianship. Its recitation should be approached with reverence and respect, calling upon the divine forces to guide and empower the departed soul as a vessel of divine protection and guardianship.

51. Incantation to invoke the blessings of the celestial rivers and their ever-flowing energy

As I stand here, a vessel of the mortal realm,
I call upon the celestial rivers, ancient and grand,
Flowing through the cosmos, across the celestial land,
With reverence and awe, I seek your blessings to command.

Oh, mighty rivers of the celestial sphere,
Your currents carry wisdom and powers revered,
Your eternal flow brings life and renewal near,
In your sacred waters, I find solace and hear.

I invoke the blessings of your ever-flowing stream,
Pour down upon me your celestial gleam,
Cleanse my spirit, make my soul beam,
With your divine energy, let my being teem.

From the celestial rivers, I seek your guidance,
Your currents hold secrets of cosmic providence,
Infuse my being with your sacred essence,
Grant me your blessings, your cosmic resonance.

May your waters cleanse and purify my soul,
Washing away all that hinders and takes its toll,
Renew my spirit, make me whole,
Let your energy within me take control.

Flow through me, celestial rivers, ever bright,
Ignite my spirit with your radiant light,
Guide me on this journey, day and night,
With your eternal wisdom, keep me in sight.

In your embrace, I find solace and peace,
Your blessings bring comfort, and my worries cease,
I offer my gratitude, my heart's release,
As I honor your power, may it never cease.

Celestial rivers, I thank you for your grace,
For the blessings bestowed in this sacred space,

May your ever-flowing energy forever embrace,
And guide me on my path with divine embrace.

So it is spoken, and so mote it be,
The blessings of the celestial rivers, I now decree,
With reverence and gratitude, I set them free,
Flowing through my spirit, for eternity.

Note: This incantation is a symbolic invocation of the blessings and energy of the celestial rivers. It is a call for their guidance, cleansing, and renewal. When reciting this incantation, it is important to visualize the majestic celestial rivers and feel their energy flowing through you, bringing forth their wisdom and blessings.

52. Ritual for the transfiguration of the deceased into a divine embodiment of sacred virtues

Step into the sacred realm of transformation,
Where the spirit transcends earthly limitations,
In this ritual, we shall invoke the divine,
To transfigure the deceased into a vessel refined.

Prepare the sacred space with reverence and care,
An altar adorned with symbols of virtues rare,
Place candles of purity, wisdom, and love,
Creating an ambiance, divine light from above.

Gather the sacred elements for this rite,
Crystals of clarity, herbs of spiritual might,
A chalice of consecrated water, pure and bright,
And incense to purify, guiding souls to new heights.

In the stillness of the chamber, let silence reign,
Invoke the presence of the divine to sustain,
With open hearts and minds, we now begin,
To transfigure the deceased, release them from sin.

Recite the ancient words, an invocation profound,
Calling upon the divine forces, in whispers resound,
"O, sacred spirits, guardians of virtue divine,
We beseech your guidance, let your light shine."

Light the candles, one by one, with reverence,
As the flames dance, invoking sacred presence,
Hold the crystals, charging them with intent,
To infuse the deceased with virtues heaven-sent.

Sprinkle consecrated water upon the altar,
Symbolizing purification, a spiritual starter,
Let the droplets fall upon the sacred ground,
Cleansing the deceased, their spirit unbound.

Ignite the incense, let its fragrance rise,
Carrying prayers heavenward, to the skies,
Waft the smoke around the sacred space,
Creating a veil, a connection to divine grace.

In the presence of the divine, speak with respect,
Address the deceased, their soul, reconnect,
"Beloved spirit, we honor your journey past,
Now transfigure, embody virtues that last."

Call forth the virtues, one by one, declare,
Compassion, courage, wisdom, and care,
Let these virtues infuse the deceased's soul,
Transfiguring their essence, making them whole.

Visualize the deceased shining with divine light,
Their form transfigured, radiant and bright,
Imbued with virtues, an embodiment divine,
Ready to guide and inspire, for all of time.

With gratitude and reverence, conclude the rite,
Expressing thanks to the divine, their eternal might,
Release the energy, let it disperse and flow,
Knowing the deceased's spirit is now aglow.

In this sacred ritual, the deceased is transformed,
Into a divine embodiment, their virtues adorned,
May their spirit guide and inspire all who see,
The transfiguration of the deceased, in eternity.

Note: This ritual is a symbolic practice to honor the deceased and invoke the divine forces to transfigure their spirit into an embodiment of sacred virtues. It is essential to approach this ritual with sincerity, reverence, and a genuine desire to honor and elevate the departed soul.

53. Spell for the reunion of the deceased's soul with their spiritual mentors and teachers

In the realm between worlds, where spirits dwell,
We seek to bridge the gap, where truths do tell,
With utmost respect and reverence, we gather here,
To call upon the spiritual mentors we hold dear.

In the sacred space, where energies align,
We invoke the spirits, wise and divine,
With love in our hearts and a focused mind,
We call upon their presence, seeking guidance kind.

Gather the tools of this sacred rite,
A candle, a photo, or an object of sight,
A piece of paper and a writing implement too,
To call forth the spirits, to connect and imbue.

Light the candle with a steady hand,
Let its flame be a beacon in this enchanted land,
Gaze upon the photo or object with intent,
Visualize the spiritual mentors, their wisdom sent.

Inscribe their names upon the paper's surface,
The mentors and teachers, who left an indelible purpose,
Write with reverence and gratitude, your intention clear,
To reunite with their wisdom, now and here.

Speak the names aloud, with reverence and care,
Calling upon their spirits, knowing they are near,
"O, spiritual mentors, guides of light,
We seek your wisdom, in this sacred night."

Close your eyes and take a deep breath in,
Feel the presence of their spirits, let the connection begin,
Visualize a doorway, opening wide,
A bridge between realms, where spirits reside.

With sincerity and respect, speak your truth,
Express your longing to reunite, to gain their reproof,
"Beloved mentors, teachers dear,
I seek your guidance, your wisdom so clear.
Reunite with me in this sacred space,
Share your knowledge, your divine grace."

Feel the energy shift, the connection ignite,
As their spirits respond to your heartfelt invite,
Sense their presence around you, their energy strong,
Guiding you forward, where you belong.

Listen carefully, in the stillness of the night,
For whispers of wisdom, shining like a light,
Receive their messages, their guidance pure,
As the reunion unfolds, your spirit will endure.

Express gratitude for their presence profound,
For the reunion of souls, in sacred ground,
Thank them for their teachings, their love, and care,
Knowing they are with you, even when unaware.

Release the energy, with love and grace,
Thanking the mentors for their divine embrace,
Extinguish the candle, with gratitude and respect,
Knowing their guidance will forever protect.

In this spell, we seek the reunion divine,
With spiritual mentors and teachers, a union so fine,
May their wisdom guide us, now and always,
As we honor their presence, in these mystic days.

Note: This spell is a symbolic practice to honor and seek guidance from spiritual mentors and teachers who have passed away. It is essential to approach this spell with reverence, sincerity, and a genuine desire to connect with their wisdom. Adapt the spell as needed, incorporating personal beliefs and cultural traditions to make it meaningful and respectful. Remember to always exercise caution and discernment when engaging in spiritual practices.

54. Invocation of the god Thoth for wisdom and understanding in the afterlife

In the realm of the beyond, where mysteries unfold,
We call upon the mighty Thoth, wise and bold,
With pen in hand and mind so keen,
Guide us in the afterlife, where knowledge is seen.

Oh, Thoth, the scribe of the gods, we implore,
Your wisdom and insight we seek to explore,
With reverence and respect, we invoke your name,
Grant us the understanding that will forever remain.

Mighty Thoth, the god of knowledge and thought,
Your presence we summon, with words well-wrought,
From the sacred depths of the cosmic sea,
Illuminate our minds and set our spirits free.

By the power of your divine essence, we beseech,
Open the gates of wisdom, within our reach,
Grant us clarity and insight in this sacred space,
As we navigate the realms of the afterlife's grace.

Oh, Thoth, the architect of cosmic design,
Guide us with your wisdom, so sublime,
Bestow upon us the gift of discernment,
To comprehend the secrets of life's eternal ascent.

As the scribe of the gods, your words hold sway,
Inscribe upon our souls the wisdom of the day,
Grant us understanding of the mysteries profound,
As we traverse the realms where knowledge is found.

Oh, Thoth, the mediator between worlds unseen,
Guide us on our journey, as we seek to glean,
The profound truths hidden in the cosmic tapestry,
Grant us the wisdom to navigate this vast mystery.

In your divine presence, we find solace and light,
Dispelling ignorance and guiding us to the right,

Oh, Thoth, the god of wisdom and insight,
Bless us with your knowledge, both day and night.

We honor you, Thoth, with reverence and awe,
For the wisdom you bestow, without a flaw,
Guide us through the afterlife's intricate scheme,
And lead us to the realms where wisdom gleams.

With gratitude in our hearts, we bid you farewell,
Knowing that your wisdom will forever dwell,
In the depths of our souls, as we continue our quest,
In the afterlife's embrace, where knowledge is blessed.

Note: This invocation is a symbolic and reverential practice to seek the guidance and wisdom of the god Thoth. It is essential to approach it with respect and sincerity. Adapt the invocation as needed, incorporating personal beliefs and cultural traditions to make it meaningful and authentic. Remember to always exercise discernment and humility when seeking wisdom from the divine.

55. Ritual of anointing with sacred herbs for spiritual healing and renewal

In this sacred ritual, we invoke the power of nature's healing gifts,
Using sacred herbs to cleanse, heal, and uplift our spirits.
With reverence and intention, we embark on this journey of renewal,
Embracing the healing energies that these herbs bestow upon us.

Prepare yourself and the sacred space for this ritual,
Creating an atmosphere of tranquility and reverence.
Gather the following sacred herbs that resonate with healing properties:
Lavender for relaxation and clarity,
Rosemary for purification and protection,
Sage for cleansing and releasing,
Chamomile for soothing and inner peace.

Create a small altar where you will place the herbs,
Arranging them in a way that feels harmonious and sacred.
Light a candle or incense to signify the sacredness of the space,
And to invite the presence of divine healing energies.

Take a moment to center yourself and connect with your breath,
Allowing any tension or distractions to melt away.
Set your intention for this ritual of anointing and healing,
Whether it be physical, emotional, or spiritual renewal.

Hold the first sacred herb in your hands, feeling its energy,
And speak words of gratitude and reverence for its healing properties.
Invoke the spirit of the herb, calling upon its healing essence,
To cleanse, heal, and renew your being.

Take the herb and gently rub it between your palms,
Releasing its aroma and essence into the air.
Bring your hands close to your face and take a deep breath,
Allowing the healing scent to fill your senses.

Now, begin anointing your body with the sacred herb,
Starting from the crown of your head and moving downward.
As you anoint each part of your body, visualize the healing energy,
Penetrating your being, bringing restoration and renewal.

Repeat this process with each sacred herb,
Honoring their unique healing properties and essence.
As you anoint yourself, you may choose to recite affirmations,
Affirming your healing and renewal in body, mind, and spirit.

Take your time with this ritual, allowing the healing energies,
To work their magic upon you, bringing balance and restoration.
When you have completed the anointing, take a moment to sit in stillness,
Feeling the effects of the sacred herbs and their healing vibrations.

Express gratitude to the divine, the herbs, and yourself,
For engaging in this sacred ritual of healing and renewal.
Extinguish the candle or incense, closing the ritual with reverence,
And carry the energy of healing and renewal with you, always.

Remember, this ritual is a personal and symbolic practice,
To connect with the healing energies of sacred herbs.
Feel free to adapt and modify it to suit your beliefs and needs,
And may it bring you profound healing and spiritual renewal.

56. Spell for the liberation of the deceased's soul from the attachments of earthly desires

In the realm beyond, where the soul journeys forth,
Bound by the chains of earthly desires it may be.
With this sacred spell, we seek liberation and release,
Freeing the departed from attachments that hinder its ascent.

Gather in a sacred space, serene and hallowed,
Where the energies of the divine may be invoked.
Light a white candle, symbolizing purity and enlightenment,
And call upon the spirits of the ancients for guidance.

Speak the words with intention, from the depths of your being,
Allowing their power to resonate through the realms.
Utter them with clarity and unwavering focus,
As you beseech the universe for the liberation of the departed.

"By the ancient forces that govern the cosmos,
I beseech thee, O divine spirits, to hear my plea.
Release the departed soul from earthly attachments,
That it may soar freely and embrace its true destiny."

Visualize the departed soul, bound by ethereal chains,
Ensnared by desires that cling tightly to its essence.
See these chains dissolve and disperse into the cosmic winds,
As the soul is liberated from their constricting grasp.

"Let go of all desires that bind and confine,
Be free, O soul, from attachments of earthly kind.
Embrace the path of enlightenment and transcendence,
And ascend to the realms of eternal existence."

Sense the energy shifting, as the spell takes effect,
Witnessing the soul's liberation and newfound freedom.
Feel a sense of lightness and liberation within your own being,
As you play a part in the soul's journey toward transcendence.

Thank the spirits for their guidance and assistance,
Expressing gratitude for their presence and blessings.

Extinguish the candle, symbolizing the completion of the spell,
And trust in the power of divine forces to bring liberation.

Remember, this spell is a sacred act of liberation,
A call to release the departed from earthly attachments.
Approach it with respect, purity of intention, and reverence,
And may it guide the soul to a realm of eternal peace and liberation.

57. Incantation to awaken the dormant spiritual wisdom within the deceased's spirit

In the realm of shadows, where spirits dwell,
I call upon the ancient wisdom that sleeps within.
By the power of divine light and celestial grace,
I awaken the dormant wisdom in the departed's spirit.

Gather in a sacred space, free from distractions,
Where the veil between worlds is thin and permeable.
Light a candle, representing the illumination of truth,
And invoke the presence of the divine and ancestral spirits.

With a voice steady and filled with reverence,
Speak the incantation, letting its essence resonate.
Let the words flow forth with clarity and intention,
As you awaken the dormant wisdom in the departed.

"Spirit of the departed, hear my call,
Awaken from slumber, arise from the depths.
Unveil the wisdom that lies dormant within,
Let it shine forth with brilliance and clarity."

Feel the energy shift, as the incantation weaves its spell,
Stirring the dormant wisdom within the departed's spirit.
Sense the ancient knowledge awakening, like a slumbering flame,
Growing brighter and fiercer with each recited verse.

"As the sun rises and illuminates the day,
So shall your wisdom shine and guide the way.
Break the chains of forgetfulness and confusion,
Embrace the knowledge that brings spiritual fusion."

Visualize the departed's spirit bathed in radiant light,
As the dormant wisdom awakens and flourishes within.
See the brilliance of their spirit, shining with insight,
As they reclaim their innate connection to divine wisdom.

Express gratitude to the spirits and deities invoked,
For their guidance and assistance in this sacred endeavor.

Blow out the candle, symbolizing the completion of the ritual,
And trust that the awakened wisdom will guide the departed.

May the dormant spiritual wisdom within the departed's spirit
Awaken and illuminate their journey in the realms beyond.
May it bring clarity, guidance, and profound understanding,
As they traverse the eternal realms with enlightened grace.

58. Ritual for the communion with the spirits of the celestial birds and their celestial melodies

Prepare a sacred space adorned with symbols of the celestial realms,
Where the veil between worlds is thin, and spirits freely roam.
Create an altar with offerings of gratitude and reverence,
Inviting the spirits of the celestial birds to join your sacred ceremony.

Light fragrant incense, carrying your intentions to the heavens,
As its smoke weaves a bridge between the earthly and divine.
Invoke the presence of the celestial birds with a humble heart,
Requesting their guidance and the gift of their celestial melodies.

Stand tall, grounding your energy deep into the earth,
As you raise your arms and open your heart to the skies above.
With eyes closed, breathe in the celestial essence surrounding you,
And feel the presence of the celestial birds drawing near.

Begin to sway gently, allowing your body to sway with the rhythm,
As the celestial melodies resound within the depths of your being.
Imagine your spirit taking flight on ethereal wings,
Guided by the harmonious songs of the celestial birds.

With each movement and step, emulate the grace and beauty of the birds,
As you honor their celestial essence and wisdom they impart.
Let their melodies penetrate your soul, awakening ancient memories,
And connecting you to the celestial realms where they freely soar.

In this sacred dance of communion, allow yourself to be carried away,
Lost in the enchanting melodies and the presence of the celestial birds.
Feel their feathers brush against your skin, their songs echoing in your ears,
As they share their celestial blessings and wisdom with your spirit.

Offer gratitude for the communion and the wisdom received,
Knowing that the celestial birds will continue to guide your journey.
Take a moment to sit in silence, feeling the echoes of their melodies,
And integrating their celestial energy deep within your being.

As you close the ritual, express gratitude to the spirits of the celestial birds,
For their presence, guidance, and the celestial melodies they shared.
Release any remaining energy to the heavens with a final prayer,
And trust that the wisdom and blessings received will continue to guide you.

In the communion with the spirits of the celestial birds and their celestial melodies,
May your spirit soar to new heights and your soul be uplifted by their divine wisdom.
May their celestial songs resonate within your being,
As you journey on the path of spiritual growth and enlightenment.

59. Spell for the transmigration of the deceased's soul into the realm of eternal bliss and happiness

Gather in a sacred space, where the veil between worlds is thin,
Where spirits dance and the energies of the divine flow within.
Light a candle, casting its gentle glow upon the sacred altar,
Creating a beacon to guide the departed soul towards eternal bliss.

Take a moment to center your being, grounding your energy to the earth,
As you prepare to perform this sacred spell of transmigration and rebirth.
Close your eyes and envision the soul of the departed before you,
Radiant and ready to embark on its journey to the realm of eternal bliss.

With focused intention, speak the sacred words with reverence and clarity:
"O departed soul, hear my voice and heed my call,
I beseech the divine powers to guide you, one and all.
Through the veil of existence, to realms of pure light,
May your journey be swift, guided by celestial might."

Visualize a path of light unfolding, leading the departed soul towards the heavens,
Illuminated by the stars, and embraced by celestial beings as its guardians.
See the soul transcending the limitations of the earthly realm,
Soaring towards the realm of eternal bliss and happiness.

Extend your hands towards the heavens, palms open and receptive,
As you continue the incantation, invoking the powers divine:
"Angels and spirits, guide this soul with grace,
Lead it to realms of eternal joy and embrace.
Release it from earthly chains and desires' strife,
Let it bask in eternal bliss, free from mortal life."

Feel the energy of the sacred words resonate within your being,
As you infuse the spell with your heartfelt intentions and purest belief.
Hold space for the departed soul, allowing it to ascend and transcend,
Leaving behind all sorrows and burdens, entering a realm of eternal serenity.

As the spell concludes, express gratitude to the divine forces above,
For their assistance in guiding the departed soul towards eternal love.

Release the energy and intention into the universe's infinite expanse,
Trusting that the soul is now embraced by eternal bliss and happiness.

With the completion of this spell, may the departed soul find eternal peace,
Bathed in the radiance of celestial light, and enveloped in divine release.
May its journey be filled with joy, love, and boundless happiness,
As it transcends into the realm of eternal bliss and sublime oneness.

60. Invocation of the goddess Nut for protection and guidance in the afterlife

In this sacred space, where realms converge,
I call upon the Goddess Nut, mighty and sublime,
Mother of the heavens, protector of souls,
I beseech your presence, O goddess divine.

Goddess Nut, whose celestial body spans the sky,
With stars as adornments, shimmering and high,
Wrap your wings around the departed soul,
Guide and protect, as it embarks on its celestial roll.

Mistress of eternity, with arms outstretched,
Embrace the soul, keep it safe and eternally fetched,
Shield it from harm and all malevolent forces,
In your divine embrace, let it find its rightful courses.

With reverence and respect, I invoke your name,
Goddess Nut, guardian of the celestial flame,
In this sacred invocation, I call upon your might,
To watch over the departed in their ethereal flight.

Grant them guidance through the astral expanse,
Illuminate their path, with your cosmic dance,
Guide them towards their destined place,
In the afterlife's realm, filled with divine grace.

Goddess Nut, with your wisdom and insight,
Bestow upon the departed soul, your celestial light,
Wrap them in your love and nurturing care,
As they navigate the realms beyond earthly fare.

In this sacred space, I offer my devotion,
To the Goddess Nut, with profound emotion,
May the departed soul find solace in your embrace,
Protected and guided in the eternal cosmic chase.

With gratitude and reverence, I honor your divine essence,
Goddess Nut, in you, I find solace and presence,

Thank you for your eternal protection and guidance,
In the afterlife's realm, may the soul find transcendence.

As I speak these words, I offer my heartfelt plea,
Goddess Nut, hear my invocation and set the soul free,
With your blessings and watchful eye,
May the departed find peace, as the stars light up the sky.

61. Ritual of purification through the sacred rituals of the eternal priesthood

In this sacred space, where time and spirit align,
We gather as vessels of the divine,
Through the ancient rituals of the eternal priesthood,
We seek purification and spiritual fortitude.

In preparation for this sacred rite,
We cleanse ourselves, body, mind, and sight,
With pure water, we wash away impurity,
Symbolic of the cleansing power of divinity.

Clothed in white, a symbol of purity and light,
We step into the role of the priestly rite,
With reverence and devotion, we begin,
To purify ourselves from within.

First, we invoke the presence of the divine,
Through prayers and invocations, we align,
Connecting with the ancient wisdom of the ages,
Seeking guidance from the immortal sages.

Next, we light the sacred incense, aromatic and pure,
Its smoke rising, carrying our intentions to the ethereal allure,
As we inhale its fragrance, we purify our breath,
Releasing all negativity, making way for spiritual depth.

The ritual tools are carefully arranged,
Symbols of power, wisdom, and change,
We consecrate them with sacred oil,
Infusing them with the divine's eternal coil.

Now, the purification ritual truly begins,
With sacred gestures and ancient hymns,
We move in harmony, invoking the sacred flame,
Cleansing ourselves of doubt and shame.

The sacred dance, rhythmic and profound,
Expresses the soul's journey, unbound,

Through fluid movements, we release and renew,
Finding solace and purpose in all that we do.

As the ritual reaches its climactic phase,
We offer prayers of gratitude and praise,
For the opportunity to commune with the divine,
To purify our spirits and realign.

In this sacred space, we leave behind,
The weight of the world, the troubles that bind,
With hearts filled with reverence and awe,
We emerge, transformed, and in spiritual awe.

May this ritual of purification be our guide,
As we navigate life's ebb and tide,
In the footsteps of the eternal priesthood,
We seek purification, wisdom, and spiritual livelihood.

With gratitude for the blessings received,
We carry the sacred flame, forever relieved,
Knowing that through these rituals divine,
We find unity, purity, and eternal shrine.

62. Spell for the transformation of the deceased into a vessel of divine light and illumination

By the powers of the cosmos, both seen and unseen,
I invoke the divine light, pure and serene,
In this sacred moment, I call upon the divine,
To transform the departed into a vessel of light, sublime.

From the depths of darkness, the soul shall ascend,
Embracing the radiance that knows no end,
With every breath and every beat of the heart,
The divine light within the deceased shall start.

O radiant light, shine upon this soul,
Illuminate their being, make them whole,
Banish the shadows that linger within,
And let the divine essence truly begin.

From the earthly constraints, they are set free,
To embrace the light, to become what they're meant to be,
A vessel of illumination, a beacon of grace,
Guiding others on their spiritual chase.

Let the divine light cleanse every part,
Mind, body, and spirit, transformed by this art,
Ignite the inner flame, awaken the divine spark,
Reveal the truth within, shining through the dark.

With every step taken in the afterlife's domain,
Let the light of wisdom guide and sustain,
In this transformation, the soul shall find,
A radiant existence, leaving all darkness behind.

So mote it be, with reverence and might,
May this spell bring forth the divine light,
May the deceased be embraced by the luminous glow,
Forever radiant, as above, so below.

As the words of this spell resound in the air,
May the transformation unfold, beyond all compare,
The deceased, now a vessel of divine light,
Radiating love, truth, and wisdom, shining bright.

In the realm of eternal existence, they shall dwell,
Embracing the divine light's enchanting spell,
Transformed, illuminated, forever sublime,
As a vessel of divine light for all time.

Note: This spell is intended as a symbolic invocation and should be performed with respect and reverence for the deceased.

63. Incantation to invoke the blessings of the celestial moon and its gentle guidance

By the powers of the night, in the celestial sphere,
I call upon the moon, radiant and clear,
With its gentle glow and soothing light,
May its blessings guide me through the darkest night.

Oh, celestial moon, with your tranquil embrace,
Shower me with your wisdom and grace,
As you wax and wane in the vast expanse,
Bestow upon me your gentle guidance and chance.

In the hushed stillness of the midnight hour,
I seek your presence, your celestial power,
Illuminate my path, reveal what's concealed,
With your luminous energy, my fate shall be revealed.

Oh, lunar goddess, with your gentle face,
Guide me through life's ever-changing pace,
Your cycles reflect the ebb and flow of life,
Teach me the lessons hidden within strife.

In your crescent, I find hope and renewal,
In your fullness, I find inspiration, so beautiful,
Your gentle guidance calms the restless mind,
Bringing clarity and peace, serenely intertwined.

Oh, celestial moon, in your ethereal glow,
Unveil the secrets that only you know,
Bless me with your intuitive sight,
As I journey through the ebony night.

With each phase you assume, your influence flows,
A beacon of solace, wherever one goes,
Your gentle guidance whispers in the breeze,
Embracing me with celestial ease.

Oh, celestial moon, I honor your might,
Guide me through the shadows, shining bright,

As I walk this earthly realm below,
With your blessings, my spirit shall grow.

In the soft radiance of your silvery beams,
I find solace, as in a nocturnal dream,
By your gentle guidance, I am inspired,
To navigate life's journey, fueled and fired.

Celestial moon, I offer my reverence and praise,
For your blessings that grace my nights and days,
Guide me, protect me, with your celestial light,
And fill my spirit with peace, throughout the night.

By the power of this incantation, may I align,
With the celestial moon, a presence so divine,
Grant me your gentle guidance, as I traverse,
Through life's phases, with reverence and purpose.

So mote it be, as above, so below,
The blessings of the celestial moon, may they bestow,
Upon my soul, this sacred connection,
Forever embraced, in celestial reflection.

Note: This incantation is a symbolic invocation of the moon's energy and should be recited with reverence and respect for the celestial forces.

64. Ritual for the transfiguration of the deceased into a divine conduit of divine messages

Prepare yourself for this sacred rite,
A ritual of transfiguration, merging dark and light,
Find a tranquil space, free from worldly noise,
Where the veil between realms is poised.

Create an altar adorned with symbols divine,
Representing the sacred, the mystical, the sublime,
Candles flickering, casting a soft glow,
Invoking spirits, both high and low.

Bathe yourself in pure water, cleansing and pure,
Let it wash away all that may obscure,
The connection to realms beyond this plane,
Where divine messages flow, without restrain.

Clothe yourself in garments of white,
Symbolizing purity and spiritual sight,
As you step into the liminal space,
Embrace the transformative embrace.

Invoke the guardians of the sacred gate,
Request their presence, their guidance so great,
Call upon the ancient spirits, wise and old,
To witness this rite, their power to unfold.

With focused intent and steady breath,
Enter into a trance, transcending life's depth,
Let go of the self, surrender to the flow,
As the divine presence begins to show.

In this state of heightened awareness,
Open yourself to receive with readiness,
Allow the deceased to merge with your soul,
Their essence blending, making you whole.

Feel their energy intertwine with yours,
Their wisdom and love, through spirit's doors,
As you become a conduit, a vessel divine,
Messages from realms beyond, align.

Words will flow, inspired and true,
As the deceased speaks through you,
Their messages of guidance and grace,
Shared with those in need, seeking solace.

Speak the words with clarity and care,
Allow the divine messages to ripple and share,
With love and compassion, convey their intent,
Guiding others, their spirits gently sent.

When the transmission is complete,
Thank the spirits for their presence, so sweet,
Close the ritual with gratitude and respect,
For the connection established, a sacred effect.

Return to the realm of the living, aware,
That you are now a divine conduit, rare,
Embrace this role with reverence and might,
Bringing forth messages of love and light.

Note: This ritual is a symbolic representation of the transfiguration of the deceased into a conduit of divine messages. It should be performed with utmost respect and sincerity, honoring the spirits involved and their messages.

65. Spell for the reunion of the deceased's soul with their spiritual allies and guardians

In this sacred space, I stand,
Seeking the presence of spirits grand,
With love and reverence, I call upon thee,
Allies and guardians, come to me.

From realms unseen and worlds afar,
Answer my call, guiding star,
Ancient spirits, wise and true,
I summon you now, to this rendezvous.

Gather around, my dear allies,
Bring forth your wisdom, let it arise,
Guardians of light, protectors divine,
Unite with the deceased, their soul entwined.

By the power of the sacred bond we share,
I beckon you, spirits, to be aware,
In this hallowed space, a reunion unfolds,
A merging of energies, as destiny beholds.

Bring forth your strength, your wisdom and might,
Guide the deceased through eternal night,
Let their soul find solace and peace,
In the loving embrace of spiritual release.

Together we form a sacred circle,
Bound by love, trust, and miracles,
Unite the realms, bridge the divide,
Let our energies intertwine and coincide.

Oh, guardians of the unseen,
Grant the deceased the solace they've been,
Guide them home, to realms sublime,
Where love and light eternally chime.

Open the gates, reveal the way,
To spiritual allies, let them sway,

May their presence be felt, their voices heard,
As the reunion unfolds, through the sacred word.

By the power vested in me,
By ancient wisdom, so mote it be,
May the reunion be blessed and true,
In the embrace of love, we now renew.

As the incantation fades away,
I release the spirits, with gratitude, I say,
Thank you for your presence, divine and kind,
Until we meet again, in realms aligned.

Note: This spell is performed with the intention to reunite the deceased's soul with their spiritual allies and guardians. It should be approached with respect and a genuine desire for the highest good of the departed.

66. Invocation of the god Horus for strength and courage in the afterlife

Mighty Horus, Falcon of the Sky,
I call upon your presence, drawing nigh.
With reverence and awe, I invoke your name,
Grant me strength and courage, I humbly claim.

Horus, son of Osiris and Isis divine,
Embodying the sun, your light shall shine.
Protector of pharaohs, guardian of the land,
Guide me through the afterlife, with a steady hand.

Winged god of power, your eyes see all,
In times of darkness, may your light not fall.
Grant me strength to face the challenges ahead,
To navigate the realms where spirits tread.

In your wings, I seek refuge and protection,
In your wisdom, I find divine direction.
Grant me the fortitude to overcome fear,
And the courage to persevere, my path to clear.

Horus, falcon-headed deity so grand,
Extend your mighty wings, where I stand.
Infuse me with your divine strength and might,
As I embark on this afterlife's sacred flight.

Fill my heart with the bravery of your gaze,
Let your courage guide me through the haze.
Empower me to face the trials that I may face,
With your blessings, I shall navigate with grace.

As I journey through the realms unseen,
May your presence be my eternal serene.
Horus, I call upon you, O god of the sky,
With your strength and courage, let my spirit fly.

So mote it be, in the name of Horus divine,
May his strength and courage forever intertwine.

I offer my gratitude for your sacred aid,
In the afterlife's journey, may I never be swayed.

Note: This invocation is performed to seek the strength and courage of the god
Horus in the afterlife. It should be conducted with respect and sincerity,
acknowledging the divine nature of Horus and his role as a guide and protector.

67. Ritual of anointing with sacred crystals for spiritual clarity and insight

Gathered here in this sacred space,
I seek the blessings of divine grace.
With crystals in hand, their energy pure,
I embark on a ritual to cleanse and restore.

In reverence, I hold each crystal dear,
Their essence radiant, shining clear.
I choose them with intention, aligned with my quest,
To bring forth clarity, and divine wisdom manifest.

First, the Amethyst, a stone of spiritual sight,
I anoint it with reverence, embracing its light.
Its purple hue, a gateway to higher realms,
Infusing my being with celestial helms.

Next, the Clear Quartz, a master healer supreme,
I anoint it gently, as in a sacred dream.
Its transparent beauty, a conduit divine,
Amplifying my intentions, aligning with the sublime.

Now, the Lapis Lazuli, a symbol of truth,
I anoint it with reverence, in eternal youth.
Its deep blue hue, a connection to the divine,
Unveiling insights, with clarity, I now align.

The Rose Quartz, a stone of love and compassion,
I anoint it tenderly, invoking divine passion.
Its gentle pink essence, a soothing balm,
Opening my heart, bringing inner calm.

Lastly, the Citrine, a stone of abundance and light,
I anoint it with reverence, shining ever bright.
Its golden glow, a beacon of inner knowing,
Illuminating my path, with wisdom growing.

With crystals anointed, their energies aligned,
I hold them close, their vibrations entwined.

I breathe in their essence, feeling their power,
As clarity and insight now start to flower.

In this ritual of anointing, I embrace,
The sacred crystals' energy, filling this space.
May their vibrations guide me, with wisdom profound,
As I walk the path of enlightenment, ever unbound.

Note: This ritual is performed to seek spiritual clarity and insight using the energy of sacred crystals. Each crystal mentioned in the ritual holds specific properties that can support the desired intention. The anointing process is a symbolic act of imbuing the crystals with one's intentions and connecting with their energies. It is important to choose crystals that resonate with you personally and to perform the ritual with reverence and respect for their spiritual significance.

68. Incantation to awaken the dormant spiritual powers within the deceased's spirit

O spirit of the departed, hear my call,
Awaken from slumber, rise and stand tall.
Within your essence lies dormant might,
Unleash your powers, embrace the light.

From realms unseen, I summon your soul,
With this incantation, I make you whole.
Arise, oh spirit, with strength and grace,
Embrace your potential, in this sacred space.

Ignite the fire within, let it burn bright,
Awaken the powers, both day and night.
Channel the energy, let it flow through,
Unleash your gifts, as I command you.

Open the gates to realms unknown,
Let your spirit soar, to heights yet shown.
Tap into wisdom from ages past,
Embrace the powers that forever last.

Awaken the sight of the inner eye,
Perceive the truth, let illusions die.
Sense the energy, both subtle and grand,
Harness your powers, take hold of your hand.

Embrace the gifts that lie deep inside,
Let them emerge, with nothing to hide.
With every breath, let your spirit soar,
Awakened and empowered, forevermore.

By the ancient forces, this spell is cast,
Awakening the dormant powers amassed.
Let the deceased's spirit shine and thrive,
As they awaken within, fully alive.

Note: This incantation is recited with the intention of awakening the dormant
spiritual powers within the deceased's spirit. It is crucial to approach this incantation

with respect and reverence, recognizing the individual journey and free will of the departed soul. The incantation calls upon the energy of the universe and higher realms to support the awakening process. It is essential to perform this incantation with pure intentions and an understanding of the responsibility that comes with harnessing spiritual powers.

69. Ritual for the communion with the spirits of the celestial rivers and their sacred currents

Prepare yourself for the sacred communion,
With celestial rivers, their currents in motion.
Find a tranquil space near flowing water,
Where spirits converge, as if drawn by an altar.

Create an offering of reverence and devotion,
To honor the spirits and elicit their emotion.
Gather petals of flowers, colorful and pure,
Symbolizing unity and the spirits' allure.

Stand by the riverbank, feet in the water's flow,
Connect with the energy, let your essence grow.
Close your eyes, breathe in the gentle breeze,
Feel the spirits' presence, as the water eases.

Recite the incantation, words whispered with care,
Calling upon the spirits, their guidance to share:
"O spirits of the rivers, hear my plea,
Come forth and commune, reveal thy mystery.
Let your sacred currents flow through my soul,
Grant me wisdom, as your secrets unfold."

Open your heart and mind to the spirits' embrace,
Feel their presence surround you, their love and grace.
Listen to the whispers carried by the water's song,
As the spirits speak to you, ancient and strong.

Dip your hands into the river's gentle stream,
Feel the sacred currents, like a divine dream.
Let the water cleanse and purify your being,
As you merge with the spirits, their essence freeing.

Offer your petals to the river's gentle tide,
A token of gratitude, let your love abide.
Watch as the petals float away with the flow,

Symbolizing unity, as above, so below.

Sit in quiet contemplation, a moment of reflection,
Absorb the wisdom shared in this sacred connection.
Thank the spirits for their presence and guidance,
As you conclude this ritual with reverence and subsidence.

Remember, this ritual for communion with the spirits of the celestial rivers is a sacred practice, requiring respect and intention. Approach it with humility and an open heart, honoring the spirits and their currents. May their wisdom and blessings flow through you, guiding you on your spiritual journey.

70. Spell for the transmigration of the deceased's soul into the realm of eternal love and compassion

In this sacred space, where worlds converge,
I call upon the powers, gentle and pure.
With heartfelt words, this spell I cast,
To guide the departed, their journey vast.

Oh, spirits of love, compassion, and grace,
I beseech you now, in this sacred place.
Wrap the departed in your tender embrace,
Guide them to the realm of eternal solace.

Let love be their guide, a guiding light,
As they traverse the realms, day and night.
Surround them with compassion, gentle and true,
In their transmigration, let love imbue.

Grant them peace, free from sorrow and pain,
In the realm of love, let them forever remain.
May their spirit be uplifted, their heart set free,
In the realm of compassion, eternally.

With each breath they take, let love expand,
Enveloping their being, like a gentle hand.
May their soul be nourished, by love's sweet song,
In the realm of compassion, where they belong.

Release them from attachments, burdens released,
In the realm of love, let their spirit find peace.
Guide them to the realm of eternal bliss,
Where love and compassion forever persist.

By the power of love, this spell is done,
As above, so below, let it be spun.
In the realm of love and compassion's embrace,
May the departed find their eternal resting place.

As you speak these words with intention and reverence,
May the spell unfold with divine benevolence.
May the departed soul find solace and eternal love,
In the realm of compassion, guided from above.

Remember, this spell is offered with respect and love,
A gift to aid the departed in their journey above.
May it bring comfort and peace to those who mourn,
As the soul transcends, into love's eternal morn.

71. Invocation of the goddess Ma'at for truth and justice in the afterlife

Oh, great Goddess Ma'at, embodiment of truth,
In this sacred moment, I call upon you.
Guide us through the realms of the afterlife,
With your scales of justice, free from strife.

Goddess of balance, your presence we seek,
In this invocation, your wisdom we speak.
Bring forth the truth, with your feather in hand,
Let justice prevail in the eternal land.

Oh, Ma'at, daughter of Ra, shining and bright,
Your light illuminates the darkest night.
With your wings unfurled, and your heart so pure,
Bring forth justice, our souls assure.

In the afterlife's realm, where spirits reside,
We seek your guidance, as we turn the tide.
May truth prevail, falsehoods be unveiled,
Let justice prevail, as your name is hailed.

Goddess of order, of harmony and right,
We invoke your presence, with all our might.
Banish deceit and bring forth clarity,
In the afterlife's realm, let truth be the key.

May the scales of justice be ever aligned,
In the realm of Ma'at, truth's light will shine.
Guide the departed with your divine hand,
To find their place in the eternal sand.

Oh, Ma'at, goddess of truth and justice fair,
We invoke your presence, with utmost care.
Bring balance and righteousness to the departed,
As they journey through the realms, uncharted.

As we speak these words, with reverence and devotion,
May Ma'at's essence flow, with utmost emotion.

In the afterlife's realm, let truth reign supreme,
With Ma'at's guidance, justice is the redeem.

Oh, Ma'at, we thank you for your eternal grace,
In the afterlife's realm, you hold a sacred space.
Guide us with truth, as we seek your light,
In the realm of justice, may we find what's right.

By the power of Ma'at, this invocation is done,
In the afterlife's realm, let justice be won.
With gratitude and reverence, we honor your name,
Oh, great Goddess Ma'at, forever may you reign.

72. Ritual of purification through the sacred dances of the eternal rhythm

In the realm of sacred dances, where rhythms intertwine,
We gather here to purify, to cleanse our spirits divine.
Through movements fluid and graceful, our souls take flight,
In this ritual of purification, guided by the eternal light.

Step into the sacred space, where music fills the air,
Feel the rhythm pulsating, flowing through your being, aware.
Let your body become an instrument, a vessel of expression,
As we embark on this journey of cleansing and progression.

Begin by centering yourself, grounding in the present moment,
Close your eyes, breathe deeply, feeling divine energy potent.
Visualize a pure light surrounding you, cleansing and renewing,
As you open yourself to the dance, your spirit it is pursuing.

With the first beat of the drum, let your body come alive,
Feel the rhythm in your limbs, let it guide you, let it drive.
Release the tensions of the day, let go of all that weighs,
Through the sacred dances, you'll find a sacred place.

As you sway and twirl, feel the purifying power grow,
Each movement a prayer, a cleansing flow.
Let the dance carry you, releasing all that is impure,
Embrace the sacredness of this dance, let your spirit soar.

With each step, imagine negativity being swept away,
Leaving you purified, renewed, in this rhythmic display.
Let your body become a channel of divine light,
As you dance, you are transmuted, shining ever bright.

As the music evolves, let your movements evolve too,
Express the depths of your soul, let your true self shine through.
Dance with passion, dance with devotion, dance with grace,
In this ritual of purification, let love's essence embrace.

As the music reaches its climax, slow your movements down,
Let the energy settle, as the sacred dances crown.

Stand tall, bask in the radiance of your purified being,
In this moment of stillness, feel the divine presence freeing.

Take a deep breath, gratitude in your heart,
For the cleansing and purification this dance imparts.
Know that you are now transformed, renewed, and whole,
Embracing the sacred dances, body, mind, and soul.

In the sacred dances of the eternal rhythm we find,
A ritual of purification, leaving no impurity behind.
Embrace this sacred dance, let it guide your way,
As you journey through life, purified day by day.

With reverence and gratitude, this ritual is now complete,
May the blessings of purification continue to repeat.
Dance in harmony with the eternal rhythm's call,
And may your spirit forever be uplifted, standing tall.

73. Spell for the transformation of the deceased into a vessel of divine healing and restoration

By the power of the sacred realms and the divine,
I invoke this spell to transform the deceased, to realign.
From the depths of sorrow and affliction, they shall be set free,
To become a vessel of healing, restoring others with divine decree.

Through the veil of transition, their spirit shall transcend,
Embracing the essence of healing, this spell shall mend.
From the realm of the departed, they emerge anew,
With healing energies flowing, radiating love and virtue.

I call upon the spirits of healing and restoration,
To infuse the deceased with divine transformation.
Let their essence be imbued with healing light,
A conduit of divine energy, shining ever bright.

From the depths of their being, let healing power arise,
Dispelling ailments, soothing pain, and wiping tears from eyes.
May their touch bring comfort, their presence be a balm,
As they embrace their purpose, bringing healing, bringing calm.

With each breath they take, let divine healing flow,
Touching hearts and souls, mending wounds, and letting go.
Grant them wisdom and intuition, the knowledge to heal,
To restore the broken, to uplift, and reveal.

Through their hands, let healing energy flow,
With every word spoken, let restoration grow.
In their presence, may peace and solace be found,
As they bring forth healing, with every sight and sound.

By the power of divine love and compassionate grace,
The deceased shall become a vessel, a healing embrace.
Empowered by the divine, they shall find their way,
A beacon of light, bringing healing each passing day.

This spell is cast with reverence and intent,
For the deceased to become a vessel, divinely sent.
May their transformation be swift and complete,
In service of healing, their purpose now concrete.

So mote it be, and let it be done,
As the deceased's transformation has just begun.
They shall embody the power of healing and restoration,
A vessel of divine love, spreading compassion without cessation.

74. Spell for the reunion of the deceased's soul with their spiritual lineage and heritage

In the realm beyond, where spirits dwell,
I call upon the powers that weave this spell.
With reverence and love, I seek to find,
The reunion of the departed with their lineage divine.

Oh ancestors of old, who came before,
I summon your presence, I open the door.
From the depths of time, across the veil so thin,
Come forth and join us, let the reunion begin.

Spirits of my bloodline, of ancient descent,
I invoke your names, with deep respect I present.
Guide the departed soul, with love and care,
Lead them to their place, in your lineage fair.

By the threads of kinship that bind us tight,
I call upon the spirits, to reunite.
May the deceased find solace, within this embrace,
Reconnecting with their roots, their ancestral grace.

Oh spirits of the past, who paved the way,
Whose wisdom and strength still shine today,
Wrap your arms around the departed soul,
Guide them home, make them whole.

In this sacred space, we gather as one,
Honoring our ancestors, their journey now done.
May the reunion be blessed, with love and light,
As the departed soul rejoins their spiritual kin tonight.

By the power of our shared bloodline and heritage,
I ask for this reunion, with deep reverence.
May the departed find comfort and belonging anew,
In the embrace of their spiritual lineage true.

So mote it be, as I speak this spell,

May the reunion unfold, all is well.
With gratitude and love, I bid farewell,
Knowing that the departed is now embraced and held.

75. Invocation of the god Osiris for resurrection and eternal life in the afterlife

Oh mighty Osiris, lord of the afterlife,
I invoke your presence with reverence and strife.
With words of power, I call upon your might,
Grant us your blessings, guide us through the eternal night.

Osiris, ruler of the realm beyond,
Protector of the souls, so despond,
I beseech you now, with humble plea,
Grant the deceased soul eternal life, set it free.

From the depths of darkness, you emerged,
A symbol of resurrection, our spirits surged.
With your wisdom and grace, you oversee,
The journey of souls to eternity.

Osiris, great judge of the departed,
We implore you, may your mercy be charted.
Grant the deceased soul a place in your domain,
A life everlasting, free from earthly pain.

In your hands lies the power of transformation,
To resurrect and grant eternal salvation.
Guide the departed soul on its sacred quest,
To dwell in your presence, forever blessed.

As the Nile floods, renewing life's cycle,
Let the deceased soul rise from the earthly trial.
Grant it eternal peace and infinite grace,
In your divine embrace, find a sacred resting place.

Oh Osiris, the god of resurrection and rebirth,
Hear our invocation, for we hold your worth.
Guide the departed soul with love and care,
To the realm of eternal life, beyond despair.

With utmost reverence and devotion, we pray,
That the soul may find solace in your divine array.

Grant resurrection, grant eternal peace,
In your presence, may the deceased soul find release.

By the power of your divine name and might,
We invoke your presence, shining bright.
Grant the gift of eternal life, we implore,
In the afterlife's realm, forevermore.

So let it be, as I call upon your name,
Osiris, mighty god, we proclaim.
Resurrect the departed, bring forth their rebirth,
Grant them eternal life in the realm of mirth.

With gratitude and reverence, we bid you farewell,
Knowing that your blessings upon the deceased soul dwell.
Guide them on their journey to the eternal shore,
Osiris, we honor you forevermore.

76. Ritual of anointing with sacred symbols for spiritual empowerment and enlightenment

In this sacred ritual of anointing,
We invoke the power of symbols, enlightening.
Gather the sacred symbols of divine grace,
To empower our spirits in this sacred space.

Prepare the altar, a place of reverence and light,
Where the sacred symbols shall come to life.
Arrange them with care, each symbol with intent,
To unlock their power and the messages they represent.

Anoint the symbols with oils of sacred scent,
To enhance their energy and make their presence potent.
With reverence and respect, apply the oil with care,
Infusing each symbol with the divine essence we share.

As you anoint each symbol, speak their name,
Connecting with their energy, invoking their flame.
Feel the power and wisdom they hold within,
As you honor them in this sacred ritual's din.

Hold each anointed symbol in your hands,
Close your eyes, breathe deep, and understand.
Feel their energy coursing through your being,
Empowering and enlightening, as you are seeing.

Invoke the sacred symbols, their meanings profound,
Channel their power, let their energy surround.
Let their wisdom guide you on your spiritual quest,
Empowering your journey, revealing what is best.

As you complete the anointing, place the symbols in view,
Creating a sacred space, where their power shines through.
Gaze upon them with reverence and awe,
Knowing that their energy supports your spiritual growth and awe.

In this ritual of anointing with sacred symbols,
We honor their power, their wisdom, and their symbols.
May they empower us on our spiritual path,
Guiding us with light, dispelling any darkness we hath.

So mote it be, as we embrace their sacred might,
Empowered and enlightened, guided by their light.
May the symbols continue to inspire and uplift,
As we walk this path of spiritual gifts.

77. Spell for the liberation of the deceased's soul from the limitations of earthly existence

In the realm of spirit, where limitations cease,
I call upon the powers of divine release.
From earthly bonds, let the soul be set free,
To soar beyond boundaries, boundless and free.

By the sacred words I now speak,
May the limitations of Earth no longer wreak.
With this spell, I break the chains that bind,
Releasing the soul to the infinite mind.

I summon the winds of freedom and flight,
To carry the soul to realms of pure light.
Let the earthly attachments dissolve and fade,
As the soul transcends this temporal shade.

Through the veil of illusions, the soul shall break,
Awakening to its true nature, wide awake.
No longer confined by worldly desire,
The soul shall ascend higher and higher.

I call upon the cosmic forces divine,
To sever the ties that anchor and confine.
Grant liberation from the earthly strife,
And guide the soul to the eternal life.

By the power of this spell and my intention pure,
I release the deceased's soul, of this I am sure.
May it soar with grace and find its true home,
Embracing the freedom from which it may roam.

As I speak these words with reverence and might,
I empower the soul to transcend the earthly plight.
May it journey with courage, love, and grace,
Liberated and free in the divine embrace.

So mote it be, in alignment with divine will,
Let the soul find liberation, its purpose fulfill.
With love and light, may it forever abide,
In realms of eternal peace, where limitations subside.

78. Incantation to awaken the dormant spiritual awareness within the deceased's spirit

By the power of the ancients and the cosmic light,
I call upon the spirits to awaken from their slumber, shining bright.
From the depths of the soul, let the awareness rise,
Awakening the dormant spirit, opening the eyes.

With sacred words and intentions pure,
I summon the divine energy to endure.
Let the veil of illusion be lifted, truth revealed,
As the dormant spirit awakens, its destiny sealed.

Awake, O spirit, from your silent sleep,
Embrace the awakening, let your consciousness leap.
Open your eyes to the wisdom of the divine,
As the dormant awareness begins to shine.

Let the illusions of the past fade away,
As the spirit awakens to a brand-new day.
Embrace the journey of self-discovery,
Reveal the truth of your divine ancestry.

With each word spoken, the awareness grows,
Expanding, evolving, as the spirit knows.
Awake, O spirit, to your true essence,
Unveil the secrets of your divine presence.

Let the spiritual awareness permeate the soul,
Rekindling the fire, making it whole.
Awake, O spirit, with purpose and grace,
Embrace the awakening, embrace the sacred space.

By the power of this incantation and divine decree,
The dormant awareness awakens, and so shall it be.
In alignment with the cosmic flow and divine plan,
Let the spirit's awareness awaken, hand in hand.

As the spirit awakens, may it find its way,
Guided by the light, in every moment, every day.
Embrace the journey, let the awakening unfold,
With spiritual awareness, the spirit is forever bold.

Awake, O spirit, with newfound sight,
Embrace the path of spiritual light.
Open your heart and let the truth be known,
As the dormant awareness within you is grown.

So mote it be, in harmony and divine grace,
Awaken, O spirit, to your sacred space.
May your spiritual awareness shine ever bright,
Guiding you on your journey, both day and night.

79. Ritual for the communion with the spirits of the celestial sun and its radiant energy

In the presence of the celestial sun's radiant light,
We gather to commune with spirits shining bright.
With hearts open and spirits aligned,
We seek the wisdom of the sun, divinely designed.

Find a sacred space where the sun's rays embrace,
A place where you feel connected to its grace.
Create an altar with symbols of the sun's power,
Golden candles, sunflowers, and crystals that glower.

Stand tall and raise your arms towards the sky,
Feel the warmth of the sun on your skin, drawing nigh.
Close your eyes and breathe in deeply,
Invoking the energy of the sun, wholly.

With gratitude and reverence, we begin,
To connect with the spirits of the sun, akin.
Recite these words with intention and might,
Invoking the communion of celestial light:

"Oh, radiant sun, source of life and fire,
I stand before you, filled with deep desire.
I call upon the spirits of your celestial domain,
To join us now in this sacred communion plain.

Spirits of the sun, so bright and grand,
I invite you here to take my hand.
Fill me with your wisdom, your radiant glow,
Guide me on this journey, as above, so below.

Grant me strength and courage, like the sun's burning flame,
Illuminate my path, and bring success to my name.
Infuse me with your energy, so warm and bright,
As I walk in alignment with your radiant light.

Spirits of the sun, I honor your power,
In this communion, may blessings shower.

Grant me clarity, vision, and divine inspiration,
As I align with your celestial congregation.

I thank you, spirits of the sun, for your presence here,
May your wisdom guide me throughout the year.
In this sacred communion, our spirits are one,
Connected to the celestial sun, until all is done."

Stand in stillness, feel the energy surround,
As the spirits of the sun make their presence profound.
Take a moment to absorb their divine light,
Feeling their blessings fill you, pure and bright.

Express your gratitude for this sacred communion,
For the wisdom received and the divine union.
Open your eyes and embrace the sun's embrace,
Knowing its energy will guide you with grace.

This ritual of communion with the celestial sun,
Connects us to spirits shining as one.
May its radiant energy continue to bless and guide,
As we walk this path, with spirits at our side.

So mote it be, in the sun's divine glow,
Communion with spirits, forever we shall know.
With hearts filled with gratitude, our spirits soar,
Aligned with the celestial sun, forevermore.

80. Spell for the transmigration of the deceased's soul into the realm of eternal harmony and balance

By the power of the realms beyond,
I call upon the spirits to respond.
For the soul departed, seeking solace anew,
To the realm of eternal harmony, I guide you.

Gather in a tranquil space, serene and still,
Where the energy flows and time stands still.
Light a candle, casting a gentle glow,
Creating a sacred space where spirits may grow.

Close your eyes and enter a state of calm,
Center your being, connecting palm to palm.
Visualize the soul of the departed one,
Hovering above, ready to journey and become.

Recite these words with reverence and intent,
As the spell for transmigration is sent:

"Spirit of the departed, listen to my call,
Embrace this journey, surrendering all.
Transcend the boundaries of earthly strife,
Into the realm of eternal harmony and life.

Let go of burdens, release all pain,
In this sacred transition, freedom you shall gain.
Unbound by limitations, liberated and free,
Into the realm of balance, may your soul be.

Through the gates of time, may you pass,
Into a realm of serenity, harmony, and vast.
Connected to the cosmic dance of the spheres,
Where peace and balance shall erase all fears.

Guided by the gentle flow of divine grace,
Embrace the eternal embrace of this sacred space.

In the realm of harmony, find solace and peace,
Where love and balance shall never cease.

With this spell, I release your soul to soar,
To embrace the beauty of eternity's door.
Transmigrate now, with spirits as your guide,
Into the realm of harmony, where peace abides.

So mote it be, let the spell be cast,
May the departed soul find peace at last.
Across the threshold, into eternal grace,
Transmigrate now, to your destined place."

Feel the energy shift as the spell takes flight,
As the departed soul embarks on their celestial flight.
Open your eyes, feeling the peace in your heart,
Knowing that their journey has now found a fresh start.

May the realm of eternal harmony embrace their soul,
As they find balance and serenity, forever whole.
In this sacred space, may they find eternal rest,
In the realm of harmony, eternally blessed.

So mote it be, as the spell completes its task,
May the departed soul find harmony that will last.
With gratitude and love, we send them on their way,
Knowing they are embraced by the eternal's sway.

81. Invocation of the goddess Hathor for beauty and joy in the afterlife

Oh, great goddess Hathor, embodiment of beauty and joy,
I invoke your presence in this sacred space, oh divine envoy.
With reverence and love, I call upon your divine grace,
To guide and bless the departed soul in their heavenly embrace.

Hathor, radiant goddess with the sun upon your brow,
Bring forth your blessings to illuminate the soul's journey now.
In the afterlife's realm, where beauty and joy reside,
Wrap the departed soul in your loving embrace, by your side.

Goddess of music and dance, bring forth your melodious tunes,
Fill the eternal realms with harmonies that soothe and commune.
Bathe the departed soul in your divine light and celestial glow,
Envelop them in the embrace of eternal beauty's vibrant flow.

Hathor, patroness of love, let your joyous energy abound,
Infuse the departed soul with the happiness that knows no bounds.
Let them dance with jubilation in the eternal cosmic sphere,
Embracing the blissful essence of your presence near.

As they journey through the realms, grant them serenity and peace,
Let them bask in the beauty that never knows decrease.
With your compassionate heart, guide them through the afterlife's way,
Surround them with love and joy every single day.

Oh, great Hathor, goddess of beauty and delight,
We honor your presence in this sacred rite.
May the departed soul find solace in your embrace,
And experience eternal beauty and joy in the heavenly space.

So, I invoke your name, Hathor, with reverence and devotion,
Asking for your blessings and grace in this sacred motion.
Guide the departed soul with your gentle hand,
To find eternal beauty and joy in the celestial land.

Hail, great goddess Hathor, in reverence we call,
Grant the departed soul beauty and joy, above all.

In the afterlife's realm, may they find eternal delight,
Blessed by your presence, shining ever so bright.

So mote it be, let the invocation be complete,
May Hathor's blessings in the afterlife sweet.
With gratitude and love, we honor your divine name,
Knowing the departed soul will never be the same.

Hail Hathor, goddess of beauty and joy,
In the afterlife's realm, your blessings we employ.

82. Ritual of purification through the sacred prayers of the eternal priesthood

The Ritual of Purification through the Sacred Prayers of the Eternal Priesthood is a solemn and reverent practice that cleanses the spirit and purifies the soul. Follow these steps to perform the ritual:

Step 1: Preparation
Create a sacred space by arranging an altar with candles, incense, and any symbols or sacred objects that hold personal significance. Light the candles and incense to set a peaceful ambiance.

Step 2: Invocation
Stand before the altar and close your eyes, taking a deep breath to center yourself. Call upon the divine presence and the eternal priesthood to witness and guide the ritual. Recite a prayer or invocation that aligns with your spiritual beliefs, expressing your intent for purification and seeking divine assistance.

Step 3: Purifying Prayer
Hold your hands over the altar and recite a purifying prayer, asking for the cleansing of your mind, body, and spirit. Let the words flow from your heart, expressing your sincere desire for purification and release from any negative energies or burdens.

Step 4: Sacred Chanting
Begin to chant sacred words or phrases that hold meaning for you. Allow the vibrations of your voice to resonate within you, filling the space with sacred energy. Focus on the intention of purifying your entire being, releasing any impurities or blockages that hinder your spiritual growth.

Step 5: Anointing
Take a small vial of sacred oil or water and dip your fingers into it. Gently anoint your forehead, heart, and palms, symbolizing the purification of your thoughts, emotions, and actions. As you do so, visualize the divine light flowing through you, washing away any negativity and bringing forth purity and clarity.

Step 6: Reflective Meditation
Sit in silence or in a comfortable position, allowing the purification energy to settle within you. Reflect upon the ritual, the prayers, and the intentions you have set. Let go of any lingering thoughts or distractions, and simply be present with your purified self.

Step 7: Gratitude and Closing

Express gratitude to the divine presence and the eternal priesthood for their guidance and assistance in the ritual. Offer any closing prayers or words of gratitude that feel appropriate to you. Extinguish the candles and allow the sacred space to return to its natural state.

Remember, this ritual is a personal and spiritual practice, so feel free to modify it according to your beliefs and preferences. The key is to approach it with reverence, sincerity, and an open heart, allowing the purification process to unfold within you.

83. Spell for the transformation of the deceased into a vessel of divine wisdom and discernment

In the realm of divine wisdom and discernment, I offer you the following spell to transform the deceased into a vessel of profound understanding and insight.

Gather in a quiet and sacred space, preferably under the night sky or within a tranquil room adorned with symbols of wisdom. Light a candle and place it before you as a representation of divine illumination. Take a moment to center yourself and connect with the energy of the departed soul.

Recite the following incantation with heartfelt intention:

"Spirits of wisdom, ancient and wise,
I call upon your power to rise.
Transform this departed soul I hold dear,
Into a vessel of wisdom, sharp and clear.

Grant them knowledge, deep and profound,
With discernment to understand the world around.
Awaken their intellect, free from all strife,
Grant them insight to navigate this life.

Infuse their spirit with divine light,
Illuminate their path, both day and night.
Guide them with wisdom from realms unknown,
As their understanding and discernment have grown.

Let their presence shine like a beacon bright,
As they radiate wisdom, pure and white.
May their words and actions inspire and uplift,
Guiding others on their own sacred drift.

By the power of the divine and the sacred flame,
I call forth this transformation in their name.
So mote it be."

As you recite the incantation, visualize the departed soul bathed in a radiant light of wisdom, their spirit expanding and embracing the profound knowledge of the universe. See them as a vessel of divine wisdom and discernment, ready to share their insights and guide others.

After completing the spell, spend a few moments in silent meditation, allowing the energy to settle and integrate. Express gratitude to the spirits of wisdom and the departed soul for their presence and participation in this transformational ritual.

Remember, this spell is intended to honor the deceased and invoke the divine wisdom within them. Approach it with respect, love, and reverence, knowing that the transformation takes place on a spiritual level.

84. Incantation to invoke the blessings of the celestial fire and its transformative power

To invoke the transformative power of the celestial fire, I present to you an incantation that calls forth its blessings. Stand before an open flame or a representation of fire, and with utmost reverence and focused intent, recite the following words:

"From the realm of celestial fire divine,
I call upon your essence to intertwine.
Bless me with your transformative might,
Ignite within me a spark of your light.

Flames that dance with passionate desire,
Consume my limitations, fuel my inner fire.
Burn away all that no longer serves,
Ignite my spirit, let it rise and observe.

In your radiant blaze, I find strength and power,
A transformative energy to shape and empower.
Guide me through challenges, lead me to the new,
With the blessings of fire, my spirit will renew.

Within this sacred space, I stand tall and true,
As I invoke the blessings of fire through and through.
May its transformative energy flow within,
Igniting my soul, releasing what has been.

By the power of celestial fire, so it shall be,
As I embrace the transformative energy set free.
With gratitude, I welcome your transformative flame,
To shape and empower, in your sacred name.

As above, so below, let it be done,
Transformative fire, let your power run.
Blessings be upon me, as I walk this path,
Aligned with celestial fire, embracing its wrath."

Feel the warmth of the flame and visualize its transformative energy surrounding you. Sense the power of the fire infusing you with vitality, passion, and the ability to let go of what no longer serves your highest good. Embrace the transformative energy and allow it to guide you on your journey.

After reciting the incantation, spend a few moments basking in the energy of the fire, allowing its transformative essence to integrate within you. Express gratitude to the celestial fire for its blessings and the transformative power it has brought forth.

Remember, when working with fire, always exercise caution and ensure you are in a safe environment. Respect the power of the flame and approach this incantation with reverence and intention.

85. Ritual for the transfiguration of the deceased into a divine messenger of divine will

To perform a ritual for the transfiguration of the deceased into a divine messenger of divine will, follow these steps:

Preparation:

Create a sacred space where you can perform the ritual undisturbed. Cleanse the area and set up an altar with symbolic representations of the divine, such as statues, candles, or sacred symbols.
Gather ritual tools and items that hold significance to the deceased or represent their connection to the divine. This can include personal belongings, photographs, or objects associated with their spiritual path.
Purification:

Begin by purifying yourself and the space. Light incense or smudge with sage, focusing on clearing any negative or stagnant energies. Visualize the space being filled with divine light and purity.
Invocation:

Stand before the altar and invoke the presence of the divine. You may use a personalized invocation or the following as a template:
"Divine [insert name of deity or higher power], I call upon your presence and guidance. Bless this sacred space and grant your divine presence to witness and guide this ritual."
Connection to the Deceased:

Take a moment to connect with the energy of the deceased. Reflect on their life, their spiritual journey, and their desire to serve as a divine messenger. Speak their name out loud and invite their presence into the ritual space.
Transfiguration:

Place the symbolic representations of the deceased on the altar, arranging them with care and intention. Light a candle to symbolize their transformation and the divine flame within them.
Focus your intention on the transfiguration of the deceased into a divine messenger of divine will. Visualize their spirit ascending, becoming radiant with divine light, and embodying the qualities of a messenger. Feel their presence and imagine their connection with the divine becoming stronger.

Invocation of Divine Will:

Speak the following invocation, or create your own, addressing the divine and expressing the deceased's willingness to serve as a messenger of divine will:
"Divine [insert name of deity or higher power], I ask that you grant [insert name of deceased] the honor and responsibility of being a messenger of your divine will. May their spirit be infused with your wisdom, guidance, and love. Allow them to be a conduit for your messages, carrying them to those who need to hear. Grant them clarity of purpose and the ability to fulfill their sacred role as a divine messenger."
Acceptance and Blessing:

Express gratitude to the divine for their presence and the opportunity to honor the deceased in this way. Offer prayers, blessings, or words of appreciation for the deceased and their willingness to serve as a divine messenger.
Closure:

Conclude the ritual by expressing your trust in the divine's guidance and thanking them for their presence. Take a few moments to ground yourself and integrate the energy of the ritual.
Remember to adapt and personalize the ritual according to your spiritual beliefs and practices. This ritual is intended as a guide, and you can modify it to align with your specific intentions and the needs of the deceased.

86. Spell for the reunion of the deceased's soul with their spiritual guides and mentors

To perform a spell for the reunion of the deceased's soul with their spiritual guides and mentors, follow these steps:

Preparation:

Find a quiet and peaceful space where you can perform the spell without interruption.
Gather items that symbolize the deceased and their spiritual guides and mentors. This can include photographs, representations of deities or spiritual figures, or objects that hold personal significance.
Cleansing and Centering:

Begin by cleansing yourself and the space. Light incense, sage, or any cleansing tool of your choice. Pass the smoke over your body and around the space, visualizing any negative energies being dispelled.
Take a few deep breaths, centering yourself and quieting your mind. Focus your intention on connecting with the spiritual realm and inviting the presence of the deceased's guides and mentors.
Invocation:

Stand before your altar or sacred space. Light a candle to represent the divine presence. Speak the following invocation, or create your own, addressing the deceased's spiritual guides and mentors:
"Spiritual guides and mentors, known and unknown, I call upon your presence. I seek your guidance and assistance in reuniting the soul of [insert name of the deceased] with your divine wisdom and support. Open the pathways between realms and facilitate their reunion. Guide and protect them on their journey of spiritual growth and enlightenment."
Connection and Reunion:

Place the items representing the deceased and their spiritual guides and mentors on the altar. Arrange them with care and intention.
Visualize a golden light enveloping the space, creating a bridge between the earthly realm and the realm of the spiritual guides and mentors. See the deceased's soul being embraced by this light, feeling the presence of their guides and mentors surrounding them with love and guidance.
Affirmation and Invitation:

Speak directly to the deceased's guides and mentors, affirming their role in the reunion process. Express your gratitude for their guidance and support.

Invite the spiritual guides and mentors to continue their connection with the deceased, offering their wisdom, guidance, and protection. Request that they assist in the deceased's spiritual journey and growth.

Gratitude and Closing:

Express your gratitude to the spiritual guides and mentors for their presence and assistance. Thank them for their ongoing support in reuniting the deceased's soul with their divine guidance.

Close the spell by extinguishing the candle or offering a final prayer or affirmation of closure. Take a moment to ground yourself and reflect on the energy and intentions of the spell.

Remember to adapt and personalize the spell based on your spiritual beliefs and practices. Feel free to modify the invocation and steps to align with your specific intentions and the spiritual guides and mentors you are invoking.

87. Invocation of the god Ra for illumination and enlightenment in the afterlife

To invoke the god Ra for illumination and enlightenment in the afterlife, you can use the following invocation:

"Great Ra, the radiant sun,
Mighty god of illumination and wisdom,
I call upon your divine presence.
As the sun rises and sets upon the world,
So may your light guide the soul of [insert name of the deceased].
In the realm of the afterlife, may their path be illuminated,
May their spirit be enlightened with your sacred knowledge.

Oh Ra, the giver of life and eternal light,
Shine your rays upon their soul,
Illuminate their path with your divine wisdom.
Grant them clarity of mind and vision,
Guide them towards the eternal truths and mysteries.

In this invocation, I honor your sacred name,
Ra, the bringer of illumination and enlightenment.
May the soul of [insert name of the deceased] be blessed,
In your radiant presence, may they find eternal peace.

Hail Ra, the sun god, I invoke your power and presence,
Illuminate the way for the departed soul,
And lead them to eternal enlightenment in the afterlife.

As I speak these words, let the connection be made,
Between the departed soul and your divine presence.
May the illumination and enlightenment of Ra
Guide and bless [insert name of the deceased]
Throughout their journey in the realm beyond.

Ra, I thank you for your divine presence and blessings,
May your light forever shine upon us all.
In the name of Ra, I seal this invocation,
So mote it be!"

Feel free to modify and personalize the invocation according to your beliefs and practices. It is essential to approach this invocation with reverence and sincerity, creating a sacred space to connect with the divine energy of Ra.

88. Ritual of anointing with sacred colors for spiritual vibrancy and manifestation

The Ritual of Anointing with Sacred Colors for Spiritual Vibrancy and Manifestation can be performed in the following steps:

Preparation:

Create a sacred space where you can perform the ritual undisturbed.
Gather the necessary materials, including sacred oils or perfumes in different colors, a small bowl, and a clean cloth.
Clear your mind and set your intention for the ritual, focusing on spiritual vibrancy and manifestation.
Invocation:

Light a candle or incense to signify the sacredness of the ritual.
Take a few deep breaths to center yourself and invoke the presence of any divine beings or energies you resonate with for guidance and support.
Color Selection:

Choose the colors that resonate with the specific qualities or intentions you wish to manifest. For example, green for abundance and growth, blue for communication and intuition, yellow for joy and creativity, and so on.
Anointing:

Take the bowl and pour a small amount of the sacred oil or perfume corresponding to the first chosen color.
Dip your fingers into the oil or perfume and gently anoint yourself with the color, starting from the forehead and moving down to the heart, arms, and hands.
As you anoint each part of your body, visualize the color infusing your being with its specific energy and qualities. Feel yourself becoming vibrant and aligned with the desired manifestation.
Affirmations:

While anointing yourself with each color, recite affirmations or intentions that align with the qualities of that color. For example, "I am open to abundance and prosperity," "I trust my intuition and communicate with clarity," "I embrace joy and express my creativity freely," and so on.
Repeat each affirmation several times, allowing the energy of the color and the power of your words to sink into your consciousness.

Repeating the Process:

Repeat steps 4 and 5 for each chosen color, anointing yourself and affirming the corresponding qualities.

Take your time with each color, fully immersing yourself in its energy and intention.

Closing:

Once you have anointed yourself with all the chosen colors and affirmed the associated qualities, take a moment to express gratitude for the experience and the divine energies that have supported you.

Extinguish the candle or incense, symbolizing the completion of the ritual.

Remember, this ritual is a sacred practice, and your intention and focus are crucial for its effectiveness. Feel free to adapt and personalize the ritual based on your own spiritual beliefs and preferences.

89. Spell for the liberation of the deceased's soul from the bonds of karmic cycles

(Perform this spell with reverence and respect for the deceased's journey.)

Preparation:

Find a quiet and sacred space where you can perform the spell without interruption.
Gather a black candle, a white candle, a small bowl of water, and a clear quartz crystal.
Take a few moments to ground yourself and center your energy.
Lighting the Candles:

Light the black candle to represent the release and transformation of negative karmic patterns.
Light the white candle to symbolize purity, light, and the divine guidance in the liberation process.
Invocation:

Close your eyes and connect with the spirit of the deceased, visualizing their presence in your mind.

Speak the following invocation or create your own heartfelt words:

"Spirits of the past, I call upon you,
Release the soul from karmic ties that bind.
Let the light of liberation shine through,
Grant freedom and peace to the soul we find."

Crystal Cleansing:

Hold the clear quartz crystal in your hands and visualize it absorbing any residual karmic energy surrounding the deceased.
Submerge the crystal in the bowl of water, symbolizing the purification and cleansing of karmic imprints.
Hold the crystal up to the black candle's flame, allowing the fire's energy to transmute and release the karmic bonds.
As you do this, focus on the intention of freeing the deceased's soul from the cycles of karma.
Affirmation:

Hold the crystal in your hands once more and speak the following affirmation:

"With this crystal's cleansing power,
I release karmic chains that bind.
The soul is liberated this hour,
Free from cycles that no longer serve or align."

Release and Closure:

Thank the spirit of the deceased for their presence and trust that the spell has set in motion the liberation of their soul.
Allow the candles to burn out on their own, symbolizing the completion of the spell.
Safely extinguish the candles once they have burned down completely.
Note: This spell is intended as a symbolic and energetic act to support the liberation of the deceased's soul from karmic cycles. It is essential to approach it with sincerity, respect, and a deep understanding of the complexities of karma and the afterlife.

90. Incantation to awaken the dormant spiritual potential within the deceased's spirit

(Perform this incantation with reverence and intention, focusing on awakening the dormant spiritual potential of the deceased.)

Preparation:

Find a quiet and sacred space where you can perform the incantation without interruption.
Light a white candle to symbolize purity, light, and divine guidance.
Take a few moments to ground yourself and center your energy.
Invocation:

Close your eyes and visualize the spirit of the deceased, sensing their presence and energy.

Speak the following incantation or create your own heartfelt words:

"Spirit of the departed, hear my call,
Awaken from slumber, arise and stand tall.
Within you lies dormant spiritual might,
Now is the time to unleash its light."

Channeling Energy:

Extend your hands towards the white candle, palms facing it, and imagine drawing in divine energy and light.
Feel the energy flowing through your hands and into the space around you, infusing it with vibrancy and spiritual power.
Affirmation:

Speak the following affirmation or create your own, directing it towards the spirit of the deceased:

"I awaken your potential, once hidden and still,
Ignite the fire within, let it glow and spill.
Unleash your gifts, your purpose, your grace,

Embrace your power, in this sacred space."

Visualization:

With eyes closed, visualize the dormant spiritual potential within the deceased awakening, like a sleeping giant coming to life.
See their spirit radiating with newfound energy, confidence, and awareness.
Gratitude and Closure:

Thank the spirit of the deceased for their presence and trust that the incantation has set in motion the awakening of their spiritual potential.
Allow the white candle to burn out on its own, symbolizing the completion of the incantation.
Safely extinguish the candle once it has burned down completely.
Note: This incantation is intended as a symbolic and energetic act to support the awakening of the deceased's dormant spiritual potential. It is important to approach it with respect, empathy, and a genuine desire to honor and uplift the spirit. Remember to adapt the incantation to suit your own beliefs and spiritual practices, as well as the specific needs and background of the deceased.

91. Ritual for the communion with the spirits of the celestial rain and its nurturing essence

(Perform this ritual with reverence and openness, seeking to connect with the nurturing essence of celestial rain and the spirits associated with it.)

Preparation:

Find a quiet outdoor space where you can perform the ritual undisturbed. If outdoor space is not available, you can adapt the ritual indoors by creating a serene and natural atmosphere.

Choose a time when rainfall is expected or use symbolic representations of rain such as a bowl of water or a misting spray.

Gather any symbolic items that represent rain and nature, such as flowers, leaves, or small stones.

Cleansing:

Begin by cleansing yourself and the space. You can do this by smudging with sacred herbs, such as sage or palo santo, or by visualizing a purifying white light surrounding you and the area.

Invocation:

Stand or sit comfortably and close your eyes. Take a few deep breaths to center yourself and quiet your mind.

Speak the following invocation or create your own words, expressing your intention to commune with the spirits of celestial rain:

"Spirits of the celestial rain, I call upon you now,
With open heart and humble soul, I seek to make a sacred vow.
Join me in this communion, bless me with your nurturing essence,
Let the divine raindrops cleanse and replenish, bringing forth your presence."

Connection with Nature:

Open your senses to the surrounding environment. Feel the air on your skin, listen to the sounds of nature, and inhale deeply, connecting with the energy of the natural world.

If it is raining, raise your hands or palms towards the sky and allow the raindrops to touch your skin, feeling the nourishing essence of the celestial rain.
Offering:

As a gesture of gratitude and respect, offer the symbolic items representing rain and nature to the earth. You can scatter the flowers, leaves, or small stones onto the ground or place them in a nearby body of water.
Meditation and Connection:

Close your eyes again and enter a meditative state. Visualize yourself standing under a gentle rainfall, feeling each raindrop as a divine blessing.
Imagine the energy of the rain seeping into your being, revitalizing and nurturing your spirit. Allow yourself to connect with the spirits of the celestial rain, feeling their presence and guidance.
Expression of Gratitude:

Express your gratitude to the spirits of the celestial rain for their presence and blessings. Offer thanks for the nourishment and rejuvenation they bring to the earth and all living beings.
Take a moment to silently or verbally express your personal gratitude and appreciation.
Closure:

Slowly bring your awareness back to the present moment. Take a few deep breaths and ground yourself by connecting with the earth beneath you.
Express a final word of gratitude and reverence, acknowledging the completion of the ritual and the connection you have made.
Note: This ritual is a way to symbolically and energetically connect with the nurturing essence of celestial rain and the spirits associated with it. It is important to adapt the ritual to your own beliefs and practices, as well as the specific natural elements available to you. Always approach nature with respect and leave the environment as you found it.

92. Spell for the transmigration of the deceased's soul into the realm of eternal peace and serenity

(Note: This spell is intended to be performed by a qualified practitioner in a respectful and sacred manner.)

Preparation:

Find a quiet and serene space where you can perform the spell without interruption. Gather items that represent peace and serenity, such as white candles, incense (such as lavender or sandalwood), and a small dish of salt.
Creating the Sacred Space:

Light the white candles and the chosen incense to cleanse and purify the space. Sprinkle a circle of salt around you to create a protective boundary and establish a sacred space.
Invocation:

Close your eyes, take a deep breath, and center yourself. Focus your intention on guiding the deceased's soul into the realm of eternal peace and serenity.

Speak the following invocation or create your own words, expressing your intention:

"By the power of light and love,
I invoke the realm of peace above.
With reverence and compassion, I call,
May [Name of the deceased] find serenity and tranquility for all."

Connection and Visualization:

Visualize the deceased's soul surrounded by a gentle, comforting light.
Envision this light guiding the soul towards a serene and peaceful realm, free from earthly worries and disturbances.
See the soul being embraced by loving and compassionate energies, bringing a deep sense of calm and tranquility.
Affirmation and Release:

Speak the following affirmation or create your own words, affirming the soul's transition into eternal peace:

"In this moment, I release [Name of the deceased] with love,
Their soul now soars to the realms above.
May peace and serenity be their eternal guide,
In the embrace of divine love, they forever reside."

Expression of Gratitude:

Express your gratitude for the opportunity to facilitate the soul's journey towards peace and serenity.
Offer thanks to any higher powers, deities, or spiritual guides you may believe in for their assistance and presence.
Closure:

Slowly bring your awareness back to the present moment, feeling the energy of peace and serenity surround you.
Thank the divine forces and the sacred space you have created for their presence and support.
Safely extinguish the candles and clear the sacred space, grounding yourself and returning to your daily life.
Remember, this spell is meant to be performed with reverence, intention, and respect. It is important to adapt it to your own beliefs and practices, and always seek guidance from experienced practitioners if needed.

93. Invocation of the goddess Sekhmet for protection and strength in the afterlife

(Note: This invocation is intended to be spoken with reverence and respect. Adjust the wording and ritual as per your personal beliefs and practices.)

Preparation:

Find a quiet and sacred space where you can perform the invocation without interruption.
Gather items that represent the power and ferocity of the Goddess Sekhmet, such as a statue or image of Sekhmet, red or gold candles, and offerings of incense or fresh flowers.
Creating the Sacred Space:

Light the red or gold candles to symbolize the strength and protection of Sekhmet.
Place the statue or image of Sekhmet in a prominent position.
Burn incense or offer fresh flowers as a gesture of devotion and purification.
Centering and Focus:

Close your eyes, take a deep breath, and center yourself. Allow your energy to align with the presence of Sekhmet.
Feel the power and protection of Sekhmet surrounding you, and know that she is listening to your invocation.
Invocation:

Speak the following invocation or create your own words, expressing your intention to invoke the protection and strength of Sekhmet:

"Mighty Sekhmet, Lioness of the Sun,
I call upon your power, fierce and strong.
In the realm of the afterlife, I seek your aid,
Protect and guide me on this sacred crusade."

Connection and Prayer:

Connect with the energy and presence of Sekhmet. Feel her power and protection envelop you.
Offer a prayer to Sekhmet, expressing your specific needs and desires for protection and strength in the afterlife.

Speak from your heart and be sincere in your requests.
Acknowledgment and Gratitude:

Express your gratitude to Sekhmet for her presence, protection, and strength.
Thank her for listening to your invocation and offering her divine assistance.
Closing:

Slowly bring your awareness back to the present moment, feeling the energy of Sekhmet's protection still surrounding you.
Safely extinguish the candles and clear the sacred space, expressing your gratitude once again.
Carry the energy and confidence of Sekhmet with you as you navigate the afterlife.
Remember, this invocation is a sacred act of connecting with the Goddess Sekhmet. Always approach it with respect, reverence, and an open heart. Adapt the words and ritual to suit your personal beliefs and practices, and feel free to seek guidance from experienced practitioners if needed.

94. Ritual of purification through the sacred offerings of the eternal altar

(Note: This ritual can be adapted to fit your personal beliefs and practices. Adjust the steps and offerings as necessary.)

Preparation:

Find a quiet and clean space where you can set up your altar.
Gather items that represent purification and sacredness, such as a bowl of water, a feather, incense, candles, and any other symbols or tools that hold personal significance to you.
Create an atmosphere of tranquility by dimming the lights or lighting a few candles.
Creating the Altar:

Set up your altar with the items you have gathered, arranging them in a way that feels harmonious to you.
Place the bowl of water at the center of the altar, symbolizing purity and cleansing.
Arrange the feather, incense, and candles around the bowl of water, creating a sacred and balanced space.
Centering and Focus:

Take a few moments to center yourself and clear your mind. Take deep breaths and allow any distractions or negative energies to dissipate.
Visualize a radiant white light surrounding you, purifying your mind, body, and spirit.
Invocation:

Stand before the altar and raise your hands in a gesture of reverence.

Speak or chant the following invocation, or create your own words to call upon the powers of purification and divine presence:

"Oh sacred altar, source of light,
I stand before you on this sacred night.
With pure intent and heart sincere,
I seek your cleansing powers to draw near."

Offering and Purification:

Take the feather and hold it over the bowl of water.

Dip the feather into the water and gently brush it over your face, arms, and body, visualizing the water washing away any impurities or negative energies.

Light the incense and let the smoke waft over your body, purifying your aura and space.

Light the candles one by one, representing the illumination of divine light and purification.

Prayer of Purification:

Offer a prayer of purification, expressing your intention to release any negative energies or impurities that may be weighing you down.

Speak from your heart and be sincere in your desire for purification and renewal.

Gratitude and Closing:

Express your gratitude to the altar, the elements, and any deities or spiritual guides you may have called upon during the ritual.

Thank them for their presence and the purification they have bestowed upon you.

Slowly extinguish the candles, offering a final prayer or affirmation of gratitude.

Integration:

Take a few moments to sit quietly, feeling the effects of the ritual and the purification process within you.

When you are ready, slowly return to your daily activities, carrying the energy of purification and sacredness with you.

Remember, this ritual is a personal practice and can be adapted to fit your own beliefs and preferences. You can perform it as often as needed to cleanse and purify your energy. Trust your intuition and modify the ritual as you see fit to create a meaningful and powerful experience.

95. Spell for the transformation of the deceased into a vessel of divine grace and compassion

(Note: This spell can be modified to suit your personal beliefs and practices. Adjust the words and intentions as necessary.)

Preparation:

Find a quiet and peaceful space where you can focus without interruptions.
Gather items that symbolize grace and compassion, such as a white candle, a rose quartz crystal, and any other objects that hold personal meaning for you.
Light the white candle, representing purity and divine energy.
Centering and Focus:

Take a few deep breaths to center yourself and clear your mind.
Visualize a serene and loving presence surrounding you, filling the space with gentle light and warmth.
Allow yourself to feel connected to the divine source of grace and compassion.
Invocation:

Stand or sit comfortably before the lit candle.

Close your eyes and speak or chant the following invocation, or create your own words to call upon the energies of divine grace and compassion:

"By the light of this candle's flame,
I call upon the divine in thy name.
Transform the deceased with love so pure,
Grant them grace and compassion, now secure."

Intention Setting:

Hold the rose quartz crystal in your hands, focusing your intention on infusing it with the energy of grace and compassion.

Speak aloud or silently affirm your intention, such as:

"With this crystal, I infuse divine grace and compassion.

May the deceased be transformed into a vessel of love and empathy,
Radiating these qualities in the realms beyond."

Visualization:

Envision the deceased surrounded by a gentle glow of divine light.
See them bathed in the energy of grace and compassion, their spirit becoming a
vessel of love and understanding.
Visualize their essence radiating compassion and extending kindness to all beings.
Blessing and Release:

Offer a prayer or blessing to the deceased, expressing your desire for their
transformation and spiritual growth.
Speak from your heart, expressing your wishes for them to embody grace and
compassion in their eternal journey.
Release the energy of the intention and visualization, trusting that it will manifest in
the realm of the divine.
Gratitude and Closing:

Express gratitude to the divine, the candle, the rose quartz crystal, and any spiritual
guides or deities you may have invoked.
Thank them for their presence and assistance in this transformative spell.
Blow out the candle, symbolizing the completion of the ritual.
Remember, this spell is a personal practice and can be adapted to suit your beliefs
and preferences. You can perform it as often as you feel called to honor the
deceased and facilitate their journey towards divine grace and compassion. Trust
your intuition and modify the spell as needed to create a meaningful and heartfelt
experience.

96. Incantation to invoke the blessings of the celestial wind and its gentle guidance

(Note: Feel free to modify and adapt this incantation to align with your personal beliefs and practices. Adjust the words and intentions as needed.)

Preparation:

Find a quiet and open space where you can connect with the energies of the wind. Stand with your feet firmly planted on the ground, allowing yourself to feel rooted and connected to the earth.
Close your eyes, take a few deep breaths, and let go of any distractions or concerns.
Invocation:

Raise your arms slightly, palms facing upwards, as if ready to receive the blessings of the celestial wind.

Speak or chant the following invocation, or create your own words to summon the energies of the celestial wind and its gentle guidance:

"O gentle wind, from realms unseen,
I call upon your guidance serene.
Flow through me, with wisdom and grace,
Bring blessings from the celestial space."

Connection:

Visualize the wind surrounding you, gently caressing your skin and filling the space around you.
Imagine the wind carrying whispers of ancient wisdom and guidance, guiding you on your spiritual path.
Affirmation:

State your intention clearly and affirm your openness to receiving the blessings and guidance of the celestial wind.

Speak aloud or silently affirm, for example:

"I open myself to the gentle wind's embrace,
I welcome its guidance with love and grace.

May its wisdom and guidance be revealed,
As I journey forward, my spirit healed."

Sensory Experience:

Tune in to your senses and feel the gentle touch of the wind on your skin.
Listen to the rustling of leaves or the sounds of nature around you, acknowledging the presence of the wind.
Gratitude and Closing:

Offer gratitude to the celestial wind and its gentle guidance.
Thank the wind for its blessings, wisdom, and the support it offers on your spiritual journey.
Slowly lower your arms, feeling grounded and connected to the earth.

Remember, this incantation is a personal practice and can be adapted to suit your beliefs and preferences. You can repeat it whenever you seek the blessings and guidance of the celestial wind. Trust your intuition and modify the incantation as needed to create a meaningful and heartfelt connection with the energies of the wind.

97. Ritual for the transfiguration of the deceased into a divine protector of sacred traditions

(Note: This ritual can be customized and adapted to your specific beliefs and practices. Modify and adjust the steps as needed.)

Preparation:

Create a sacred space where you can perform the ritual. This can be indoors or outdoors, as per your preference.
Gather items and symbols that represent sacred traditions, such as religious artifacts, ancestral relics, or symbolic objects.
Setting the Intention:

Light a candle or an incense stick to signify the presence of divine energy.
Take a moment to center yourself and set your intention for the ritual. Focus on the transfiguration of the deceased into a divine protector of sacred traditions.
Invocation:

Call upon the presence of divine beings or deities associated with the protection of sacred traditions.

Speak or chant an invocation to invite their presence and assistance in the ritual. For example:

"Divine protectors of sacred traditions,
Hear my call and guide my actions.
By the power of (name of deity/deities),
I seek the transfiguration of the deceased."

Anointing and Symbolism:

Take the symbolic objects representing sacred traditions and hold them in your hands.
With reverence, anoint the objects with consecrated oil or water, symbolizing their spiritual power and significance.
Visualize the deceased individual transforming into a divine protector, dedicated to upholding and safeguarding sacred traditions.

Affirmation:

Speak aloud or silently affirm your intentions for the transfiguration of the deceased. For example:

"By this ritual and sacred intention,
I transfigure (name of deceased) into a divine protector.
May their spirit be dedicated and empowered,
To preserve and uphold sacred traditions forever."

Offering and Blessing:

Offer a heartfelt prayer or blessing to the deceased, expressing gratitude for their presence and dedication to sacred traditions.
Present an offering such as food, drink, or flowers, symbolizing your respect and honor for their role as a divine protector.
Closing:

Express gratitude to the divine beings or deities you invoked at the beginning of the ritual.
Extinguish the candle or incense, symbolizing the completion of the ritual.
Take a moment to reflect on the energy and intention set during the ritual, and visualize the deceased as a divine protector of sacred traditions.

Remember, this ritual is a personal practice and can be adjusted according to your beliefs and preferences. Adapt the steps and wording to resonate with your spiritual path. Focus on the intention of transfiguring the deceased into a divine guardian and protector, upholding the sacred traditions that hold significance to you and your community.

98. Spell for the remembrance of the deceased's name throughout eternity

(Note: This spell can be customized and adapted to your specific beliefs and practices. Modify and adjust the steps as needed.)

Preparation:

Create a sacred space where you can perform the spell. This can be indoors or outdoors, as per your preference.
Gather items that hold significance to the deceased, such as photographs, personal belongings, or objects associated with their life.
Setting the Intention:

Light a candle or an incense stick to signify the presence of divine energy.
Take a moment to center yourself and set your intention for the spell. Focus on ensuring the remembrance of the deceased's name throughout eternity.
Invocation:

Call upon the presence of divine beings or deities associated with memory, remembrance, or ancestral connections.

Speak or chant an invocation to invite their presence and assistance in the spell. For example:

"Divine beings of memory and eternity,
Hear my plea and lend me your power.
By the strength of (name of deity/deities),
I seek the remembrance of (name of deceased) throughout eternity."

Name Enshrinement:

Place the items representing the deceased in a prominent location within your sacred space.
Speak aloud the full name of the deceased, with love and reverence, ensuring each syllable resonates deeply.
Intention and Symbolism:

Visualize the name of the deceased being inscribed or engraved on a timeless monument or within the eternal realm.

Envision the name shining with a radiant light, ensuring its remembrance throughout eternity.

Affirmation:

Speak aloud or silently affirm your intentions for the remembrance of the deceased's name. For example:

"By this spell and sacred intention,
I ensure the remembrance of (name of deceased) throughout eternity.
May their name be spoken and honored,
Forever imprinted upon the fabric of existence."

Offering and Blessing:

Offer a prayer or blessing to the deceased, expressing your love, gratitude, and the desire for their name to endure forever.

Present an offering such as incense, flowers, or a personal memento, symbolizing your respect and reverence for their memory.

Closing:

Express gratitude to the divine beings or deities you invoked at the beginning of the spell.

Extinguish the candle or incense, symbolizing the completion of the spell.

Take a moment to reflect on the energy and intention set during the spell, and trust that the name of the deceased will be remembered throughout eternity.

Remember, this spell is a personal practice and can be adjusted according to your beliefs and preferences. Adapt the steps and wording to resonate with your spiritual path. Focus on the intention of ensuring the eternal remembrance of the deceased's name, honoring their memory and the impact they had in life.

99. Incantation to invoke the protection of the sacred scarab beetle

(Note: This incantation can be customized and adapted to your specific beliefs and practices. Modify and adjust the words as needed.)

Preparation:

Create a sacred space where you can perform the incantation. This can be indoors or outdoors, as per your preference.
Find a representation of the scarab beetle, such as a carved statue or an image, to serve as a focal point.
Centering:

Take a few deep breaths and allow yourself to become present in the moment.
Close your eyes and visualize a golden light surrounding you, radiating warmth and protection.
Invocation:

Begin by raising your hands towards the representation of the scarab beetle, or simply hold it in your hands.

Speak or chant the following incantation:

"Oh, sacred scarab, guardian of the Sun,
In your wings, protection is won.
With your strength and ancient might,
I call upon your power this night."

Visualize Protection:

Envision a vibrant, shimmering green light surrounding you, symbolizing the energy and protection of the scarab beetle.
See this protective light forming a shield around you, warding off negativity and offering guidance and strength.
Affirmation:

Speak aloud or silently affirm your intention for invoking the protection of the sacred scarab beetle. For example:

"By the power of the sacred scarab,
I am shielded and protected from all harm.
Like the scarab's resilience and transformative nature,
I am guided towards growth and renewal."

Gratitude and Closing:

Express gratitude to the sacred scarab beetle for its presence and protection.
Lower your hands or gently place the representation of the scarab beetle back in its place.
Take a moment to ground yourself, feeling the connection to the earth beneath you.

Remember, this incantation is a personal practice and can be adjusted according to your beliefs and preferences. Adapt the words and visualization to resonate with your spiritual path. Focus on invoking the protective energies of the sacred scarab beetle, recognizing its symbolism of transformation and guidance. Embrace the feeling of being shielded and empowered as you continue your spiritual journey.

100.   Ritual for the liberation of the deceased's spirit from the shackles of fear

(Note: This ritual can be customized and adapted to your specific beliefs and practices. Modify and adjust the steps as needed.)

Preparation:

Find a quiet and sacred space where you can perform the ritual without distractions. Gather items that symbolize release and freedom, such as a white candle, a feather, and a piece of paper and pen.
Setting Intentions:

Light the white candle, representing purity and clarity of intention.
Take a moment to center yourself and focus on your intention to help liberate the deceased's spirit from fear.
Writing the Fear:

Take the piece of paper and pen, and write down any fears or negative emotions you believe may be holding the deceased's spirit captive.
Encourage a free flow of thoughts and emotions, allowing any fears to be expressed without judgment.
Burning the Fear:

Hold the paper over the flame of the candle, carefully allowing it to catch fire.
As the paper burns, visualize the fears transforming into wisps of smoke, dissipating into the air and being released.
Affirmation of Liberation:

Hold the feather in your hand, symbolizing lightness, freedom, and the ability to soar above fear.

Speak or chant an affirmation, such as:

"By the power within and the grace of divine love,
I release the deceased from the shackles of fear.
May their spirit be liberated, free to transcend
and embrace the boundless realms of peace."

Meditation and Visualization:

Close your eyes and enter a meditative state.

Visualize the deceased's spirit surrounded by a radiant light, gently guiding them away from the grip of fear.

See the spirit becoming lighter, growing in strength, and ascending towards a state of serenity and liberation.

Gratitude and Closing:

Express gratitude to the divine or any spiritual beings you believe in for their assistance in this ritual.

Blow out the candle, symbolizing the completion of the ritual and the release of fear.

Take a few moments to reflect on the ritual and its purpose, allowing a sense of peace and healing to fill the space.

Remember, this ritual is a personal practice and can be adapted to your beliefs and preferences. Trust your intuition and modify the steps or add any additional elements that feel right for you. The goal is to create a sacred space where the deceased's spirit can be freed from fear and find peace and liberation in the afterlife.

101. Invocation of the goddess Bastet for the preservation of the deceased's essence

(Note: This invocation can be personalized and adjusted according to your beliefs and practices. Adapt the wording and steps as desired.)

Preparation:

Find a quiet and sacred space where you can perform the invocation without distractions.

Gather items that symbolize the essence of the deceased, such as a photograph or an object that holds sentimental value.

Setting Intentions:

Hold the photograph or object in your hands, connecting with the essence and memory of the deceased.

Take a moment to center yourself and focus on your intention to invoke the presence and protection of the goddess Bastet for the preservation of the deceased's essence.

Calling upon Bastet:

Begin by lighting a candle or an incense stick as an offering to Bastet.

Close your eyes and take a deep breath, envisioning a warm and loving energy surrounding you.

Speak or chant the following invocation, or create your own heartfelt words:

"Oh mighty Bastet, feline goddess of love and protection,
I call upon your divine presence in this sacred hour.
Preserve and safeguard the essence of [name of the deceased],
May their spirit be embraced and cherished in your loving care.

Bastet, guardian of life and keeper of the sacred flame,
I beseech you to watch over [name of the deceased],
Shield them from harm, negativity, and spiritual decay,
Let their essence remain pure, radiant, and whole in eternity."

Visualization and Connection:

Envision the presence of Bastet standing before you, emanating a gentle and nurturing energy.

Imagine her extending her protective embrace around the essence of the deceased, forming a shield of light and love.

Visualize the essence of the deceased glowing with a vibrant and radiant energy, preserved and safe under the watchful care of Bastet.

Gratitude and Closing:

Express your gratitude to Bastet for her presence and protection.

Offer a heartfelt prayer, expressing your thanks for her assistance in preserving the essence of the deceased.

Extinguish the candle or incense, symbolizing the completion of the invocation and the continued presence of Bastet's protection.

Remember, this invocation is a personal practice and can be tailored to your beliefs and preferences. Trust your intuition and modify the words or steps as needed. The goal is to invoke the divine presence of Bastet and seek her protection for the preservation of the deceased's essence, allowing their spirit to be embraced and cherished in eternity.

102.   Spell for the reunion of the deceased's soul with their beloved departed ones

(Note: This spell can be adapted and personalized according to your beliefs and practices. Feel free to modify the wording and steps to align with your intentions.)

Preparation:

Find a quiet and peaceful space where you can perform the spell without distractions. Gather items that represent the deceased and their departed loved ones, such as photographs or sentimental objects.
Creating Sacred Space:

Place the photographs or objects in a circle or arrangement, representing the connection between the deceased and their departed loved ones.
Light a candle or an incense stick as a symbol of spiritual presence and connection.
Centering and Intentions:

Take a few moments to ground yourself and enter a calm and focused state of mind. Set your intention clearly in your mind: to create a space for the reunion and connection of the deceased's soul with their beloved departed ones.
Reciting the Spell:

Speak or chant the following spell, or create your own words from the depths of your heart:

"By the power of love that transcends the realms,
I call upon the spirits of departed ones,
Those beloved to [name of the deceased],
Come forth now and join this sacred circle.

Across the veil that separates our worlds,
I invite you to bridge the gap and reunite,
Let the love and memories shared be a beacon,
Guiding [name of the deceased] to your embrace.

Spirits of the departed, hear my call,
Open the gates and welcome [name of the deceased],

Let their souls intertwine once more,
In a bond that transcends time and space."

Visualizing the Reunion:

Close your eyes and visualize the presence of the departed loved ones gathering around the circle, their energy and love enveloping the space.
See the deceased's soul approaching the circle, greeted by their beloved departed ones with open arms and loving smiles.
Imagine a warm and comforting energy enveloping the deceased, as they are reunited with their loved ones, sharing in the joy of their presence.
Offering Gratitude and Closing:

Express your gratitude to the departed loved ones for their presence and assistance in the reunion.
Offer a heartfelt prayer or words of thanks, acknowledging their continued connection and support.
Blow out the candle or incense, symbolizing the completion of the spell and the ongoing bond between the deceased and their beloved departed ones.
Remember, this spell is a personal practice and can be tailored to your beliefs and preferences. Trust your intuition and modify the words or steps as needed. The intention is to create a space for the reunion and connection of the deceased's soul with their beloved departed ones, allowing their spirits to come together and share in the love and memories that transcend the physical realm.

103.   Ritual of anointing with sacred water for purification and renewal of the spirit

(Note: This ritual can be adapted and personalized according to your beliefs and practices. Feel free to modify the wording and steps to align with your intentions.)

Preparation:

Find a quiet and serene space where you can perform the ritual undisturbed.
Gather a bowl or container of clean, pure water. You may choose to infuse the water with herbs or essential oils that are symbolic of purification and renewal.
Setting the Intention:

Take a few moments to center yourself and set your intention for the ritual. Visualize the water as a potent source of spiritual purification and renewal.
Purification Bath:

If possible, begin by taking a ritual bath or shower to cleanse your own physical and energetic body. This will help you enter the ritual with a clear and focused mindset.
Blessing the Water:

Hold the bowl or container of water in your hands and close your eyes.

Speak or silently offer a prayer or blessing, invoking the sacredness of the water for purification and renewal. You may say something like:

"By the sacred power of water, I invoke its cleansing and purifying essence. May this water be imbued with divine energy to cleanse and renew my spirit. May it wash away any negativity, purify my being, and prepare me for spiritual growth and transformation."

Visualize the water being infused with divine light and energy, becoming charged with the intention of purification and renewal.

Anointing the Body:

Dip your fingers into the blessed water and gently anoint yourself with small droplets, starting from the top of your head and moving downwards. You may touch your forehead, heart, and other significant areas as you feel guided.

As you anoint yourself, focus on the intention of purifying and renewing your spirit. Feel the water washing away any stagnant energy or impurities, leaving you refreshed and revitalized.

Affirmations and Intentions:

While anointing yourself, recite affirmations or intentions that resonate with your spiritual goals. For example:

"I release all that no longer serves me. I cleanse my spirit of negativity and open myself to divine love and light. I am purified and renewed, ready to embrace spiritual growth and transformation."

Repeat these affirmations or intentions several times, allowing their energy to resonate within you.

Gratitude and Closing:

Once you have completed the anointing, take a moment to express gratitude for the purification and renewal you have experienced.
Thank the sacred water and any spiritual beings or guides you feel connected to for their assistance in the ritual.
Pour the remaining water onto the earth or a plant as an offering of gratitude.
Remember, this ritual is a personal practice and can be adapted to suit your beliefs and preferences. Trust your intuition and modify the steps or words as needed. The intention is to use the sacred water as a tool for spiritual purification and renewal, allowing its transformative energy to cleanse and refresh your spirit, preparing you for spiritual growth and transformation.

104.   Incantation to awaken the dormant memories within the deceased's spirit

(Note: This incantation is designed to help awaken the dormant memories within the deceased's spirit. It can be adapted and personalized according to your beliefs and practices. Feel free to modify the wording and intentions to align with your specific needs and intentions.)

Preparation:

Find a quiet and sacred space where you can perform the incantation without distractions.
Light a candle or create a serene ambiance to create a focused and peaceful atmosphere.
Centering and Grounding:

Take a few deep breaths and center yourself. Allow any distractions or thoughts to fade away as you focus on the intention of awakening the dormant memories within the deceased's spirit.
Invocation:

Begin by calling upon the spiritual energies or deities you believe can assist in this process. You may address them by name or use general terms such as "Spirit of Remembrance" or "Divine Guardians of Memory."

Speak or chant the following incantation, or create your own based on your beliefs and practices:

"By the power of sacred invocation,
I call upon the dormant memories of (name of the deceased),
Awaken from slumber, arise from the depths,
Let the veil of forgetfulness be lifted.
Ancient wisdom and memories deep,
Come forth, be revealed, in this sacred keep.

(Name of the deceased), remember your journey, remember your truth,
Your memories hold treasures, from days of yore,
Awaken now, as I implore.
Let the past unfold, in vivid detail,
Memories rise, without fail.

Spirits of guidance, ancestors dear,
Aid us now, with love sincere.
Open the gates, unlock the door,
Let the memories flow, forevermore.

With love and reverence, I call upon thee,
Awaken the dormant memories, set them free."

Repeat the incantation multiple times, allowing the words to resonate within the space and in your heart.

Visualization and Connection:

Close your eyes and visualize a gentle light surrounding you and the spirit of the deceased.
Envision the light gently permeating the spirit, slowly awakening the dormant memories and bringing them to the surface.
Allow yourself to feel a deep connection with the spirit, as if you are assisting in the process of remembering and rediscovering.
Openness and Patience:

After completing the incantation, remain open and receptive to any messages, images, or sensations that may arise. Trust in the process and allow the memories to unfold naturally.
Gratitude and Closing:

Once you feel complete, express gratitude to the spiritual energies or deities you invoked, as well as to the deceased spirit, for their presence and assistance.
Blow out the candle or extinguish any flames to symbolize the completion of the ritual.
Remember, this incantation is meant to assist in awakening the dormant memories within the deceased's spirit. It is important to approach this practice with reverence, love, and patience, allowing the memories to unfold naturally and respecting the boundaries of the deceased spirit. Adapt the incantation and steps as necessary to align with your beliefs and intentions.

105. Ritual for the communion with the spirits of the celestial constellations

(Note: This ritual is designed to help establish a connection and communion with the spirits associated with the celestial constellations. You can adapt and personalize it according to your beliefs and practices. Feel free to modify the wording and steps to align with your specific intentions and preferences.)

Preparation:

Choose a quiet and open space where you can perform the ritual without disturbances.
Set up your ritual space with meaningful items such as candles, crystals, or representations of the celestial constellations.
Centering and Grounding:

Take a few moments to center yourself and ground your energy. Focus on your breath, allowing any distractions or thoughts to fade away.
Invocation:

Stand or sit comfortably and begin by invoking the spirits of the celestial constellations. You may address them collectively or individually, depending on your purpose.

Speak or chant the following invocation, or create your own based on your beliefs and practices:

"Spirits of the celestial constellations,
Guardians of the vast cosmic realms,
I call upon you with reverence and respect.
Open the gates between our worlds,
And grant me communion with your presence.

(Name the constellations you wish to connect with),
Your shining patterns illuminate the night,
Your stories etched upon the tapestry of the sky.
I seek to understand your wisdom and guidance,
To commune with your celestial essence.

As above, so below,
May our spirits align and flow.

Grant me insight, clarity, and connection,
As I enter this sacred communion."

Repeat the invocation multiple times, allowing the words to resonate within the space and in your heart.

Celestial Alignment:

Close your eyes and visualize the celestial constellations above, their patterns and stars shining brightly.
Imagine a bridge of light extending from your heart to the heavens, connecting you to the spirits of the constellations.
Feel the energy of the constellations flowing through this bridge, merging with your own energy and consciousness.
Communion and Guidance:

Once you feel connected, express your intentions and desires to commune with the spirits of the constellations.
Open yourself to receive their guidance, wisdom, and insights. Be receptive to any messages, images, or sensations that may come through.
Meditation and Contemplation:

Enter into a state of meditation or contemplation, allowing yourself to be in the presence of the celestial spirits.
Ask any questions or seek clarity on specific areas of your life or spiritual journey.
Listen attentively for any responses or insights that may arise.
Gratitude and Closing:

Offer gratitude to the spirits of the celestial constellations for their presence and guidance.
Slowly bring your awareness back to the present moment, gently disconnecting from the celestial energies.
Express gratitude for the experience and close the ritual in a way that feels appropriate to you. This may include extinguishing candles, offering a final prayer, or any other closing gesture.
Remember, this ritual is intended to establish a connection and commune with the spirits of the celestial constellations. Approach it with reverence, openness, and respect for the energies involved. Adapt the steps and wording as necessary to align with your beliefs and intentions.

106. Spell for the transmigration of the deceased's soul into the realm of eternal wisdom

Preparation:

Create a sacred space where you can perform the spell undisturbed.
Place a white candle in the center of the space, symbolizing purity and divine light.
Gather any items that hold significance for the deceased, such as photographs or personal belongings.
Centering and Intent:

Take a few deep breaths and focus your mind on the intention of guiding the deceased's soul towards eternal wisdom and understanding.
Visualize the soul of the departed, envisioning them surrounded by a warm, comforting light.
Invocation:

Light the white candle, representing the divine presence and illumination.

Speak or chant the following invocation, or create your own based on your beliefs and practices:

"In this sacred space, I call upon the realms of wisdom,
I invoke the eternal knowledge that transcends time.
With love and reverence, I guide the soul of [Name of the deceased],
To the realm of eternal wisdom, where understanding shines.

May their spirit be embraced by divine enlightenment,
May their journey be guided by the luminous path.
Through the gateways of wisdom, their soul shall transcend,
Gaining insight and knowledge, forever unbound.

As their soul traverses the realms of eternity,
Grant them the treasures of profound clarity.
Let wisdom fill their essence, forevermore,
A beacon of enlightenment, their spirit shall soar."

Repeat the invocation as many times as you feel necessary, allowing the words to resonate with your intentions and reach the soul of the departed.

Communion and Release:

Reflect on the memories and experiences shared with the deceased. Feel a deep connection with their spirit.
Offer words of love, gratitude, and encouragement, letting them know it is safe to embark on their journey towards eternal wisdom.
Farewell and Blessing:

Thank the soul of the departed for their presence in your life and for the lessons they brought.
Blow out the candle, symbolizing the completion of the spell and the release of the deceased's soul to the realm of eternal wisdom.
Closing:

Take a moment to ground yourself, allowing any residual energies to dissipate.
Express gratitude for the experience and the opportunity to honor the departed's journey.
Close the ritual in a way that feels appropriate to you, such as offering a final prayer, a moment of silence, or a personal gesture.
Remember, this spell is intended to assist the transmigration of the deceased's soul into the realm of eternal wisdom. Approach it with love, respect, and reverence.
Customize the spell to align with your beliefs and practices, and adapt the wording and steps as necessary to suit the occasion.

107.   Invocation of the god Anubis for guidance and protection in the afterlife

Preparation:

Find a quiet and sacred space where you can focus your energy and connect with the divine.
Place a statue or image of Anubis on your altar or in front of you.
Light a candle or incense as an offering and to create an atmosphere of reverence.
Centering and Intent:

Take a few deep breaths to center yourself and bring your focus to the purpose of the invocation.
Visualize a connection with Anubis, the guardian of the afterlife, and feel his presence around you.
Invocation:

Stand or kneel before the image or statue of Anubis and recite the following invocation, or create your own based on your beliefs and practices:

"Great Anubis, Guardian of the Afterlife,
I invoke your presence and seek your guidance.
You, who holds the keys to the realm beyond,
I call upon your wisdom and protection profound.

O Anubis, guide the departed soul's journey,
Safeguard them through the trials and challenges they face.
Grant them clarity of mind and spirit,
As they navigate the realms with your divine grace.

Protector of souls, weigh their heart with care,
Lead them towards the eternal realms of peace.
Shield them from harm and darkness that may arise,
Surround them with your vigilance that will never cease.

Anubis, I honor your sacred role,
I offer my respect and gratitude to you.
May your presence bring solace and strength,
As you guide the departed soul on their path anew."

Repeat the invocation as many times as you feel necessary, allowing your words to carry your intentions and connection with Anubis.

Connection and Offering:

Visualize a golden light emanating from the image or statue of Anubis, enveloping you and creating a sacred bond.
Offer your heartfelt prayers and intentions for the departed soul, expressing your trust in Anubis's guidance and protection.
Gratitude and Farewell:

Express your gratitude to Anubis for his presence and assistance.
Close the invocation by offering a final prayer or personal words of thanks and respect.
Take a moment to reflect and honor the connection you have established with Anubis and the assistance sought for the departed soul.
Remember, this invocation is a means of seeking the guidance and protection of Anubis in the afterlife. Approach it with sincerity, respect, and reverence. Adapt the invocation to suit your personal beliefs and practices, and feel free to add any additional elements or gestures that resonate with you.

108.   Ritual of purification through the sacred flames of transformation

Preparation:

Find a quiet and safe space where you can perform the ritual undisturbed.
Set up an altar or a designated area for the ritual. Place a fireproof bowl or cauldron at the center.
Gathering the Elements:

Collect the following items: a white candle, matches or a lighter, a small bowl of salt, and a feather or smudging tool (such as sage or palo santo).
Place these items on your altar or near the fireproof bowl.
Centering and Intent:

Close your eyes, take several deep breaths, and focus your attention on your intention for the ritual.
Visualize yourself surrounded by a bright and purifying light, ready to release anything that no longer serves you.
Lighting the Sacred Flame:

Light the white candle using the matches or lighter, symbolizing the sacred flame of transformation.
As you light the candle, affirm your intention for purification and transformation, speaking your desires aloud or silently.
Purification with Salt:

Take a small pinch of salt from the bowl and sprinkle it into the fireproof bowl or cauldron, representing the cleansing and purifying energy of salt.
Visualize the salt absorbing any negativity or impurities, purifying your energy and creating a sacred space.
Smudging and Cleansing:

Take the feather or smudging tool and light it using the sacred flame.
Allow the flame to extinguish, leaving behind a smoldering smoke.
Move the smudging tool around your body, starting from your feet and moving upward, envisioning the smoke purifying and cleansing your energy field.
Releasing and Letting Go:

Take a moment to reflect on anything you wish to release and let go of. This could be negative emotions, limiting beliefs, or any attachments that no longer serve you. Speak your intentions aloud or silently, expressing your desire to release these burdens and embrace personal transformation.

Offering to the Flames:

Take a piece of paper and write down any specific thoughts, emotions, or attachments you wish to release.

Safely light the paper using the sacred flame, allowing it to burn in the fireproof bowl or cauldron.

As the paper burns, visualize the flames transmuting your intentions into pure energy, releasing them into the universe.

Affirmations and Gratitude:

Close the ritual by expressing gratitude for the purification and transformation that has taken place.

Speak affirmations or prayers of gratitude, acknowledging the cleansing of your spirit and welcoming positive energies and new beginnings.

Extinguishing the Sacred Flame:

Gently blow out the white candle, symbolizing the completion of the ritual.

Take a moment to observe the residual energy and bask in the sense of purification and renewal.

Remember to approach this ritual with reverence and respect. Adapt and modify it as needed to align with your personal beliefs and practices. Take the time to set your intentions and truly connect with the transformative energies of the sacred flames.

109.　Spell for the transformation of the deceased into a vessel of divine balance

Preparation:

Find a quiet and peaceful space where you can perform the spell without interruption.
Gather the following items: a white candle, a black candle, matches or a lighter, a small bowl of water, and a representation of balance (such as a yin-yang symbol or a scale).
Centering and Intent:

Take a few deep breaths to center yourself and focus your intention on invoking divine balance for the deceased.
Visualize the deceased's spirit surrounded by a radiant light, and hold the representation of balance in your hands.
Lighting the Candles:

Place the white candle on the right side and the black candle on the left side of your workspace.
Light the white candle first, representing the light and purity of divine balance.
Light the black candle second, symbolizing the shadows and contrast that bring equilibrium.
Invocation and Affirmation:

Stand before the candles and hold the representation of balance in your hands.
Speak the following invocation or create your own heartfelt words:
"By the power of divine balance, I call upon the forces of light and darkness. May the deceased's spirit be transformed into a vessel of harmony and equilibrium. May all imbalances be resolved, and may divine balance prevail in their eternal journey."
Blessing of Water:

Take the small bowl of water and hold it up to the light of the white candle.
Visualize the water being infused with the energy of divine balance.
Say the following affirmation or adapt it to your own words:
"I bless this water with the essence of divine balance. May its purity and fluidity bring harmony and equilibrium to the spirit of the deceased."
Anointing with Water:

Dip your fingers into the blessed water and gently sprinkle or anoint the representation of balance.

As you do so, visualize the divine energy of balance infusing the symbol and radiating outward.

Closing and Gratitude:

Express gratitude for the divine balance invoked and for the transformation of the deceased's spirit.

Blow out the candles, starting with the black candle and then the white candle, symbolizing the completion of the spell.

Take a moment to reflect on the energy created and the potential for divine balance in the afterlife.

Remember, this spell is intended as a symbolic ritual and a way to focus your intention. Adapt it to your beliefs and practices, and feel free to add any additional elements that resonate with you. Offer your sincere intentions and trust in the power of divine balance to support the transformation of the deceased's spirit.

110.　Incantation to invoke the blessings of the celestial lotus and its purity

Eternal lotus, flower of divine grace,
From celestial realms, I seek your embrace.
With petals pristine and radiant light,
Bless me with purity, shining so bright.

Oh, sacred lotus, pure and serene,
Bearer of blessings, gentle and pristine.
From celestial waters, you gracefully rise,
An embodiment of beauty, that none can deny.

With each petal's touch, may purity unfold,
A cleansing essence, purifying the old.
In your delicate form, divine wisdom resides,
Guiding me on a path where love abides.

Celestial lotus, I call upon your power,
To bring forth purity in this sacred hour.
May your blessings flow, like gentle streams,
Washing away impurities, like fleeting dreams.

By your essence, may my spirit rise,
In purity and grace, reaching the skies.
Let your sacred energy permeate my being,
Awakening purity, from within and foreseeing.

Oh, celestial lotus, I offer my devotion,
Embracing your purity, with heartfelt emotion.
With gratitude and reverence, I embrace your touch,
May your blessings guide me, I thank you so much.

As I speak these words, may your blessings pour,
Infusing my spirit, forevermore.
Celestial lotus, in your purity I trust,
Bless me with your grace and divine love, I must.

Take a moment to meditate or reflect upon the energy invoked by the incantation.
Visualize the celestial lotus blooming within you, radiating pure light and bestowing

its blessings upon you. Embrace the purity and grace that it symbolizes, allowing it to fill your spirit with divine love and purity.

Remember, this incantation is a tool to connect with the energy and symbolism of the celestial lotus. Embrace its essence and trust in its power to bring forth purity and blessings into your life.

111. Ritual for the transfiguration of the deceased into a divine conductor of cosmic energies

Invoke the sacred script of cosmic metamorphosis,
To elevate the departed into a divine conductor of cosmic might.
With ancient wisdom, we unravel the steps of this transformative rite,
Guiding the soul through the veils, beyond mortal sight.

First, cleanse the sacred space with purifying flame,
As incense rises, let the ethereal essence proclaim.
Prepare the altar with offerings, both precious and rare,
For the celestial beings, their favor we seek to ensnare.

Gather the faithful priests, adorned in sacred vestments,
Chanting hymns of old, invoking celestial segments.
With reverence, approach the blessed coffin of the departed,
Assembled in solemnity, with the gods' blessings imparted.

The chief priest, bearer of life's eternal symbol,
With measured steps, approaches the celestial threshold.
Anoint the vessel of the soul with fragrant oils divine,
Infusing the essence with blessings, an alchemical sign.

Bring forth the vessel of holy water, blessed by sacred hands,
With measured pour, let the divine essence expand.
As droplets cascade upon the departed's form,
Purification commences, as earthly bonds transform.

Recite the sacred texts, inscribed on scrolls of ancient lore,
Their mystic power unveiled, the soul to restore.
With fervent invocation, the priest's voice shall resound,
Calling upon cosmic forces to gather and surround.

"O, revered deities, guardians of celestial spheres,
Descend upon this soul, release it from earthly fears.
Transmute the essence, let it merge with the divine,
A conductor of cosmic energies, eternally entwined."

With the final incantation echoing through the air,
Raise your hands in reverence, as cosmic energies flare.
Feel the presence of celestial beings drawing near,
Their gentle touch upon the departed, sacred and clear.

As the ritual concludes, a profound silence prevails,
The soul, transfigured, beyond mortal trails.
Released from earthly bounds, it ascends with grace,
A divine conductor of cosmic energies, in infinite space.

"O, departed soul, journey with celestial might,
Conduct the cosmic symphony, shining with eternal light.
Guide the celestial orchestra, harmonizing the spheres,
A divine entity, connected through cosmic years."

Thus, the ritual completes, its purpose fulfilled,
As the departed transcends, the cosmic realms are thrilled.
May their transfiguration be a beacon of divine grace,
Forever conducting the cosmic energies, in sacred embrace.

112.   Spell for the reunion of the deceased's soul with their spiritual kindred

By the power of ancient sorcery, we gather here,
To weave a spell of reunion, beyond death's frontier.
With utmost reverence, let the ritual commence,
To unite the departed's soul with their spiritual kindred hence.

Prepare the sacred chamber, adorned with symbols profound,
Inscribed upon the walls, the names of those renowned.
Let the fragrance of myrrh and lotus permeate the air,
Invoking the presence of ancestral spirits with utmost care.

Ignite the sacred fire, its flickering flames aglow,
Casting shadows dancing, as energies ebb and flow.
Within its radiant warmth, let the departed's essence dwell,
Drawing forth the spiritual kindred, their stories to tell.

Invoke the names of the departed's forebears, long since gone,
Their spirits, awakened, shall heed the sacred summon.
With solemn words, address the ancestral lineage,
"O revered spirits, we beseech your divine patronage."

Bring forth the offerings, symbols of earthly connection,
Bread, water, and wine, a gesture of affection.
Place them upon the altar, with reverence and grace,
An invitation extended to the spiritual kindred's embrace.

Recite the incantations, passed down through time,
Words imbued with power, their rhythm and rhyme.
Call upon the guardians of the threshold, steadfast and true,
To guide the departed's soul to the reunion anew.

"O spirits of the ancient ones, whose blood runs in their veins,
Hear our invocation, release them from mortal chains.
Guide their wandering soul, let it find its destined path,
To the realm where kindred spirits converge, without wrath."

As the incantations reach their zenith, their echoes fade,
A sacred silence envelopes the chamber's hallowed shade.

Observe the signs and omens, the veil thinning before our eyes,
As the spiritual kindred draw near, a reunion in the skies.

In the presence of the departed's spiritual kin,
The soul finds solace, transcending realms akin.
Memories intertwine, stories shared in ethereal communion,
Uniting the living and deceased, in a timeless union.

With gratitude and reverence, bid farewell to the spirits' domain,
Knowing the departed's soul has found solace and refrain.
May they find eternal comfort in the company they keep,
United with their spiritual kindred, in a bond so deep.

Thus, the spell for reunion concludes its sacred quest,
The departed's soul embraced by the spiritual crest.
May they find eternal peace, amidst kindred souls,
Forever united, as the cosmic destiny unfolds.

113.   Invocation of the goddess Hathor for joy and celebration in the afterlife

Hear, ye gods and spirits, as we invoke the goddess divine,
Hathor, the Lady of Joy, her radiance shall forever shine.
With offerings of music and dance, let the ritual commence,
To bring joy and celebration to the departed's afterlife hence.

Gather in the sacred hall, adorned in colors vibrant and bright,
Symbolizing the zest for life, an everlasting delight.
With tambourines and harps, let melodies fill the air,
Awakening the soul to Hathor's presence, beyond despair.

Raise your voices in jubilation, sing praises to her name,
Goddess Hathor, the bringer of joy, forever shall we acclaim.
In rhythmic steps and graceful movements, let the dance unfold,
A celebration of life's splendor, in stories yet untold.

Invoke the goddess with words of reverence and respect,
"O Hathor, radiant goddess, in your grace we reflect.
Bestow upon the departed your blessings of mirth,
That their afterlife be filled with joy, a celestial rebirth."

Offer libations of sweet wine, poured in her sacred name,
An elixir of bliss, to ignite the spirit's eternal flame.
Fragrant incense rises, filling the sacred space,
A symphony of scents, invoking Hathor's embrace.

Call upon her divine presence, as the ritual intensifies,
Her essence descending from the celestial skies.
Feel her divine energy, filling every corner of the room,
As the departed's soul basks in Hathor's celestial bloom.

"O Hathor, joyous goddess, fill the afterlife with glee,
Let music and laughter echo through eternity.
Grant the departed eternal jubilation and merriment,
In the realm beyond, a joyous testament."

With hearts uplifted and spirits renewed,
Dance with exuberance, expressing gratitude.

Let the rhythms and melodies ignite the soul's delight,
In Hathor's presence, a timeless celebration takes flight.

As the ritual draws to a close, offer thanks and praise,
To Hathor, the goddess who blesses all our days.
May the departed find everlasting joy in her divine embrace,
Their afterlife adorned with celebrations, a celestial space.

Thus, the invocation of Hathor concludes its sacred decree,
May her blessings of joy endure for all eternity.
In the afterlife's realm, let jubilation forever prevail,
As the departed's soul dances with Hathor, beyond the mortal veil.

114. Ritual of anointing with sacred incense for the elevation of consciousness

Preparation:
Gathering the Elements:
In the sacred chamber, gather the elements with care,
The vessel of sacred incense, a fragrance rare.
Select resins, herbs, and oils, blended with intention,
To create a potent elixir for consciousness' ascension.

Centering and Intent:
Find a quiet space within, let the mind be still,
Center your being, align with divine will.
Set the intent for this ritual, a quest for higher states,
To elevate consciousness, transcending earthly rates.

Lighting the Sacred Flame:
Ignite the sacred flame, its flickering glow,
Symbolizing the inner spark, the divine's sacred flow.
Invoke the presence of the eternal flame's light,
Guiding the anointing ritual, in its luminous sight.

Purification with Salt:
Take the purifying salt, a symbol of earthly purity,
Sprinkle it upon your palms, a sacred security.
Rub your hands together, cleansing with intention,
Releasing impurities, creating a sacred dimension.

Smudging and Cleansing:
Take the sacred incense, carefully lit with the flame,
Let its smoke rise, the chamber's energy to reclaim.
Walk around the sacred space, in clockwise rotation,
Cleansing the atmosphere, purifying with dedication.

Anointing with Sacred Incense:
Hold the vessel of sacred incense, its aroma divine,
Dip your fingers into its essence, an anointing sign.
Trace the symbol of the divine upon your forehead,
Inviting the elevation of consciousness, a journey spread.

Inhale the sacred fragrance, allowing it to infuse,
Elevating your senses, awakening higher views.
Let the smoke envelop your being, as consciousness expands,
Connecting with cosmic wisdom, held in divine hands.

Closing:
Offer gratitude to the cosmic forces that guided your way,
To the sacred flame, the incense, and the realms astray.
As the ritual concludes, feel the transformation within,
Elevated consciousness, a gift that shall not thin.

Remember:
Carry the wisdom gained, let it guide your path,
In every moment, connect to the divine's sacred bath.
Elevate your consciousness, embrace the divine light,
Unveiling mysteries, in the depths of cosmic night.

115.   Incantation to awaken the dormant powers within the deceased's spirit

In the realm of spirits, where the veil is thin,
We gather to awaken the dormant powers within.
With sacred words and intention sincere,
Let the deceased's spirit rise, its true essence to appear.

Invoke the ancient forces, the guardians of might,
To stir the dormant powers, hidden out of sight.
In the presence of celestial beings, both fierce and kind,
Let the incantation weave its transformative bind.

"O spirits of the departed, hear this sacred call,
Awaken from slumber, rise and stand tall.
Within your essence lies untapped strength and power,
Unleash it now, in this transformative hour."

With each repetition, the incantation gains force,
Vibrating through realms, taking its cosmic course.
Let the words resonate with ancient energy,
Stirring the dormant powers, setting the spirit free.

Whispers of the ancestors lend their ethereal support,
As the dormant powers awaken, like a celestial port.
Feel the surge of energy, coursing through the spirit's core,
Igniting the latent abilities, long silenced before.

"Arise, dormant powers, from the depths of sleep,
Unleash your potential, let the celestial secrets seep.
Embrace your true essence, with strength and might,
Transcend the boundaries, ascend to cosmic height."

As the incantation reaches its zenith, its power unleashed,
The dormant powers surge forth, no longer peace breached.
The deceased's spirit, now ablaze with cosmic fire,
Embraces its latent powers, its true self to acquire.

Witness the transformation, as the spirit awakens,
A radiant being, its dormant powers unshaken.

With newfound strength, it navigates the celestial realm,
Guided by ancestral wisdom, at the helm.

In this awakened state, the spirit's essence soars,
Unveiling hidden talents, unlocking cosmic doors.
Embrace the potential, let the powers unfold,
A testament to the spirit's journey, both new and old.

With gratitude and reverence, conclude the sacred rite,
Thank the celestial forces for their divine light.
May the awakened powers guide the spirit's ascent,
In the realms of eternity, their purpose be spent.

Thus, the incantation to awaken dormant powers finds its end,
May the deceased's spirit embrace its true self, ascend.
With newfound strength and cosmic energy as their guide,
May they soar through the realms, forever unified.

116.   Ritual for the communion with the spirits of the celestial mountains and their majesty

In the sacred sanctuary, we gather as one,
To commune with spirits of mountains, where they've spun
Their majestic tales, reaching heights divine,
Unveiling their wisdom, in this sacred shrine.

Prepare the ritual space, adorned with reverence and grace,
Symbols of mountains, a reflection of their celestial embrace.
Let the scent of earth and pine fill the air,
Invoking the presence of spirits, with utmost care.

Light the sacred flame, its flickering glow,
Illuminating the path to the spirits' abode.
With hearts open wide, offer words of invocation,
To beckon the mountain spirits, their majestic manifestation.

"O spirits of the celestial mountains, ancient and grand,
We seek communion with your presence, by sacred command.
Unveil your majesty, share your wisdom profound,
Guide us through your realms, where mysteries abound."

Sit in silent contemplation, attuning to the mountain's call,
Feel the energies shift, as the spirits stand tall.
Sense their presence, as they draw near,
With reverence and awe, let their essence appear.

Speak from the heart, with words sincere and true,
Address the mountain spirits, as they come into view.
Express gratitude for their towering might,
For the lessons they bestow, in nature's wondrous light.

In this communion, seek their wisdom deep,
Ask questions, ponder mysteries, their secrets to reap.
Listen for whispers in the wind, echoes of ancient lore,
As the mountain spirits guide you, to realms unexplored.

Feel the currents of energy, flowing through your being,
As the spirits of mountains impart what they're foreseeing.
Their wisdom, like peaks, reaching skies above,
Elevating consciousness, expanding hearts with love.

Offerings of gratitude, extend with reverence,
Gifts to the spirits, in humble deference.
Sacred water, crystals, or fragrant flowers,
Tokens of appreciation, acknowledging their powers.

With deep respect, bid farewell to the mountain's domain,
Knowing the communion's imprint shall forever remain.
Carry their wisdom within, in heart and mind,
Guiding your journey, their presence intertwined.

In closing, express gratitude for their celestial grace,
For the communion shared, in this sacred space.
May the spirits of the celestial mountains forever inspire,
Guiding us to heights grand, our souls reaching higher.

Thus, the ritual for communion with the spirits finds its conclusion,
May the majestic mountains' wisdom be forever an infusion.
With reverence and awe, embrace their celestial majesty,
As we traverse the realms, connected eternally.

117.   Spell for the transmigration of the deceased's soul into the realm of eternal beauty

In the realm between realms, where spirits traverse,
We gather to enact a spell, a solemn verse.
To guide the deceased's soul, with utmost care,
Into the realm of eternal beauty, beyond worldly glare.

Create a sacred space, adorned with symbols of grace,
An altar of reverence, where the spell finds its place.
Surround it with candles, their flames flickering bright,
Illuminating the path, guiding the soul's flight.

Invoke the spirits of guidance and light,
To aid the transmigration, to ensure it's right.
Call upon the guardians, both gentle and wise,
To accompany the soul, as it journeys to the skies.

"With love and respect, we gather here today,
To guide the departed's soul, on its destined way.
Transcend the earthly realm, to realms serene,
To the realm of eternal beauty, forever to gleam."

Offer prayers of peace, serenity, and hope,
Visualize the soul's transition, a seamless slope.
Envision the soul, shedding its earthly ties,
Embracing its divine essence, as it soars and flies.

Let the incantation flow, words of power and might,
Echo through the veil, igniting the soul's light.
"O departed soul, released from earthly strife,
Transmigrate with ease, to the realm of eternal life.
Leave behind the sorrows, the burdens of the past,
Embrace the eternal beauty, where love shall forever last."

Feel the presence of celestial beings, as they draw near,
Embracing the departed soul, removing all fear.
Their gentle touch guides the soul's journey ahead,

Transcending earthly bounds, to realms where beauty spreads.

As the spell reaches its peak, the soul begins to transcend,
Its essence expanding, its earthly ties to mend.
Witness its departure, as it fades from sight,
Into the realm of eternal beauty, clothed in ethereal light.

Offer gratitude to the spirits, for their guiding embrace,
For assisting the soul in its transmigration, with grace.
May the departed find solace in the realm serene,
In eternal beauty, where their spirit shall forever preen.

With reverence and gratitude, conclude the sacred rite,
Knowing the soul's journey is guided by celestial light.
May the departed find peace and eternal bliss,
In the realm of eternal beauty, where love's eternal kiss.

Thus, the spell for the transmigration finds its closure,
May the departed's soul find eternal beauty's composure.
Guided by celestial beings, bathed in radiant light,
Forever embraced in the realm where beauty takes flight.

118.   Invocation of the god Ptah for craftsmanship and creation in the afterlife

In the realm of eternal existence, where spirits thrive,
We call upon Ptah, the god of craftsmanship, to arrive.
With reverence and awe, we gather in this sacred space,
Invoking Ptah's presence, his divine artistry to embrace.

Prepare the altar with tools of creation, symbols of skill,
Representing the mastery and craftsmanship we instill.
Place offerings of paint, chisel, and precious metals,
Honoring Ptah's domain, where creation settles.

Light the flame, symbolizing Ptah's divine spark,
Illuminating the path to creation's embark.
With the flickering light as our guide and companion,
We invoke Ptah's essence, his craftsmanship champion.

"Ptah, the divine artist, we call upon you this day,
Master of creation, guide us on our creative way.
Bless our hands with skill, our minds with inspiration,
As we journey in the afterlife, a realm of eternal creation."

Feel the presence of Ptah, his energy drawing near,
His divine essence imbued with craftsmanship clear.
Open your heart and mind to his guiding hand,
As his creative influence envelops the sacred land.

Invoke Ptah's power, his mastery and expertise,
To awaken the artist within, the creative energies.
"Ptah, grant us your vision, your creative insight,
Illuminate our minds, with inspiration's light."

Feel Ptah's divine touch upon your hands,
Guiding them with skill, as creation expands.
In this afterlife realm, let craftsmanship unfold,
With Ptah as our muse, our creations taking hold.

As you work with your chosen medium, whether paint or stone,
Feel Ptah's presence beside you, never feeling alone.

Let his creative essence flow through your very being,
As you bring forth beauty, in this realm of seeing.

Express gratitude to Ptah for his divine inspiration,
For guiding your artistic journey, with elation.
May your creations in the afterlife shine with grace,
A testament to Ptah's craftsmanship and embrace.

With reverence and gratitude, conclude the invocation,
Knowing Ptah's presence lingers, a source of inspiration.
May your craftsmanship and creations forever thrive,
In the realm of eternal existence, where Ptah's energies survive.

Thus, the invocation of Ptah, the god of craftsmanship, finds its end,
May his divine essence guide your artistic endeavors, and extend
Your creative reach in the afterlife's realm divine,
Crafting masterpieces, an eternal legacy to intertwine.

119. Ritual of purification through the sacred chants of divine hymns

In the sacred space, where spirits entwine,
We embark on a ritual of purification divine.
Through sacred chants and melodic hymns,
Let the soul's cleansing and purity begin.

Prepare the ritual space, adorned with care,
Symbols of divinity, serenity in the air.
Light the candles, their flickering flames,
Guiding the path to spiritual reclaims.

Invoke the presence of the divine,
With hearts open wide, let the chants intertwine.
Breathe in deeply, feel the sacred sound,
As the vibrations purify, soul and spirit bound.

Begin with a chant, pure and clear,
A mantra of cleansing, removing all that's drear.
Let the words resonate, with each sacred tone,
As they penetrate, purifying to the bone.

As the chant reverberates, energy aligns,
Cleansing the soul, like celestial signs.
Feel the burdens release, as the sound unfolds,
Purification deepening, as each verse unfolds.

Invoke the divine beings, with hymns of grace,
Their presence embraces, in this sacred space.
Chant their names, with reverence and devotion,
In harmonious union, experiencing divine motion.

Let the sacred hymns fill the atmosphere,
Creating a vessel, pure and clear.
As the melodies rise, soul and spirit ascend,
Transcending limitations, to realms that transcend.

Release all impurities, doubts, and fears,
Through the sacred chants, let them disappear.

Feel the purity infusing every cell,
In this ritual of purification, where blessings dwell.

Continue the chants, building in intensity,
As the purification deepens, soul's clarity.
With each repetition, the energy amplifies,
Raising vibrations, as the chant intensifies.

Bathe in the divine melodies, like a gentle rain,
Purifying the spirit, washing away all stain.
Let the sacred sound cleanse and restore,
Leaving the soul radiant, forevermore.

In the closing of the ritual, express gratitude profound,
For the purification experienced, in this sacred ground.
May the sacred chants continue to resonate,
Guiding us to purity, in our spiritual state.

Thus, the ritual of purification through sacred chants finds its completion,
May the soul be cleansed and renewed, embracing divine transformation.
As the melodies fade, may the spirit's radiance shine,
Purified and awakened, in the realms of the divine.

120.   Spell for the transformation of the deceased into a vessel of divine protection

In the realm of spirits, where the ancient sleep,
We cast a spell, profound and deep.
To transform the deceased, with sacred grace,
Into a vessel of divine protection, in this sacred space.

Prepare the ritual space, adorned with symbols bold,
An altar of reverence, where protection unfolds.
Surround it with candles, their flames burning bright,
Invoking the divine presence, to guide us through the night.

Light the sacred flame, a beacon of divine light,
Igniting the path to transformation's might.
With focused intention, channel the ancient power,
To envelop the deceased, in a protective tower.

"Goddess of protection, I invoke your name,
Wrap the deceased in your shield, free from harm and blame.
Transform their essence, into a vessel secure,
A guardian of strength, steadfast and pure."

Call upon the celestial forces, both fierce and kind,
To infuse the deceased with protection aligned.
Let their energy merge, with the soul's essence,
Creating a shield, a divine presence.

Speak the incantation, with words potent and clear,
Allow the transformation to draw near.
"O ancient spirits, guardians of the divine,
Bestow upon the deceased your protective sign.
Transform their being, into a vessel of might,
Shielded from darkness, radiant with light."

Feel the currents of energy, flowing through the air,
As the transformation occurs, with utmost care.
Witness the deceased's essence, transmuted and changed,
Into a vessel of protection, divinely arranged.

Envision a shield, radiant and strong,
Surrounding the deceased, all their life long.
A shield of light, impenetrable and true,
Guarding them from harm, both old and new.

Offer gratitude to the divine forces at play,
For their transformative power on this sacred day.
May the deceased find solace and peace,
Protected and guided, their spirit released.

With reverence and gratitude, conclude the sacred rite,
Knowing the deceased is enveloped in protective light.
May they navigate the realms, secure and free,
A vessel of divine protection, for all eternity.

Thus, the spell for the transformation into a vessel of divine protection finds its end,
May the deceased be shielded and guided, their spirit forever on the mend.
Embraced by celestial forces, their protective presence strong,
As they journey through the realms, shielded from all wrong.

121.   Incantation to invoke the blessings of the celestial rivers and their life-giving flow

In the realm of spirits, where secrets reside,
We invoke the blessings of celestial rivers wide.
Their life-giving flow, their sacred embrace,
We call upon their essence, in this sacred space.

Raise your voice in reverence, let the incantation begin,
To awaken the rivers, their blessings to bring in.
Speak with authority, with words strong and clear,
Summon the currents, their presence drawing near.

"O celestial rivers, flowing with grace,
Carriers of life, in this sacred place.
I call upon your blessings, your divine flow,
Bestow upon us your abundance, in waters that glow."

Visualize the rivers, winding and free,
Their waters glistening, connecting you and me.
See the life force they carry, the vitality they bring,
Invoking their essence, the blessings they sing.

Feel the gentle caress of the rivers' touch,
As their currents surround you, a divine clutch.
Their waters cleanse and nourish, with every drop,
Revitalizing the spirit, never to stop.

Invoke the blessings of the rivers' might,
Their healing waters, a source of delight.
"Flow through our lives, with your sacred stream,
Renew our spirits, in waters pristine."

In gratitude and awe, offer your appreciation,
For the blessings bestowed, a divine manifestation.
May the rivers' flow guide you on your way,
Bringing abundance and renewal, day by day.

With reverence and gratitude, conclude the incantation,
Knowing the celestial rivers' blessings in creation.

May their life-giving flow continue to bestow,
Abundance and vitality wherever you go.

Thus, the incantation to invoke the blessings of the celestial rivers finds its end,
May their life-giving flow forever be your faithful friend.
In their embrace, may you find renewal and bliss,
Connected to their sacred essence, their eternal kiss.

122.   Ritual for the transfiguration of the deceased into a divine conduit of divine energy

In the realm of spirits, where mysteries unfold,
We gather to enact a ritual, potent and bold.
To transfigure the deceased, with divine grace,
Into a conduit of energy, a celestial embrace.

Prepare the sacred space, adorned with symbols divine,
An altar of reverence, where energies intertwine.
Surround it with candles, their flames dancing bright,
Illuminating the path to transfiguration's light.

Center your being, align with cosmic flow,
Open your heart, let divine energies grow.
Invoke the presence of celestial forces grand,
To witness and bless this ritual at hand.

"Divine energies, I call upon you this day,
Transfigure the deceased in a wondrous way.
Grant them the honor, to become a conduit true,
A vessel of divine energy, vibrant and anew."

Elevate your voice, with words of power and might,
Resonating through the realms, piercing the night.
Speak with reverence, with intentions pure,
Calling forth the transfiguration, to ensure.

Envision the deceased, their essence aglow,
As divine energy engulfs them, a celestial show.
See their form shifting, their spirit expanding,
Into a conduit of energy, divine power commanding.

Feel the currents of cosmic energy, swirling around,
As the transfiguration deepens, profound.
Witness the deceased's transformation unfold,
As they become a conduit, their spirit bold.

With each breath, inhale the celestial energy bright,
Allow it to flow through you, merging with their light.
Channel the divine essence, with utmost care,
Infusing the deceased's being, a conduit rare.

Offer gratitude to the celestial forces above,
For their presence and blessings, for their love.
May the deceased serve as a conduit pure,
A vessel of divine energy, forever to endure.

With reverence and gratitude, conclude the sacred rite,
Knowing the transfiguration has taken flight.
May the deceased's spirit shine with celestial power,
A conduit of divine energy, in this afterlife hour.

Thus, the ritual for the transfiguration into a divine conduit finds its conclusion,
May the deceased's spirit radiate with divine energy, their eternal fusion.
Embraced by celestial forces, their essence forever enshrined,
A conduit of divine energy, transcending all confines.

123. Spell for the reunion of the deceased's soul with their spiritual ancestors

In the realm of spirits, where connections span,
We weave a spell to unite the departed with their spiritual clan.
To bring forth the reunion, with ancestors of old,
Guiding the deceased's soul, in this sacred fold.

Create a sacred space, adorned with reverence deep,
An altar of remembrance, where the ancestors' presence seep.
Surround it with candles, their flames steady and bright,
Inviting the ancestral spirits, to join us in this rite.

Invoke the presence of the spiritual ancestors dear,
Their wisdom and guidance, drawing near.
With heartfelt intention, call upon their name,
To guide the departed soul, their reunion to reclaim.

Speak with sincerity, with words profound,
Addressing the ancestral spirits, their presence unbound.
"Ancestors of old, hear our plea,
Guide the departed soul, set their spirit free.
In this sacred reunion, let love abound,
Bring them home, to the ancestral ground."

Visualize the departed soul, surrounded by light,
As the ancestral spirits gather, shimmering and bright.
Feel their embrace, their love and protection strong,
Guiding the departed soul, where they belong.

Open your heart, invite the ancestral energies in,
To bridge the divide, let the reunion begin.
Feel their presence, as they surround the departed soul,
Nurturing and comforting, making them whole.

Let the ancestral spirits share their wisdom and grace,
Guiding the departed soul in this ethereal space.
Through whispers of insight, in whispers unknown,
They bring solace and clarity, as their love is shown.

Offer gratitude to the ancestral spirits above,
For their presence and blessings, for their eternal love.
May the departed soul find solace and peace,
Reunited with ancestors, their spiritual release.

With reverence and gratitude, conclude the sacred spell,
Knowing the reunion has been achieved, all is well.
May the departed soul find eternal connection and bliss,
Guided and embraced by the ancestral spirits' gentle kiss.

Thus, the spell for the reunion of the deceased's soul with their spiritual ancestors finds its end,
May the departed soul be surrounded by love, their reunion forever transcend.
In the realm of spirits, united with ancestors of old,
Their spirits entwined, a sacred bond to hold.

124.   Spell for Protection

In the realm of spirits, where powers intertwine,
I call upon the divine, this spell to design.
To shield and safeguard, with mystical art,
A potent protection, for mind, soul, and heart.

Gather your focus, let intentions align,
For this spell of protection, pure and divine.
Draw upon the energies, ancient and strong,
To shield from harm, all that may go wrong.

"By the forces of light, I call upon thee,
Guardians of protection, come forth and see.
Wrap me in your cloak, a shield so grand,
Shield me from harm, with your guiding hand."

Visualize a radiant light, surrounding your being,
A shield of protection, bright and all-seeing.
See it grow stronger, as your words unfold,
An impenetrable barrier, protecting from all that's untold.

Invoke the guardians, beings of might,
To stand by your side, both day and night.
Their presence brings comfort, their power secure,
Protecting your essence, keeping darkness obscure.

"Guardians of the unseen, I call upon your grace,
Wrap me in protection, in this sacred space.
Shield me from negativity, from harm and ill will,
With your divine power, may I be shielded still."

Feel the warmth of their embrace, as the spell takes hold,
A shield of protection, strong and bold.
Know that you are safe, wrapped in their care,
Shielded from dangers, with strength beyond compare.

With gratitude and trust, conclude the spell,
Knowing the protection is cast, all is well.
May this shield of light guide you each day,
Keeping you safe, on life's mystical way.

Thus, the spell for protection finds its end,
May you be guarded, forever on the mend.
In the realm of spirits, protected and strong,
Shielded from harm, as you journey along.

125.　Ritual of Opening the Mouth

The Ritual of Opening the Mouth was a sacred ceremony performed in ancient Egypt to awaken the senses of a statue or mummy, allowing it to partake in the offerings and rituals. It involved specific steps and gestures believed to restore the life force and grant the entity the ability to receive nourishment and engage with the spiritual realm. The following are the steps taken to perform the ritual:

Preparation:

Create a sacred space within the temple or burial chamber, adorned with symbolic objects and representations of deities associated with life and death.
Gather the necessary tools and offerings, including the Opening of the Mouth instrument (a special adze or utensil) and various ritual implements.
Purification:

Perform ablutions and purify yourself and the ceremonial tools with water, incense, and natron, symbolizing the cleansing of impurities and the readiness for the sacred act.
Invocation of Deities:

Call upon the protective and funerary deities, such as Anubis, Osiris, and Thoth, to witness and bless the ritual, guiding the deceased's spirit through the journey of awakening.
Opening the Mouth:

Holding the Opening of the Mouth instrument, the officiant (often a priest or family member) would approach the statue or mummy, focusing their intention on restoring the senses.
The officiant would then touch the instrument to the mouth and eyes of the entity, symbolically opening its faculties to receive offerings and engage with the spiritual realm.
This act was believed to restore the life force and enable the entity to breathe, eat, see, hear, and speak in the afterlife.
Offerings and Ritual Gestures:

Offer various food and drink items, such as bread, fruits, and libations, to the statue or mummy, representing the sustenance needed for the entity's journey.
Perform ritual gestures, such as the pouring of libations and the burning of incense, to purify and consecrate the offerings, allowing their spiritual essence to nourish the entity.

Ritual Utterances:

Recite specific prayers and utterances, invoking the power of the deities and affirming the entity's rejuvenation, renewed life, and connection to the divine realms.
These utterances often included the names of the deities involved and references to the ancient mythologies and cosmology of Egypt.
Conclusion:

Express gratitude to the deities, acknowledging their presence and assistance in the ritual.
Offer final prayers and blessings for the entity's continued journey in the afterlife, expressing hopes for eternal life, protection, and spiritual guidance.
The Ritual of Opening the Mouth was a solemn and profound ceremony, believed to bridge the gap between the physical and spiritual realms, ensuring the entity's continued existence and engagement in the afterlife.

126.   Incantation for Healing

In the realm of ancient wisdom and light,
I invoke the healing power, strong and bright.
With words of potency, this incantation unfolds,
To mend the body, to restore what was untold.

By the spirits of healing, known in old lore,
By Ra's golden rays and the Nile's sacred shore,
I call upon the forces, divine and pure,
To bring forth healing, a remedy sure.

"From the depths of the universe, healing flows,
Through the channels of life, let it transpose.
By the sacred breath, the essence of air,
May healing energy flow, beyond compare."

Visualize a gentle glow, surrounding the afflicted,
A soothing embrace, where pain is evicted.
See the light penetrating, each cell it will touch,
Restoring balance, vitality, and such.

Invoke the healers of old, the spirits renowned,
Imhotep's wisdom and Sekhmet's power profound,
May their essence infuse, every word that is spoken,
Healing energies released, their blessings unbroken.

"With each word I utter, with each sound I voice,
May healing vibrations, restore and rejoice.
By the spirits of the herbs and waters pure,
May the body's harmony, now endure."

Feel the energy shifting, as the incantation takes hold,
A surge of healing power, strong and bold.
Know that within, the body mends and mends,
A journey to wellness, where pain soon transcends.

With gratitude and trust, conclude the sacred chant,
Knowing the healing energy remains, ever so grand.
May this incantation's power bring comfort and grace,
Restoring the body's health, at its own perfect pace.

Thus, the incantation for healing finds its end,
May it bring restoration, to the one on whom it descends.
In the realm of ancient wisdom and light,
May healing prevail, shining pure and bright.

127.   Ritual of Offering

In the realm of ancient reverence and grace,
We gather in sacred space, a hallowed place.
With hearts aflame and intentions clear,
We perform the ritual of offering, held dear.

Preparation:

Create a sacred altar, adorned with symbols of the divine,
representing the gods and goddesses, both near and far.
Arrange offerings of food, drink, flowers, and incense,
chosen with care and devotion, each with its own significance.
Invocation of Deities:

Call upon the presence of the honored gods and goddesses,
who govern the realms of sky, earth, and the afterlife.
Recite their names, with reverence and respect,
inviting their divine presence to bless the ritual and accept the offering.
Presentation of Offerings:

With hands outstretched, present each offering one by one,
to the unseen realms and the deities who reside there.
Express gratitude and devotion, as you offer the gifts,
acknowledging the abundance and blessings bestowed upon you.
Uttering of Prayers:

Recite prayers and invocations, praising the deities,
acknowledging their divine qualities and powers.
Seek their favor and blessings, for yourself and your community,
and ask for guidance, protection, and abundance in return.
Sharing the Offering:

After the ritual, partake in a communal meal,
sharing the blessed offerings with all who gathered.
Experience the sacred connection, as the divine nourishment
is shared and enjoyed, fostering unity and spiritual communion.
Expression of Gratitude:

Offer heartfelt thanks to the deities for their presence,
their guidance, and the acceptance of the offerings.

Express gratitude for the blessings received,
and the opportunity to connect with the divine.
Closing:

Close the ritual by extinguishing the sacred flame,
symbolizing the completion of the offering.
Express a final prayer or blessing, asking for the continued
presence and favor of the deities in your life.
In this sacred act of offering, we connect with the divine,
Nourishing our souls, as we seek blessings to align.
May the gods and goddesses receive our devotion and praise,
Guiding us on our journey, through life's ever-changing maze.

Thus, the ritual of offering finds its end,
Leaving us blessed, by the gods we commend.
In the realm of ancient reverence and grace,
May the spirits embrace us, in every sacred space.

128.   Spell for Abundance

In the realm of ancient mystic lore,
I call upon abundance, evermore.
With words of power, this spell I cast,
To bring forth blessings, prosperity vast.

Preparation:

Create a sacred space, cleansed and clear,
Where the energies of abundance may appear.
Gather symbols of wealth, such as coins or grains,
And any objects that embody prosperity's gains.
Alignment:

Align your thoughts and intentions,
With the frequency of abundance's dimensions.
Believe in your worth and the universe's flow,
Trusting that abundance will soon bestow.
Invocation of Deities:

Call upon the gods and goddesses of plenty,
Such as Hathor, Isis, and Ptah, so mighty.
Seek their favor and assistance,
To manifest abundance with divine persistence.
Incantation:

Recite words of power, with conviction and might,
Calling forth abundance, day and night.
"By the forces of the cosmos, by the ancient lore,
I summon abundance, now and evermore.
From earth and sky, let prosperity flow,
Manifesting riches, wherever I go."
Visualization:

Envision the abundance you desire,
See it manifesting, reaching higher and higher.
Feel the joy and gratitude within,
As if the abundance has already begun to spin.
Offering:

Present an offering to the deities you invoke,
A token of gratitude, from the depths of your hope.
Give thanks for their guidance and assistance,
And for the blessings that will soon commence.
Release:

Let go of any doubts or fears,
Release them now, let abundance draw near.
Trust in the universe's infinite supply,
Knowing that abundance is your birthright, no deny.
Gratitude:

Express gratitude for the abundance bestowed,
For the riches that come, like rivers that flowed.
Give thanks for the blessings, big and small,
And share your abundance, for the good of all.
In the realm of ancient mystic lore,
May this spell for abundance open every door.
May blessings flow, and prosperity find its way,
Bringing abundance to you, each and every day.

Thus, the spell for abundance finds its end,
May prosperity to your life forever attend.
In the realm of dreams turned into reality,
May abundance be yours, eternally free.

129.   Incantation for Safe Journey

In the realm of ancient wisdom and might,
I call upon protection for a journey so bright.
With words of power and intention pure,
I summon safety and guidance to endure.

Preparation:

Find a quiet space, free from worldly noise,
Where you can connect with ancient joys.
Gather a symbol of protection, such as a talisman or stone,
Something to carry with you, wherever you may roam.
Invocation of Deities:

Invoke the deities of travel and protection,
Such as Horus, Bastet, and Thoth, with affection.
Seek their watchful eyes and divine care,
As you embark on your journey, so fair.
Incantation:

Speak the words of power, with faith and might,
Calling upon the forces that guard day and night.
"By the ancient powers that govern the way,
I summon protection for my journey today.
From start to end, may safety prevail,
Guided by light, may perils be curtailed."
Visualization:

Envision a radiant light surrounding you,
A shield of protection, steadfast and true.
See it extending, forming a bubble of divine grace,
Guarding you against any harm or trace.
Offering:

Present an offering to the deities you invoke,
A token of gratitude, from the depths of your hope.
Seek their favor and blessings on your path,
As you navigate the journey, free from wrath.
Trust:

Release any worries or fears from your mind,

Trusting in the guidance you will surely find.
Have faith in the unseen forces at play,
Knowing that safety will be with you each day.
Gratitude:

Express gratitude to the deities for their presence,
For their protection and unwavering essence.
Give thanks for the safe journey ahead,
And for the blessings received in this sacred thread.
In the realm of ancient wisdom and might,
May this incantation guide you through the night.
May your journey be safe, filled with joy and delight,
Protected and guarded, from morning to twilight.

Thus, the incantation for safe journey finds its end,
May it be your guiding light, a true and loyal friend.
In the realm of travel, both far and near,
May every step be blessed, banishing any fear.

130.   Ritual of the Opening of the Year

The Ritual of the Opening of the Year was a significant ceremony in ancient Egypt, marking the beginning of a new year and the renewal of cosmic and earthly cycles. This ritual was performed with great reverence and involved various symbolic actions and offerings. The following are the steps taken to perform the Ritual of the Opening of the Year:

Preparation:

The ritual would take place in a sacred temple, dedicated to a specific deity associated with the new year, such as Ra or Amun.
The temple would be adorned with colorful decorations, sacred symbols, and representations of the deities.
Priests and priestesses would undergo purification rites, ensuring their spiritual readiness to perform the ritual.
Awakening of the Deity:

The officiating high priest or priestess would approach the shrine or statue of the presiding deity.
With ceremonial gestures and offerings, they would awaken the deity from slumber, symbolizing the rejuvenation and renewal of cosmic energies.
Opening of the Temple Gates:

The high priest or a designated representative would ceremoniously open the temple gates, inviting the divine presence and cosmic energies to enter.
This act represented the connection between the earthly realm and the divine realm, facilitating the flow of blessings and abundance.
Offerings and Invocations:

Various offerings, including food, drink, incense, and precious items, would be presented to the deity.
Prayers and invocations would be recited, expressing gratitude for the past year's blessings and seeking divine guidance and protection for the year ahead.
The offerings would be believed to sustain the deity's energies and maintain cosmic order.
Processions and Celebrations:

Colorful processions would take place, featuring priests, priestesses, and devotees, adorned in ceremonial attire and carrying sacred objects and symbols.

Music, chants, and dances would fill the air, symbolizing the joyful celebration of the new year and the harmonious rhythm of the cosmos.

Proclamations and Declarations:

The high priest or a designated authority figure would make proclamations and declarations, affirming the renewal of cosmic cycles and the divine order for the new year.

These statements would reestablish the principles of justice, harmony, and balance in society and reaffirm the role of the pharaoh as the earthly representative of divine power.

Blessings and Dispensation of Amulets:

The high priest or priestess would bestow blessings upon the assembled devotees, offering prayers for their well-being, protection, and prosperity in the coming year. Amulets and talismans, believed to carry the divine blessings and provide spiritual and physical protection, would be distributed among the faithful.

Closing:

The high priest or designated authority figure would offer a closing prayer, expressing gratitude to the deities for their presence and blessings.

The temple gates would be ceremoniously closed, symbolizing the conclusion of the ritual and the containment of divine energies within the sacred space.

The Ritual of the Opening of the Year was a profound and joyous ceremony, embodying the cyclical nature of time and the eternal renewal of life. It served as a communal celebration, reaffirming the bond between humanity, the gods, and the cosmic forces that governed the universe.

131. Spell for Divine Guidance

In the realm of ancient mystic lore,
I seek divine guidance, forevermore.
With words of power, this spell I weave,
To connect with wisdom, I do believe.

Preparation:

Find a quiet space, serene and still,
Where you can commune with higher will.
Light a candle or burn sacred incense,
Creating an atmosphere of spiritual presence.
Centering and Intent:

Close your eyes and take deep breaths,
Clearing your mind from daily quests.
Focus your intention on seeking guidance,
Opening your heart to divine providence.
Invocation of Deities:

Call upon the gods and goddesses wise,
Such as Thoth, Ma'at, or Isis in the skies.
Request their presence and divine insight,
To shed light on your path, both day and night.
Incantation:

Speak the words of power, with reverence and trust,
Invoking the divine to guide you, both humble and just.
"By the ancient wisdom that spans the ages,
I summon divine guidance through eternal pages.
Illuminate my path, with clarity and grace,
Lead me to the truth, in every time and space."
Meditation and Stillness:

Enter a meditative state, calm and serene,
Open yourself to the guidance unseen.
Listen to the whispers of your intuition,
Allowing divine messages to spark recognition.
Signs and Symbols:

Be attentive to signs and symbols around,
Messages from the universe, profound.
Pay heed to synchronicities and dreams,
Where guidance often silently streams.
Gratitude and Trust:

Offer gratitude for the guidance received,
For the wisdom shared, helping you succeed.
Trust in the divine's loving embrace,
Knowing that guidance is present in every space.
Closing:

Give thanks to the deities for their presence,
For their guidance, wisdom, and essence.
Slowly open your eyes, feeling renewed,
Connected to the divine, your path imbued.
In the realm of ancient mystic lore,
May this spell for guidance forevermore,
Lead you on a path of truth and light,
Guided by wisdom, day and night.

Thus, the spell for divine guidance finds its end,
May you find wisdom, on which to depend.
In the realm of mysteries, both known and unseen,
May divine guidance bless your journey serene.

132. Ritual of Ancestor Worship

The Ritual of Ancestor Worship was a revered practice in ancient Egypt, honoring and paying homage to one's ancestors who had passed away. It was believed that the spirits of the deceased ancestors continued to exist and could provide guidance, blessings, and protection to their living descendants. The following are the steps taken to perform the Ritual of Ancestor Worship:

Setting:

Create a sacred space within the home or a designated ancestral shrine.
Place a representation or image of the ancestral spirits, such as a portrait, statue, or personal belongings.
Purification:

Begin with personal purification, cleansing the body and mind through ritual bathing or purifying gestures.
Light incense or burn sacred herbs, creating a spiritually pure atmosphere.
Offerings:

Prepare offerings of food and drink, including the favorite dishes and beverages of the deceased ancestors.
Arrange the offerings on an altar or table before the ancestral representation.
Include symbolic offerings, such as flowers, candles, and incense, to honor and appease the ancestral spirits.
Invocations and Prayers:

Invoke the names of the honored ancestors, speaking their names aloud with respect and love.
Offer prayers and heartfelt expressions of gratitude, acknowledging the guidance, protection, and blessings received from the ancestors.
Request continued guidance, blessings, and assistance in daily life and important endeavors.
Communion:

Sit or kneel before the ancestral representation, creating a connection with the spirits.
Engage in quiet meditation or reflection, allowing for a sense of communion and communication with the ancestors.
Listen attentively, with an open heart, for any messages or guidance that may be conveyed.
Sharing and Remembrance:

Share stories, memories, and anecdotes about the ancestors, keeping their legacies alive.

Reflect upon the qualities, virtues, and lessons learned from the ancestors, seeking to embody their positive traits.

Express love, honor, and respect for the ancestral lineage, acknowledging the interconnectedness of past and present.

Closing:

Express gratitude to the ancestral spirits for their presence and blessings.

Offer a final prayer or blessing, asking for the continued protection, guidance, and support of the ancestors.

Extinguish any candles or incense, signaling the completion of the ritual.

The Ritual of Ancestor Worship served as a profound and meaningful way to maintain a deep connection with one's ancestral lineage. It fostered a sense of belonging, gratitude, and reverence for the wisdom and guidance passed down through generations. It was a reminder that the spirits of the ancestors were always present, offering their love and support to their living descendants.

133. Incantation for Love and Harmony

In the realm of ancient mystic arts,
I invoke love's power to mend all hearts.
With words of enchantment, pure and true,
I call forth harmony, between me and you.

Preparation:

Find a peaceful space, free from strife,
Where you can harness love's transformative life.
Light a pink or red candle, symbolizing love's flame,
Illuminating the path for hearts to reclaim.
Centering and Intent:

Close your eyes and breathe deeply in,
Focus your thoughts, let love begin.
Set your intention for love and harmony,
A union of souls, bound eternally.
Invocation of Love Deities:

Invoke the deities of love and compassion,
Such as Hathor, Isis, or Aphrodite in their fashion.
Call upon their grace and divine embrace,
To infuse your life with love's enchanting grace.
Incantation:

Speak the words of power, with heartfelt desire,
Harnessing love's energy to ignite love's fire.
"By the ancient bonds that connect all hearts,
I invoke love's magic, where healing starts.
Let love's light shine upon us, bright and clear,
Creating harmony and joy, banishing all fear."
Visualization:

Envision love's radiant energy surrounding you,
Embracing your being, pure and true.
See it radiating outward, touching all around,
Filling hearts with love's harmonious sound.
Affirmations:

Repeat affirmations of love and harmony,
Declaring intentions with sincerity.
Speak words of kindness, compassion, and care,
Planting seeds of love, everywhere.
Sending Love:

Extend love's energy to those near and far,
To friends, family, and even those who scar.
Send love's healing vibrations to the world,
Creating a ripple effect, as love unfurled.
Gratitude and Release:

Express gratitude to the deities for their love,
For guiding your intentions from realms above.
Release the incantation to the universe's care,
Trusting love's power to manifest and share.
In the realm of ancient mystic arts,
May this incantation bind all broken parts.
May love's energy flow, abundant and true,
Creating harmony and joy, for me and you.

Thus, the incantation for love and harmony finds its end,
May it bring love's blessings, on which to depend.
In the realm of hearts united, both near and far,
May love's magic reign, forever shining like a star.

134.   Spell for Success in Business

In the realm of ancient mystic lore,
I seek success in business, forevermore.
With words of power, this spell I weave,
To attract prosperity and blessings to receive.

Preparation:

Find a quiet space, free from distraction,
Where you can focus on your business attraction.
Light a green or gold candle, symbolizing wealth,
Igniting the energy to boost business health.
Centering and Intent:

Close your eyes and take deep breaths,
Centering your mind from worldly tests.
Focus your intention on business success,
Visualize achievements and progress.
Invocation of Prosperity Deities:

Invoke the deities of abundance and prosperity,
Such as Osiris, Ptah, or Lakshmi with sincerity.
Call upon their blessings and financial grace,
To assist you in business endeavors you embrace.
Incantation:

Speak the words of power, with unwavering belief,
Channeling the energy to overcome any grief.
"By the ancient forces of wealth and gain,
I call forth success in my business domain.
Let opportunities flow and abundance grow,
May my ventures prosper, both high and low."
Visualization:

Envision your business flourishing and thriving,
Seeing it expanding and steadily thriving.
Picture satisfied customers and growing demand,
Visualize prosperity flowing in like a golden band.
Action and Strategy:

Combine the spell with diligent work,
Taking practical steps to achieve and perk.
Set goals, create plans, and take action,
Aligning your efforts with magical traction.
Networking and Connections:

Engage in networking, forming strong alliances,
Building relationships that foster business advancements.
Seek collaborations and mutually beneficial ties,
Expanding your reach and widening your skies.
Gratitude and Manifestation:

Express gratitude for the blessings to come,
Thanking the universe for what's already begun.
Believe in your success, hold it in your heart,
Manifesting abundance as a sacred art.
In the realm of ancient mystic lore,
May this spell for business success open the door.
May prosperity and abundance flow ceaselessly,
Bringing success and fulfillment, abundantly.

Thus, the spell for success in business finds its end,
May it bring prosperous ventures around the bend.
In the realm of business triumph, both near and far,
May this spell's magic guide you to reach your star.

135.   Ritual of Divination

The Ritual of Divination was a sacred practice in ancient Egypt used to seek guidance and insight into the past, present, and future. It allowed individuals to connect with the divine and receive messages from the spiritual realms. Here are the steps taken to perform the Ritual of Divination:

Preparation:

Find a quiet and serene space, free from distractions.
Gather divination tools such as oracle cards, scrying mirrors, or casting stones.
Light a candle or burn incense to create a sacred atmosphere.
Centering and Focus:

Take deep breaths and clear your mind of mundane thoughts.
Enter a state of deep relaxation and focus your attention on the purpose of the divination.
Invocation of Deities:

Call upon the gods and goddesses associated with divination, such as Thoth or Isis.
Request their presence and guidance in the divination process.
Connection with Higher Self:

Close your eyes and visualize a connection with your higher self or spiritual guides.
Invite their assistance and wisdom in interpreting the messages received.
Choosing the Method:

Select the divination method that resonates with you, such as tarot cards, runes, or pendulum.
Hold the chosen tool and imbue it with your intention and energy.
Formulating the Question:

Clearly formulate the question or topic for the divination.
Focus on the specific aspect you seek guidance or insight into.
Performing the Divination:

Follow the specific method's instructions for conducting the divination.
Shuffle or arrange the cards, cast the stones, or engage in the chosen practice.
Allow your intuition to guide you in the interpretation of the symbols and messages received.
Reflecting and Recording:

Take time to reflect on the insights and messages revealed.
Record the details of the divination, including the cards drawn or symbols observed.
Consider the broader meanings and potential implications of the divination results.
Gratitude and Closing:

Express gratitude to the deities and spiritual guides for their assistance.
Thank the divination tools for their cooperation in revealing the messages.
Blow out the candle or extinguish the incense to signify the end of the ritual.
The Ritual of Divination was a sacred endeavor, allowing individuals to tap into higher realms of knowledge and receive guidance for their lives. It provided a connection to the divine and an opportunity to gain deeper insights into the mysteries of existence.

136.   Incantation for Fertility

In the realm of ancient rites of old,
I call upon the powers that unfold.
With words of magic, potent and pure,
I invoke the blessings of fertility, sure.

Preparation:

Find a tranquil space in nature's embrace,
Where fertile energies freely interlace.
Light a green or white candle, symbolizing life,
Igniting the energy to bring forth fertility rife.
Centering and Intent:

Close your eyes, connect with the earth's core,
Grounding yourself, feeling its fertile lore.
Focus your intention on fertile abundance,
Visualize growth and life in every nuance.
Invocation of Fertility Deities:

Invoke the deities of fertility and creation,
Such as Isis, Hathor, or Demeter in dedication.
Call upon their power and nurturing grace,
To bless your life with fertility's embrace.
Incantation:

Speak the words of power, with passion and belief,
Channeling the energy to manifest relief.
"By the ancient forces of life's sacred flow,
I call forth fertility's blessings to bestow.
Let fertile energies blossom and grow,
Bringing forth life's wonders, to us all show."
Visualization:

Envision a lush garden, vibrant and green,
Where life flourishes in a magical scene.
Picture seeds sprouting, plants reaching high,
Imagining fertility's abundance drawing nigh.
Connection with Nature:

Spend time in nature, embracing its cycles,
Observing the beauty and miracles it encircles.
Engage with the earth, planting seeds with care,
Honoring the cycle of life, nurturing it with prayer.
Nurturing Self and Environment:

Nurture your body, mind, and spirit as well,
Providing a fertile ground for life to dwell.
Create a nurturing environment at home,
Harmonizing energies to fertility's dome.
Gratitude and Manifestation:

Express gratitude to the deities for their blessings,
Thanking them for the abundant fertility's dressings.
Embrace the belief that fertility is yours to receive,
Manifesting its blessings, with trust and conceive.
In the realm of ancient rites of old,
May this incantation's power forever hold.
May fertility's abundance grace your days,
Bringing forth life's wonders in miraculous ways.

Thus, the incantation for fertility finds its end,
May it bring blessings of life, on which to depend.
In the realm of fertile creation, both near and far,
May this spell's magic guide you to embrace the star.

137.Spell for Protection Against Evil Spirits

In the realm where darkness and light collide,
I seek protection from spirits that hide.
With words of power, this spell I cast,
To shield me from evil's grip, steadfast.

Preparation:

Find a quiet and sacred space to perform the spell.
Gather protective items such as a white candle, salt, and a small mirror.
Centering and Focus:

Take deep breaths to calm your mind and center your energy.
Visualize a radiant sphere of white light surrounding you, creating a protective barrier.
Invocation of Protection Deities:

Call upon deities associated with protection, such as Isis, Anubis, or Horus.
Request their presence and assistance in warding off evil spirits.
Incantation:

Speak the words of power, with conviction and strength,
Banishing evil spirits, protecting at length.
"By ancient forces of light and divine might,
I ward off evil spirits, banishing their blight.
With this spell, I create a shield so strong,
Protecting me from harm, all night long."
Symbolic Protection:

Light the white candle, symbolizing purity and protection.
Sprinkle a circle of salt around you, forming a barrier against negative energies.
Place the small mirror facing outward, reflecting away any malevolent forces.
Visualization and Intention:

Visualize a bubble of radiant light expanding from your core.
See it growing and encompassing your entire being, forming an impenetrable shield.
Intentionally project thoughts of protection, affirming your safety and repelling negativity.
Setting Boundaries:

Establish energetic boundaries, clearly stating what is allowed and what is not.

Command any malevolent spirits to depart, firmly asserting your protected space.
Gratitude and Closure:

Express gratitude to the deities for their presence and protection.
Extinguish the candle, symbolizing the completion of the spell.
Remove the salt and mirror, cleansing them for future use.
In the realm where darkness and light collide,
May this spell's protection forever abide.
May evil spirits be banished far and wide,
Leaving you safe, with peace as your guide.

Thus, the spell for protection against evil spirits finds its end,
May it shield you, your energy it will defend.
In the realm of divine protection, both near and far,
May this spell's magic guard you like a shining star.

138.   Ritual of Marriage

The Ritual of Marriage was a sacred ceremony in ancient Egypt, symbolizing the union of two individuals in love and commitment. It celebrated the bond between a couple and invoked the blessings of the gods for a harmonious and fruitful partnership. Here are the steps taken to perform the Ritual of Marriage:

Preparations:

Select a sacred space or temple for the ceremony, adorned with flowers and symbols of love.
Seek the presence and blessings of deities associated with love and marriage, such as Hathor or Osiris.
Gather family, friends, and witnesses to witness and participate in the ceremony.
Purification:

Both the bride and groom undergo a purification ritual, symbolizing the cleansing of past energies and preparing for a fresh start.
This may involve bathing in sacred water or receiving blessings from a priest or priestess.
Exchange of Vows:

The couple stands before an altar, facing each other, and declares their vows of love, commitment, and partnership.
They express their intentions to honor and support one another through the journey of life.
Exchange of Rings or Tokens:

The couple exchanges rings or other symbolic tokens, representing their eternal love and commitment.
These objects are blessed and imbued with the divine energy of the ceremony.
Invocation and Blessings:

A priest or priestess invokes the presence of the deities and seeks their blessings upon the couple.
Prayers and invocations are offered, asking for the gods' guidance, protection, and abundance in their marital union.
Offering and Unity Ritual:

The couple presents offerings to the deities, expressing their gratitude for the blessings bestowed.

They may also engage in a unity ritual, such as lighting a unity candle or pouring sand into a single vessel, symbolizing their unity as one.

Sacred Rituals and Symbolism:

The couple may participate in rituals specific to their cultural traditions, such as the binding of hands, sharing of a cup of wine, or the tying of a ceremonial knot.
These rituals deepen the symbolic significance of their union and strengthen their bond.

Pronouncement and Celebration:

The priest or priestess declares the couple as husband and wife, affirming their union before the gods and the gathered community.
Joyous celebrations, feasts, music, and dance follow, marking the beginning of their shared life together.
The Ritual of Marriage was a sacred and joyous occasion in ancient Egypt, uniting two souls in a lifelong partnership. It honored the gods and sought their blessings for a harmonious and prosperous union. It symbolized the joining of two paths into one, with love, commitment, and shared dreams for a fulfilling future.

139.   Incantation for Wisdom and Knowledge

In the realm of ancient wisdom's allure,
I seek the guidance of knowledge pure.
With words of power, this incantation I say,
To invoke wisdom's light, illuminating my way.

Preparation:

Find a serene and quiet space to perform the incantation.
Light a candle or burn incense, creating an atmosphere of focused energy.
Centering and Focus:

Close your eyes and take deep, calming breaths.
Still your mind and release any distractions, allowing space for wisdom to enter.
Invocation of Wisdom Deities:

Call upon deities associated with wisdom and knowledge, such as Thoth or Seshat.
Request their presence and guidance on your quest for enlightenment.
Incantation:

Speak the words of power, with reverence and intention,
Invoking wisdom's essence, beyond comprehension.
"By ancient forces of knowledge's embrace,
I summon wisdom's light, in this sacred space.
Grant me insight, clarity, and understanding deep,
Illumine my path, wisdom's secrets to keep."
Opening the Mind:

Visualize a beam of light entering the crown of your head,
Filling your mind with a radiant glow of wisdom's thread.
Feel the energy expanding, awakening dormant knowledge,
Embracing the pursuit of wisdom with fervor and courage.
Seeking Knowledge:

Engage in activities that nurture wisdom and knowledge,
Whether reading sacred texts, studying, or exploring college.
Embrace lifelong learning, seeking answers to your questions,
Cultivating a thirst for knowledge in all its expressions.
Reflection and Contemplation:

Take time to reflect upon the insights gained,
Meditate on the teachings, allowing wisdom to be retained.
Journal your thoughts, record profound revelations,
Allowing wisdom to be integrated into your daily observations.
Gratitude and Closing:

Express gratitude to the wisdom deities for their presence and guidance.
Blow out the candle or extinguish the incense, signifying the completion of the incantation.
Carry the intention of seeking wisdom and knowledge in your heart as you move forward.
In the realm of ancient wisdom's allure,
May this incantation's power forever endure.
May wisdom's light guide you on your way,
Revealing profound truths each and every day.

Thus, the incantation for wisdom and knowledge finds its end,
May it lead you to wisdom's depths, where insights transcend.
In the realm of divine enlightenment, both near and far,
May this spell's magic guide you like a shining star.

140.   Spell for Prosperity

In the realm where abundance takes its hold,
I call forth prosperity, shining gold.
With words of power, this spell I weave,
Invoking blessings to flourish and receive.

Preparation:

Find a peaceful and undisturbed space to perform the spell.
Gather symbols of abundance, such as coins, seeds, or green candles.
Centering and Focus:

Close your eyes, take deep breaths, and center your energy.
Clear your mind of doubts and fears, focusing solely on prosperity's sphere.
Invocation of Prosperity Deities:

Call upon deities associated with prosperity, such as Isis, Osiris, or Hathor.
Request their presence and blessings to amplify your abundance.
Incantation:

Speak the words of power, with unwavering belief,
Manifesting prosperity, bringing relief.
"By ancient forces of abundance and wealth,
I summon prosperity's blessings, with spiritual stealth.
Let my fortunes expand, let success unfold,
May abundance be mine, as the story is told."
Symbolic Actions:

Light green candles, representing the energy of prosperity.
Hold the symbols of abundance in your hands, infusing them with your intentions.
Visualize yourself surrounded by wealth, envisioning the life you desire.
Gratitude and Affirmation:

Express gratitude for the blessings already present in your life.
Affirm your worthiness of abundance and your readiness to receive.
Repeat affirmations such as, "I am open to receive abundance in all its forms."
Generosity and Giving:

Embrace the spirit of generosity and giving.

Share your wealth, whether through acts of kindness, donations, or supporting others in need.
Action and Opportunity:

Take inspired action towards your goals and aspirations.
Seize opportunities that align with your vision of prosperity.
Stay open to new ideas, collaborations, and avenues for financial growth.
Gratitude and Closing:

Offer gratitude to the prosperity deities for their blessings.
Express thanks for the abundance that flows into your life.
Close the ritual with a sense of optimism and anticipation.
In the realm where abundance takes its hold,
May this spell's power forever unfold.
May prosperity's blessings come your way,
Enriching your life, day by day.

Thus, the spell for prosperity finds its end,
May it bring abundance, around the bend.
In the realm of divine wealth, both near and far,
May this spell's magic guide you like a shining star.

141. Ritual of Renewal

The Ritual of Renewal was a sacred ceremony in ancient Egypt, performed to rejuvenate the mind, body, and spirit, and to invite the blessings of the gods for a fresh start. It was a ritual of purification and regeneration, symbolizing the cycles of life, death, and rebirth. Here are the steps taken to perform the Ritual of Renewal:

Preparations:

Find a serene and private space for the ritual, preferably near natural elements like water or plants.
Gather items such as white robes, flowers, herbs, and a small vessel of pure water.
Purification:

Begin the ritual by purifying yourself physically and mentally.
Take a cleansing bath or shower, focusing on releasing negative energies and thoughts.
Put on clean white robes, symbolizing purity and readiness for renewal.
Centering and Focus:

Sit in a comfortable position, close your eyes, and take deep breaths.
Quiet your mind, let go of distractions, and focus on the present moment.
Invocation of Renewal Deities:

Call upon deities associated with renewal and rebirth, such as Osiris or Nut.
Invite their presence and ask for their blessings in the ritual of renewal.
Ritual Cleansing:

Take the vessel of pure water and sprinkle or pour it over yourself.
Visualize the water washing away any stagnant energy or impurities, leaving you refreshed and renewed.
Offering and Affirmation:

Offer flowers or herbs as symbols of new beginnings and growth.
Hold them in your hands and affirm your intention for renewal and transformation.
Repeat affirmations such as, "I release the old and embrace the new. I am ready for renewal."
Meditation and Inner Reflection:

Enter into a meditative state and reflect on areas of your life that need renewal.

Visualize a golden light surrounding you, purifying and revitalizing every aspect of your being.

Allow any emotions or thoughts that arise to be acknowledged and released.

Rebirth and Celebration:

Imagine yourself emerging from a cocoon or stepping into a new dawn.

Embrace the sense of rebirth, envisioning a fresh start filled with positivity and opportunities.

Express gratitude for the blessings of renewal and celebrate this transformative moment.

Closing and Integration:

Thank the deities for their presence and blessings throughout the ritual.

Take a few moments to ground yourself and integrate the energies of renewal.

Carry the essence of renewal with you, knowing that you have embarked on a new chapter of growth and transformation.

The Ritual of Renewal was a sacred practice in ancient Egypt, symbolizing the power of transformation and the eternal cycles of life. It offered an opportunity to release the old, embrace the new, and invite divine blessings for a fresh start. By participating in this ritual, individuals sought to purify their beings, rejuvenate their spirits, and align themselves with the natural forces of renewal.

142. Incantation for Protection During Sleep

In the realm of dreams, where shadows creep,
I call forth protection, both strong and deep.
With words of power, this incantation I say,
To safeguard my slumber, until the break of day.

Preparations:

Find a calm and quiet space where you can lie down comfortably for sleep.
Dim the lights or light a soothing candle to create a peaceful ambiance.
Centering and Focus:

Lie down on your bed and close your eyes.
Take several deep breaths to relax your body and quiet your mind.
Visualize a serene and protective energy enveloping you.
Invocation of Protective Deities:

Call upon deities associated with protection, such as Isis or Horus.
Request their presence and blessings to shield you during sleep.
Incantation:

Speak the words of power, with intention and conviction,
Invoking protection's strength, a secure haven.
"By ancient forces, protect me while I sleep,
Shield me from harm, my slumber to keep.
May no ill enter, nor any dark entity,
I am safe and secure, in divine tranquility."
Sacred Symbols:

Place a protective amulet or talisman near your bedside, such as an Eye of Horus or
an ankh.
These symbols act as a physical reminder of your intention for protection.
Visualization and Affirmation:

Imagine a bright, radiant light surrounding your sleeping area.
Visualize this light forming a shield, impenetrable by negative or harmful energies.
Repeat affirmations such as, "I am safe and protected during my sleep. I am
surrounded by divine light."

Gratitude and Trust:

Express gratitude to the protective deities for their presence and guidance.
Trust in their power and the strength of your intention for protection.
Release any worries or concerns, knowing that you are safe and secure.
Drifting into Sleep:

Allow yourself to drift into a state of relaxation and surrender.
Release control and trust that you are being watched over and protected.
Drift into sleep with a sense of peace and assurance.
In the realm of dreams, where shadows creep,
May this incantation's power forever seep.
May protection surround you through the night,
Safeguarding your slumber until the morning light.

Thus, the incantation for protection during sleep finds its end,
May it bring peace and security, a trusted friend.
In the realm of divine rest, both near and far,
May this spell's magic guide you like a shining star.

143.　　Spell for Emotional Healing

In the realm where emotions reside,
I seek healing, a soothing tide.
With words of power, this spell I weave,
To mend my heart, and pain relieve.

Preparations:

Find a quiet and comfortable space where you can be alone.
Gather items that bring you comfort, such as a soft blanket, crystals, or a journal.
Centering and Focus:

Sit or lie down in a relaxed position.
Close your eyes, take deep breaths, and center your energy.
Allow yourself to let go of any tension or distractions.
Invocation of Healing Deities:

Call upon deities associated with healing and emotional well-being, such as Isis or Sekhmet.
Invite their presence and ask for their guidance in the process of emotional healing.
Incantation:

Speak the words of power, with sincerity and intention,
Invoking emotional healing, a divine intervention.
"By ancient forces of love and light,
I summon healing energy, pure and bright.
Mend my heart, soothe my soul,
Restore my emotions, make me whole."
Emotional Release:

Allow yourself to feel the emotions that need healing.
Cry, scream, or express your emotions in a safe and healthy way.
Release any pent-up feelings and let them flow out of you.
Comfort and Self-Care:

Wrap yourself in a soft blanket or hold comforting objects.
Engage in self-care activities that nurture your emotional well-being, such as taking a bath, writing in a journal, or listening to calming music.
Visualization and Affirmation:

Visualize a gentle, healing light surrounding you, entering through your heart.
Imagine this light dissolving any emotional pain or wounds, replacing them with love and healing energy.
Repeat affirmations such as, "I release past pain and embrace emotional healing. I am worthy of love and peace."
Gratitude and Acceptance:

Express gratitude to the healing deities for their presence and assistance.
Embrace acceptance of your emotions and the healing process.
Trust that emotional healing is unfolding in divine timing.
Integration and Growth:

Take moments throughout your day to reflect on your emotions and the progress of your healing.
Practice self-compassion and patience as you continue on your journey of emotional healing.
Seek support from loved ones or professionals if needed.
In the realm where emotions reside,
May this spell's power forever provide.
May your heart find solace, wounds mend,
Emotional healing, a journey to transcend.

Thus, the spell for emotional healing finds its end,
May it bring peace and wholeness, around the bend.
In the realm of divine emotional well-being, both near and far,
May this spell's magic guide you like a shining star.

144.   Ritual of Purification

The Ritual of Purification was a sacred ceremony in ancient Egypt, performed to cleanse the body, mind, and spirit from impurities and negative energies. It was a ritual of renewal and preparation for engaging with the divine. Here are the steps taken to perform the Ritual of Purification:

Preparations:

Find a sacred space, preferably near water or in a serene environment.
Gather items such as water, natron (a type of salt), oils, and clean linen.
Centering and Focus:

Stand or sit in a comfortable position and take a few deep breaths.
Clear your mind of distractions and focus on the intention of purification.
Invocation of Purification Deities:

Call upon deities associated with purification, such as Hapi or Ma'at.
Request their presence and blessings for the ritual of purification.
Cleansing the Body:

Begin by washing your hands and face with clean water.
Stand or sit near a basin of water and cleanse your body, starting from the head and working down to the feet.
As you cleanse, visualize the impurities and negative energies being washed away.
Purification with Natron:

Prepare a mixture of natron and water in a sacred vessel.
Dip a clean linen cloth or sponge into the natron water and gently rub it over your body.
As you do so, imagine the natron purifying and purging any impurities from your being.
Anointing with Oils:

After the natron purification, apply scented oils to your body.
Choose oils that are associated with purification and spiritual upliftment, such as lotus or frankincense.
Rub the oils into your skin, focusing on areas like the forehead, chest, and hands.
Affirmations and Prayers:

Speak affirmations or prayers that reflect your desire for purification.

Express gratitude for the cleansing process and ask for continued guidance and protection.
Visualization and Energy Alignment:

Close your eyes and visualize a radiant white light surrounding you.
Imagine this light purifying and harmonizing your body, mind, and spirit.
Feel the energy of purification flowing through every part of your being.
Gratitude and Release:

Offer gratitude to the purification deities for their presence and blessings.
Express your intention to release any lingering impurities or negative energies.
Visualize these energies dissipating and being replaced by divine purity and light.
Integration and Renewal:

Take a moment to absorb the energies of purification and renewal.
Reflect on the experience and set intentions for maintaining a purified state of being.
Carry the essence of purification with you, knowing that you have cleansed and prepared yourself for divine connection.
The Ritual of Purification was a sacred practice in ancient Egypt, symbolizing the cleansing and preparation of the body, mind, and spirit for sacred engagement. It offered an opportunity to release impurities, negative energies, and blockages, creating a state of receptivity and alignment with the divine. By participating in this ritual, individuals sought to purify their beings, renew their connection to the divine, and walk the path of spiritual growth and transformation.

145.   Incantation for Rain and Fertility

In the realm where heavens meet the earth,
I invoke the powers that bring forth rebirth.
With words of power, this incantation I cast,
To summon rain's blessings, fertility unsurpassed.

Preparation:

Find a serene outdoor space, preferably during a time of need for rain and fertility.
Take a moment to connect with nature and the elements around you.
Centering and Focus:

Stand tall with your feet firmly planted on the ground.
Close your eyes, take deep breaths, and feel your connection to the earth.
Invocation of Rain and Fertility Deities:

Call upon deities associated with rain and fertility, such as Tefnut or Osiris.
Invite their presence and ask for their assistance in bringing forth rain and abundance.
Incantation:

Speak the words of power, with conviction and reverence,
Summoning rain's blessings, fertility's deliverance.
"By ancient forces of sky and earth,
I call upon rain's gift, fertility's rebirth.
Let the heavens open, let the waters flow,
Bless us with rain, let fertility grow."
Visualize Rain and Fertility:

Envision dark clouds gathering in the sky above.
See the rain pouring down, nourishing the earth and bringing life to the land.
Imagine plants growing, blossoming, and bearing abundant fruits.
Connection and Gratitude:

Extend your arms upward, embracing the energy of the heavens.
Express gratitude to the rain and fertility deities for their presence and blessings.
Thank them for the abundant rains and fertility that will manifest.
Offerings:

Prepare offerings of water, fruits, or flowers to honor the rain and fertility deities.
Place these offerings in a sacred space, inviting their acceptance and appreciation.

Trust and Release:

Trust in the power of the incantation and the blessings it has invoked.
Release any doubts or worries, knowing that rain and fertility will come in divine timing.
Have faith in the cycle of nature and the abundance it brings.
In the realm where heavens meet the earth,
May this incantation's power bring forth rebirth.
May rain's blessings fall, and fertility grow,
Nurturing the land, abundance to bestow.

Thus, the incantation for rain and fertility finds its end,
May it bring forth life, renewal, and blend.
In the realm of nature's bounty, both near and far,
May this spell's magic guide you like a shining star.

146.   Spell for Banishing Negativity

In the realm where light overcomes the dark,
I call upon the powers to make negativity depart.
With words of power, this spell I cast,
To banish negativity, ensuring it shall not last.

Preparation:

Find a quiet and peaceful space where you can focus without distractions.
Gather items that symbolize positivity and protection, such as a white candle, a black tourmaline crystal, and purifying herbs like sage or rosemary.
Centering and Focus:

Sit or stand in a comfortable position and take a few deep breaths.
Close your eyes, allowing yourself to become present in the moment.
Clear your mind and focus on your intention to banish negativity.
Invocation of Protective Deities:

Call upon deities associated with protection and purification, such as Bastet or Ra.
Invite their presence and ask for their assistance in banishing negativity from your life.
Lighting the White Candle:

Light the white candle as a symbol of purity, light, and positivity.
As the flame grows, visualize it radiating a bright and powerful light that dispels darkness and negativity.
Cleansing and Purification:

Use the purifying herbs, such as sage or rosemary, to smudge yourself and the space around you.
Wave the smoke over your body, focusing on areas where negativity may linger.
Envision the smoke purifying and cleansing your energy field, removing any traces of negativity.
Empowering Affirmations:

Speak empowering affirmations that reinforce your intention to banish negativity.
Repeat affirmations such as, "I release all negativity from my life. I am surrounded by positivity and light. I attract only positive energies."
Visualization and Energy Release:

Close your eyes and visualize a dark cloud of negativity hovering around you.

See the cloud being dispersed by a gust of wind or dissolved by the radiant light of the white candle flame.

As the negativity dissipates, imagine a clear and vibrant energy enveloping you, filling the space with positivity.

Protection and Seal:

Hold the black tourmaline crystal in your hands, infusing it with your intention to protect against negativity.

Visualize a shield of protective energy forming around you, creating a barrier that repels negativity.

Place the crystal near your workspace or carry it with you as a talisman of protection.

Gratitude and Closure:

Express gratitude to the protective deities for their presence and assistance in banishing negativity.

Thank the elements and energies that have supported you throughout the spell.

Close the spell with words of gratitude and affirmation, knowing that you are now free from negativity.

In the realm where light overcomes the dark,
May this spell's power create a vital spark.
May negativity be banished, never to return,
Positivity and light within you eternally burn.

Thus, the spell for banishing negativity finds its end,
May it protect and uplift, around the bend.
In the realm of positive energy, both near and far,
May this spell's magic guide you like a shining star.

147.   Ritual of Harvest Blessing

The Ritual of Harvest Blessing was a sacred ceremony in ancient Egypt, performed to give thanks for a bountiful harvest and to invoke blessings for future abundance. It celebrated the cycle of growth and the abundance provided by the land. Here are the steps taken to perform the Ritual of Harvest Blessing:

Preparation:

Find a suitable outdoor location, preferably near a field or garden.
Gather symbols of the harvest, such as grains, fruits, and vegetables.
Centering and Focus:

Stand or sit in a comfortable position, grounding yourself.
Take a few deep breaths, quieting your mind and connecting with the energy of the earth.
Invocation of Harvest Deities:

Call upon deities associated with harvest and abundance, such as Osiris or Hathor.
Invite their presence and blessings for the harvest ritual.
Harvest Offering:

Arrange the symbols of the harvest, such as grains, fruits, and vegetables, in a decorative manner.
Place the offering in a sacred space, representing the abundance of the harvest.
Gratitude and Reflection:

Take a moment to reflect on the bountiful harvest and the gifts of the earth.
Express gratitude for the abundance and the sustenance it provides.
Blessing the Harvest:

Extend your hands over the offering, symbolizing the transfer of energy and blessings.
Speak words of blessing and gratitude, acknowledging the earth's generosity and abundance.
Pray for continued fertility and a prosperous future.
Sharing and Celebration:

Share the harvest offering with others present, symbolizing the communal celebration of abundance.
Enjoy a meal together, incorporating the harvested ingredients, and savor the flavors and nourishment.

Offering of Thanks:

Offer a final prayer of thanks to the harvest deities for their presence and blessings. Express appreciation for the cycle of growth and the abundance received.
Closing:

Conclude the ritual by expressing gratitude to the earth and the harvest deities. Offer a gesture of farewell and honor to the spirits of the land.
The Ritual of Harvest Blessing celebrated the connection between humans and the earth, expressing gratitude for the bountiful harvest and invoking blessings for continued abundance. It was a time of communal celebration and appreciation for the gifts of nature. By participating in this ritual, individuals honored the land, acknowledged the cycle of growth, and expressed gratitude for the nourishment provided by the harvest.

148.   Incantation for Rebirth and Transformation

In the realm where souls are born anew,
I call upon the powers to transform and renew.
With words of power, this incantation I cast,
To invoke rebirth and transformation that shall last.

Preparation:

Find a quiet and sacred space where you can focus without distractions.
Light a white or blue candle to symbolize the transformative energy you seek.
Centering and Focus:

Sit or stand in a comfortable position and take a few deep breaths.
Close your eyes and visualize yourself surrounded by a warm, radiant light.
Feel the energy flowing through your body, awakening your spirit.
Invocation of Rebirth Deities:

Call upon deities associated with rebirth and transformation, such as Isis or Phoenix.
Invite their presence and ask for their guidance in your journey of rebirth.
Incantation:

Speak the words of power, with intention and conviction,
Invoking the forces of transformation and rebirth.
"From the ashes of the past, I rise anew,
Transforming, evolving, my spirit true.
Like a phoenix, I soar, reborn with might,
Embracing change, transforming darkness into light."
Visualize Rebirth and Transformation:

Envision yourself shedding old patterns and limitations.
See yourself rising like a phoenix, renewed and transformed.
Picture the qualities and aspects you wish to embody in your rebirth.
Affirmations:

Speak affirmations that align with your desire for rebirth and transformation.
Repeat statements such as, "I release the old and welcome the new. I embrace
positive change and growth. I am reborn, transformed, and empowered."
Embrace the Energy:

Allow the energy of the incantation and your intentions to permeate your being.
Feel the transformative energy flowing through you, igniting your spirit.
Embrace the emotions and sensations that arise, knowing that transformation is underway.
Gratitude and Integration:

Express gratitude to the deities for their presence and guidance in your journey of rebirth.
Thank them for the transformative energy that will continue to support and uplift you.
Take a moment to integrate the experience, grounding yourself and embracing your newfound empowerment.
In the realm where souls are born anew,
May this incantation's power bring forth what's true.
May rebirth and transformation be yours to hold,
As you journey onward, empowered and bold.

Thus, the incantation for rebirth and transformation finds its end,
May it guide you on a path of growth, around the bend.
In the realm of endless possibilities, both near and far,
May this spell's magic guide you like a shining star.

149.   Spell for Safe Childbirth

In the realm of life's sacred creation,
I call upon the powers of protection.
With words of power, this spell I cast,
To ensure safe childbirth, holding fear in the past.

Preparation:

Create a calm and nurturing environment in the birthing space.
Light a white or pink candle to symbolize purity and love.
Centering and Focus:

The expectant mother should find a comfortable position and take slow, deep breaths.
Close the eyes, focusing on the connection with the baby and the energy of love.
Invocation of Protective Deities:

Call upon deities associated with motherhood and childbirth, such as Isis or Hathor.
Invite their presence and ask for their guidance and protection throughout the birthing process.
Blessing of the Birthing Space:

Take a moment to bless the birthing space and create a sacred atmosphere.
Use sacred water or a sprig of lavender to sprinkle or cleanse the area, symbolizing purity and protection.
Affirmations of Safety and Strength:

Speak affirmations that reinforce a sense of safety, strength, and trust in the birthing process.
Repeat statements such as, "I am safe, strong, and supported. My body knows how to birth my baby with ease. Love and protection surround us."
Visualize a Smooth and Safe Birth:

Encourage the expectant mother to visualize a smooth and safe childbirth experience.
See the baby descending through the birth canal, supported by the gentle guidance of the mother's body.
Envision a warm and loving atmosphere, with the presence of protective energies surrounding both mother and baby.
Prayers and Requests:

Offer prayers for the well-being and safety of the mother and baby.

Request the assistance and protection of the protective deities, asking them to guide the birthing process.
Healing and Calming Energy:

Place hands gently on the mother's belly, radiating love and calmness.
Imagine a soothing energy flowing through the hands, promoting relaxation and reducing any discomfort.
Gratitude and Trust:

Express gratitude to the protective deities for their presence and guidance throughout the birthing process.
Trust in the innate wisdom of the body and the natural process of childbirth.
In the realm of life's sacred creation,
May this spell bring forth safe childbirth, a blessed sensation.
May love and protection encompass mother and child,
Guided by deities, serene and mild.

Thus, the spell for safe childbirth finds its end,
May it bring peace and assurance, around the bend.
In the realm of new beginnings, both near and far,
May this spell's magic guide you like a shining star.

150. Ritual of Funeral Procession

In the solemn realm of the departed's farewell,
The Funeral Procession begins, a ritual to dwell.
With reverence and honor, we gather today,
To escort the departed on their sacred way.

Preparation:

Prepare a sacred space for the Funeral Procession.
Decorate the area with symbols of mourning and remembrance, such as black drapes
and floral arrangements.
Gathering of Mourners:

Mourners assemble at the designated location, dressed in somber attire.
Each person carries a token of remembrance, such as a flower or a small item
symbolizing the deceased.
Invocation of Ancestral Spirits:

Call upon the ancestral spirits to guide and protect the departed soul.
Offer prayers or incantations to honor and seek their presence during the procession.
Formation of the Procession:

Arrange the mourners in a line, with the closest family members and loved ones at
the forefront.
Hold hands or link arms, symbolizing the collective support and unity in grief.
Funeral Chants:

Begin the procession with funeral chants or hymns, expressing sorrow and
remembrance.
Sing or recite verses that honor the life of the departed and evoke a sense of
reverence.
The Departed's Journey:

Carry or transport the casket or symbolic representation of the deceased at the head
of the procession.
Walk slowly and solemnly, paying respect to the departed's final journey.
Moments of Reflection:

Pause at significant points along the procession route to allow for moments of
reflection and remembrance.

Share memories or stories about the departed, honoring their life and legacy.
Offerings and Prayers:

At designated intervals, pause to offer prayers, incantations, or other forms of spiritual offerings.
Express gratitude for the departed's life, seek blessings for their journey, and offer comfort to the grieving.
Arrival at the Final Resting Place:

Reach the final destination, such as the burial site or the crematorium.
Gather around the gravesite or designated area, creating a circle of support and love.
Closing Ritual:

Conclude the Funeral Procession with a final prayer or closing ritual.
Express gratitude for the presence of the mourners and the guidance of the ancestral spirits.
In the solemn realm of the departed's farewell,
We complete the Funeral Procession, a sacred spell.
With reverence and honor, we bid our adieu,
Guided by spirits, our love and grief true.

Thus, the Ritual of Funeral Procession finds its end,
May it honor the departed and bring solace, my friend.
In the realm of remembrance, both near and far,
May this ritual's essence comfort, like a guiding star.

151. Incantation for Communication with the Dead

In the realm where spirits dwell,
I call upon the departed, I cast my spell.
With reverence and intent, I seek to commune,
To bridge the realms and hear their whispered tune.

Preparation:

Find a quiet and sacred space where you can focus without distractions.
Light a candle or incense to create an atmosphere conducive to spiritual communication.
Invocation of Ancestral Spirits:

Call upon the ancestral spirits, invoking their presence and guidance.
Speak their names or offer words of invitation, inviting them to communicate with you.
Centering and Focus:

Sit or stand in a comfortable position and take a few deep breaths.
Close your eyes and visualize a connection between your heart and the realm of the spirits.
Incantation:

Speak the words of power, with clarity and sincerity,
Invoking the spirits and opening the channels of communication.
"O spirits of the departed, I call upon thee,
With respect and reverence, I seek to see.
Bridge the realms, let our communication flow,
Share your wisdom and guidance, here below."
Silence and Receptivity:

After speaking the incantation, maintain a receptive state of mind.
Be open to signs, messages, or sensations that may come from the spirit realm.
Listen attentively and trust your intuition.
Questions and Requests:

If you have specific questions or requests for the departed, speak them aloud or silently in your mind.

Be clear and concise in your intentions, allowing space for the spirits to respond.
Signs and Messages:

Pay attention to any signs or messages that may manifest during the communication.
These may include dreams, synchronicities, or subtle sensations that indicate a
response from the spirits.
Gratitude and Farewell:

Express gratitude to the ancestral spirits for their presence and willingness to
communicate.
Thank them for any messages or guidance received during the interaction.
Bid farewell with respect and love, acknowledging the temporary nature of the
connection.
In the realm where spirits dwell,
May this incantation's power weave its spell.
May communication with the departed be clear,
Their wisdom and guidance, to our hearts, draw near.

Thus, the Incantation for Communication with the Dead finds its end,
May it open the channels and messages, spirit to friend.
In the realm of unseen connection, both near and far,
May this incantation's magic guide you like a shining star.

152.   Spell for Removing Curses

In the shadowed realm of lingering hex,
I cast this spell to remove the vex.
With power and intent, I break the curse,
Releasing its hold, invoking blessings' verse.

Preparation:

Create a sacred space where you can perform the spell without interruptions.
Gather items that symbolize purification and protection, such as salt and a white candle.
Centering and Focus:

Take a moment to ground yourself and center your energy.
Close your eyes and breathe deeply, allowing your mind to become focused and clear.
Invocation of Divine Assistance:

Call upon the divine forces or deities that resonate with you for assistance in removing the curse.
Speak their names or offer prayers, requesting their aid in breaking the negative energy.
Cleansing Ritual:

Light the white candle, symbolizing purity and divine intervention.
Sprinkle salt around the area or create a salt circle to create a protective barrier.
Incantation:

Speak the words of power, with conviction and authority,
Breaking the curse's hold and restoring harmony.
"By the power of light and the forces divine,
I break this curse, its grip unbind.
Negative energies, away you disperse,
I call upon blessings, in this universe."
Visualization:

Visualize the curse unraveling and dissipating, like dark clouds dispersing.
See yourself surrounded by a protective shield of light, shielding you from any remaining negative influences.
Symbolic Action:

Take a symbolic action to represent the breaking of the curse.
This could include snapping a twig, tearing a piece of paper with the curse written on it, or extinguishing the candle.
Gratitude and Closure:

Express gratitude to the divine forces or deities for their assistance in removing the curse.
Thank them for their guidance and protection throughout the process.
Close the ritual with a prayer or affirmation of positive energy and blessings.
In the shadowed realm of lingering hex,
May this spell remove the curse's vex.
May negative energies scatter and disperse,
Replaced by blessings, in this universe.

Thus, the Spell for Removing Curses finds its end,
May it bring relief and protection, on which you depend.
In the realm of renewed positivity, both near and far,
May this spell's magic guide you like a shining star.

153. Ritual of Temple Dedication

In the realm where gods reside,
We gather to dedicate, side by side.
With reverence and awe, we consecrate,
This sacred temple, a divine estate.

Preparation:

Prepare the temple space, ensuring cleanliness and readiness for dedication.
Decorate the altar and sacred areas with symbols representing the gods and their attributes.
Purification:

Begin the ritual with a purification ceremony, using water or incense to cleanse the space and participants.
Sprinkle or wave the purifying element while reciting prayers or incantations of purification.
Invocation of Deities:

Call upon the gods and goddesses who will preside over the temple.
Invoke their names and attributes, inviting their presence and blessings.
Presentation of Offerings:

Offer gifts and sacrifices to the deities as a sign of devotion and gratitude.
These offerings may include food, drink, flowers, incense, or other items that hold symbolic significance.
Blessing and Consecration:

Invoke the divine blessings upon the temple and its sacred spaces.
Use sacred oils or water to anoint the temple walls, statues, and altar, infusing them with divine energy.
Prayers and Chants:

Recite prayers and chants that honor the deities and express devotion.
Engage in communal singing or chanting to create an atmosphere of reverence and spiritual connection.
Ritual Actions:

Perform symbolic actions that represent the purpose and essence of the temple.

This may include lighting candles, ringing bells, or performing specific gestures that hold spiritual significance.
Oath and Dedication:

Make a solemn oath or vow to uphold the sanctity of the temple and its rituals.
Declare your commitment to the service of the deities and the spiritual community associated with the temple.
Communion and Celebration:

Share in communal feasting and celebration to honor the temple dedication.
Partake in food and drink as a symbol of unity and divine communion.
Closing and Blessing:

Conclude the ritual with a final prayer or blessing, expressing gratitude to the gods and goddesses.
Ask for their ongoing presence and guidance in the temple's sacred work.
In the realm where gods reside,
We dedicate this temple with reverence and pride.
May divine blessings forever flow,
In this sacred space, where gods bestow.

Thus, the Ritual of Temple Dedication finds its end,
May it be a sanctuary where gods and mortals blend.
In the realm of divine connection, both near and far,
May this ritual's essence guide you like a guiding star.

154.   Incantation for Protection of the Home

In the sanctuary of our humble abode,
I cast this incantation, to protect the abode.
With ancient words of power and sacred might,
I summon guardians to keep our home alight.

Preparation:

Find a quiet and comfortable space within your home to perform the incantation.
Light a white or protective-colored candle to create a sacred atmosphere.
Centering and Focus:

Close your eyes and take a few deep breaths to calm your mind.
Visualize a shield of protective energy enveloping your home, warding off negative influences.
Invocation of Guardians:

Call upon the guardians or deities associated with home protection.
Speak their names or offer prayers, inviting their presence and assistance in safeguarding your home.
Incantation:

Speak the words of power, with conviction and belief,
Invoking protection and security, to bring relief.
"By the strength of ancient magic and divine might,
I call upon guardians, to keep our home tight.
Shield us from harm, both seen and unseen,
Protect our sanctuary, where love and joy convene."
Visualization:

Visualize a brilliant light surrounding your home, forming a protective barrier.
See this light growing stronger and brighter, emanating a sense of safety and security.
Symbolic Action:

Take a symbolic action to enhance the incantation's power.
This could involve sprinkling salt at entrances, drawing protective symbols on windows or doors, or placing protective amulets in key areas.
Gratitude and Closure:

Express gratitude to the guardians or deities for their protection and assistance.
Thank them for their presence and ongoing support in safeguarding your home.
Extinguish the candle, symbolizing the completion of the ritual.
In the sanctuary of our humble abode,
May this incantation protect the abode.
May guardians stand watch, with steadfast might,
Keeping our home safe, in day and night.

Thus, the Incantation for Protection of the Home finds its end,
May it shield your dwelling, your refuge, and your friend.
In the realm of secure living, both near and far,
May this incantation's magic guide you like a shining star.

155.   Spell for Strength and Courage

In times of challenge, I cast this spell,
To summon strength and courage, deep and well.
With inner power and resilience untold,
I rise above, brave and bold.

Preparation:

Find a quiet and peaceful space where you can focus without distractions.
Light a candle or use a symbol that represents strength and courage.
Centering and Focus:

Take a few deep breaths to calm your mind and center your energy.
Close your eyes and visualize a flame within you, growing brighter with each breath.
Invocation of Inner Strength:

Call upon your inner strength and resilience, acknowledging the power within.
Speak words of affirmation, recognizing your own capabilities and courage.
Incantation:

Speak the words of power, with conviction and determination,
Invoking strength and courage to face any situation.
"By the strength of my spirit, I summon might,
Courage flows within me, shining bright.
I rise above challenges, fearless and strong,
In my heart and soul, resilience belongs."
Visualization:

Visualize yourself surrounded by a radiant aura of strength and courage.
See yourself standing tall, facing challenges with confidence and unwavering resolve.
Symbolic Gesture:

Make a symbolic gesture that represents your intention to embody strength and
courage.
This could include raising your fist, standing in a power pose, or holding a talisman
that represents bravery.
Affirmations:

Repeat affirmations or mantras that reinforce your strength and courage.
Speak them aloud or silently, allowing their positive energy to resonate within you.

Gratitude and Empowerment:

Express gratitude for the strength and courage that resides within you.
Embrace this power, knowing that you are capable of overcoming any obstacle.
Carry this sense of empowerment with you into your daily life.
In times of challenge, may this spell be your guide,
May strength and courage in you forever reside.
Rise above, with resilience untold,
Bold and brave, as you unfold.

Thus, the Spell for Strength and Courage finds its end,
May it empower you, your spirit to transcend.
In the realm of unwavering bravery, both near and far,
May this spell's magic guide you like a shining star.

156. Ritual of Solar Adoration

In the presence of the radiant sun's glow,
We gather to perform this ritual, to let it show.
With reverence and awe, we adore the solar might,
Basking in its warmth, embracing its light.

Preparation:

Choose an outdoor space where the sun's rays can reach you directly.
Set up a small altar or sacred space facing the direction of the rising or setting sun.
Centering and Focus:

Stand or sit in a comfortable position, facing the sun.
Close your eyes and breathe deeply, connecting with the energy of the sun and the world around you.
Invocation of Solar Energy:

Raise your arms in a welcoming gesture, facing the sun.
Call upon the solar energy, speaking words of praise and gratitude for its life-giving power.
Sun Salutation:

Perform a series of physical movements or yoga postures known as a sun salutation.
Flow gracefully from one posture to another, honoring the sun's energy with each movement.
Chanting and Singing:

Offer chants or songs that celebrate the sun's majesty and life-affirming qualities.
Let your voice carry the vibration of gratitude and adoration.
Meditation and Visualization:

Close your eyes and visualize the sun as a brilliant ball of golden light.
Imagine its warm rays permeating every cell of your being, filling you with vitality and positive energy.
Offering of Light:

Light a candle or hold a symbol of light, dedicating it to the sun.
Express your gratitude for the sun's presence and its role in sustaining life on Earth.
Closing and Benediction:

Lower your arms and offer a final prayer or blessing of thanks to the sun.
Express your intention to carry the energy and warmth of the sun within you
throughout the day.
In the presence of the radiant sun's glow,
We adore its brilliance, let it show.
May its energy fill us, vibrant and bright,
Guiding our steps, with its celestial light.

Thus, the Ritual of Solar Adoration finds its end,
May it inspire you, its energy to transcend.
In the realm of divine illumination, both near and far,
May this ritual's essence guide you like a shining star.

157.   Incantation for Protection During Travel

In journeys afar, where paths unfold,
I cast this incantation, to protect the traveler bold.
With words of power and ancient might,
I summon guardians to guide through day and night.

Preparation:

Find a quiet and calm space where you can focus without distractions.
Light a candle or use a symbol that represents safe travel.
Centering and Focus:

Take a few deep breaths to center your energy and clear your mind.
Visualize a shield of protective light surrounding you and your travel companions.
Invocation of Travel Guardians:

Call upon the guardians or deities associated with safe travel.
Speak their names or offer prayers, inviting their presence and protection during your journey.
Incantation:

Speak the words of power, with intention and belief,
Invoking protection and guidance to relieve.
"By the strength of ancient magic and divine care,
I summon guardians, to keep me safe in air or lair.
Surround me with their watchful eyes,
Shield me from perils as I traverse the skies."
Symbolic Action:

Take a symbolic action to enhance the incantation's power.
This could involve carrying a protective amulet, tying a blessed cord around your wrist, or placing a travel talisman in your bag.
Visualization:

Envision a luminous sphere of protective energy surrounding you and your traveling companions.
See this sphere expanding to encompass your vehicle or mode of transportation.
Gratitude and Assurance:

Express gratitude to the guardians or deities for their protection and guidance.
Thank them for their presence and their commitment to ensuring your safe travels.
Trust in their watchful care and feel assured that you are protected.
In journeys afar, where paths unfold,
May this incantation protect the traveler bold.
Guided and guarded, through day and night,
Safe and secure, till journey's delight.

Thus, the Incantation for Protection During Travel finds its end,
May it be a shield, your travels to defend.
In the realm of secure journeys, both near and far,
May this incantation's magic guide you like a shining star.

158. Spell for Dream Interpretation

In the realm of dreams, where messages reside,
I cast this spell to unlock the truths they hide.
With clarity and insight, I seek to discern,
The wisdom within, for knowledge I yearn.

Preparation:

Find a quiet and comfortable space where you can focus on your dreams.
Create a dream journal or have a notebook and pen ready to record your dream
interpretations.
Centering and Focus:

Close your eyes and take a few deep breaths to center your mind and body.
Visualize a serene and peaceful space where you can explore the realm of dreams.
Invocation of Dream Guidance:

Call upon your inner wisdom and intuition to guide you in interpreting your dreams.
Speak words of intention, inviting clarity and insight into your dream interpretations.
Incantation:

Speak the words of power, with openness and curiosity,
Invoking understanding and unraveling dream mystery.
"By the power of dreams, I seek to understand,
Unveil their meanings, like grains of sand.
Grant me insight, to unravel the dream's thread,
Illuminate the symbols, the messages unsaid."
Dream Recall and Reflection:

Reflect on the dreams you have had recently or recall a specific dream that you wish
to interpret.
Write down the details of the dream, including symbols, emotions, and any
significant events or interactions.
Symbolic Analysis:

Analyze the symbols and themes present in your dream.
Research their potential meanings in dream interpretation guides or consult with
experts in dream analysis.
Intuitive Reflection:

Tune into your intuition and inner knowing as you contemplate the dream's significance.
Trust your instincts and allow your intuition to guide you in understanding the deeper layers of your dream.
Journaling and Recording:

Write down your interpretations and insights in your dream journal or notebook.
Reflect on how the dream may relate to your waking life and what lessons or messages it may hold for you.
Gratitude and Integration:

Express gratitude for the wisdom and guidance received through dream interpretation.
Embrace the insights gained and carry them into your waking life for personal growth and understanding.
In the realm of dreams, where secrets reside,
May this spell be your key, your trusted guide.
Unlocking meanings, with clarity and insight,
Revealing truths, in the dreams' sacred light.

Thus, the Spell for Dream Interpretation finds its end,
May it unveil wisdom, your dreams to transcend.
In the realm of profound insights, both near and far,
May this spell's magic guide you like a shining star.

159.   Ritual of Coronation

In the realm of power and royal might,
We gather to perform this sacred rite.
With regal splendor and divine decree,
A monarch crowned, for all to see.

Preparation:

Choose a grand and ceremonial location for the coronation.
Decorate the space with symbols of royalty, such as banners, regalia, and a throne.
Centering and Focus:

Begin the ritual with a moment of silence and reflection.
Clear your mind and open your heart to the significance of the coronation ceremony.
Invocation of Divine Blessings:

Call upon the gods and goddesses associated with kingship and leadership.
Offer prayers or invocations to seek their blessings and guidance for the new monarch.
Anointing with Sacred Oil:

Prepare a vessel of sacred oil, symbolizing the divine authority bestowed upon the monarch.
With a ceremonial brush or finger, anoint the monarch's forehead, hands, and heart, while reciting words of blessing and consecration.
Placing of the Crown:

Bring forth the crown, a symbol of the monarch's authority and sovereignty.
Place the crown upon the monarch's head, affirming their role as the rightful ruler.
Oath of Allegiance:

Lead the monarch in reciting an oath of allegiance to their people and their kingdom.
This oath should express their commitment to justice, prosperity, and the well-being of their subjects.
Acclamation and Celebration:

The assembled dignitaries and witnesses rejoice and applaud, hailing the newly crowned monarch.
Festivities ensue, such as music, dancing, feasting, and other joyful expressions of celebration.

Benediction and Proclamation:

Offer a final blessing, invoking divine protection and guidance upon the monarch's reign.
The monarch delivers a proclamation, addressing their subjects and outlining their vision for the kingdom.
In the realm of power and royal might,
May this coronation shine with divine light.
A new monarch crowned, with grace and poise,
Guided by wisdom, their kingdom to rejoice.

Thus, the Ritual of Coronation finds its end,
May it bless the monarch, their rule to transcend.
In the realm of majestic sovereignty, both near and far,
May this ritual's essence guide them like a shining star.

160. Incantation for Protection Against Disease

In the realm of health and well-being,
I cast this incantation, protective and freeing.
With words of power and healing grace,
I ward off illness, in every time and space.

Preparation:

Find a quiet and peaceful space where you can focus on the incantation.
Light a white or green candle to symbolize healing and purity.
Centering and Focus:

Take a few deep breaths to center your energy and clear your mind.
Visualize a sphere of radiant light surrounding you, representing your protective
shield against disease.
Invocation of Healing Deities:

Call upon the deities associated with health and healing.
Speak their names or offer prayers, inviting their presence and assistance in warding
off disease.
Incantation:

Speak the words of power, with conviction and belief,
Invoking protection, a shield of relief.
"By ancient forces and divine decree,
I call upon protection to surround me.
Shield me from illness, both known and unknown,
May disease be banished, far from my zone."
Visualization:

Envision a radiant light emanating from within you, purifying and protecting your
body and spirit.
See this light expanding outward, forming a shield that repels any harmful energies or
disease-causing agents.
Symbolic Action:

Take a symbolic action to enhance the incantation's power.

This could involve carrying a protective amulet or talisman, placing healing crystals nearby, or anointing yourself with a healing oil.
Gratitude and Assurance:

Express gratitude to the healing deities for their protection and assistance.
Thank them for their presence and their commitment to safeguarding your health.
Trust in their healing powers and feel assured that you are shielded from disease.
In the realm of health and well-being,
May this incantation's power be freeing.
Protected and shielded, in every time and space,
Guarded from disease, in divine embrace.

Thus, the Incantation for Protection Against Disease finds its end,
May it be a shield, your health to defend.
In the realm of wellness, both near and far,
May this incantation's magic guide you like a shining star.

161. Spell for Breaking Bad Habits

In the realm of transformation and self-mastery,
I cast this spell to break the chains of a harmful decree.
With inner strength and resolve, I now proclaim,
The end of this habit, no longer to be the same.

Preparation:

Find a quiet and comfortable space where you can focus on the spell.
Create a sacred atmosphere by lighting a candle or burning incense.
Centering and Focus:

Take a few deep breaths to center your energy and clear your mind.
Focus on the habit you wish to break, recognizing its negative impact on your life.
Invocation of Personal Power:

Call upon your inner strength and determination to overcome the habit.
Affirm your commitment to change and reclaim your power over your actions.
Naming the Habit:

Speak the name of the habit out loud, acknowledging its hold on you.
Understand that by speaking its name, you are taking the first step towards releasing
its grip.
Affirmation of Release:

Declare your intention to break free from the habit and replace it with healthier
choices.
Speak words of affirmation, such as, "I release this habit from my life, embracing
positive change."
Symbolic Action:

Perform a symbolic action that represents your release from the habit.
This could involve tearing up a written representation of the habit or disposing of an
object associated with it.
Visualization of Transformation:

Close your eyes and visualize yourself free from the habit's influence.
See yourself engaging in positive behaviors and making choices that align with your
well-being.
Support and Accountability:

Seek support from loved ones or join a support group to help you on your journey of breaking the habit.
Share your intention with someone you trust and ask for their encouragement and accountability.
Daily Affirmations and Reminders:

Create daily affirmations or reminders that reinforce your commitment to breaking the habit.
Repeat them each day, emphasizing your determination and the positive changes you are making.
In the realm of transformation and self-mastery,
May this spell dissolve the habit's decree.
Breaking free, with strength and resolve,
Embracing a new path, our spirits evolve.

Thus, the Spell for Breaking Bad Habits finds its end,
May it empower you, your will to transcend.
In the realm of transformation, both near and far,
May this spell's magic guide you like a shining star.

162.   Ritual of River Blessing

In the realm of flowing waters, pure and divine,
We gather for this ritual, a sacred intertwine.
With reverence and gratitude, we honor the river's might,
Blessing its waters, bringing harmony and light.

Preparation:

Choose a location along the banks of the river, where you can perform the ritual.
Bring offerings such as flowers, herbs, or small gifts to express gratitude to the river.
Centering and Focus:

Stand by the river's edge and take a moment to connect with its energy.
Close your eyes, feel the gentle breeze, and listen to the soothing sound of the
flowing water.
Invocation of Water Deities:

Call upon the water deities associated with rivers, such as Hapi or Khnum.
Offer prayers or invocations, inviting their presence and blessings for the ritual.
Offering and Gratitude:

Select one of the offerings and hold it in your hands.
Express your gratitude to the river for its life-giving and cleansing qualities.
Place the offering gently into the river, symbolically giving back and honoring its
importance.
Chanting and Blessing:

Begin chanting or reciting words of blessing for the river.
Speak words that convey appreciation, harmony, and abundance for the river's
ecosystem and all beings who rely on it.
Water Anointing:

Dip your hands into the river's water, cupping it in your palms.
Slowly bring your wet palms to your face, forehead, and heart, anointing yourself with
the river's blessings.
Unity and Oneness:

Extend your arms out towards the river, visualizing a connection between your
energy and the river's energy.

Feel the unity and oneness with the flowing waters, recognizing that you are a part of the larger natural world.
Closing and Gratitude:

Offer a final prayer of gratitude to the river and the water deities.
Thank them for their presence and blessings, and express your commitment to protect and honor the river in your daily life.
In the realm of flowing waters, pure and divine,
May this river blessing eternally shine.
Harmony and gratitude, in each sacred rite,
Uniting us with the river's wisdom and light.

Thus, the Ritual of River Blessing finds its end,
May it honor the river, our guide and friend.
In the realm of flowing waters, both near and far,
May this ritual's essence guide us like a shining star.

163.   Incantation for Protection in Battle

In the realm of strife and conflict's roar,
I call upon the spirits to shield me evermore.
With words of power, my armor strong,
Protect me in battle, as I journey along.

Preparation:

Find a quiet and focused space where you can perform the incantation.
Light a candle or place a symbol of protection nearby.
Centering and Focus:

Take a deep breath and close your eyes, centering your energy.
Visualize a shield of divine light surrounding you, ready to protect you in battle.
Invocation of Warrior Deities:

Call upon the warrior deities, such as Horus or Sekhmet.
Offer prayers or invocations, requesting their presence and assistance in battle.
Incantation:

Speak the words of power with strength and conviction,
Invoking protection in this fierce affliction.
"By ancient forces, I call upon thee,
Shield me in battle, protect and set me free.
Grant me courage, strength, and valor untold,
May I emerge victorious, brave and bold."
Visualization:

Envision a shining aura of protection surrounding your body.
See the armor of light forming a shield, deflecting any harm or danger that may come
your way.
Symbolic Action:

Take a symbolic action to enhance the incantation's power.
This could involve wearing or holding a talisman or weapon of protection.
Assurance and Confidence:

Feel a surge of confidence and assurance as you embrace the protection granted by
the incantation.

Trust in your abilities and the support of the warrior deities as you face the challenges ahead.
Gratitude and Farewell:

Express gratitude to the warrior deities for their presence and protection.
Thank them for their guidance and strength, and bid them farewell until their aid is needed once more.
In the realm of strife and conflict's roar,
May this incantation protect me evermore.
Shielded in battle, with courage and might,
I emerge victorious, guided by divine light.

Thus, the Incantation for Protection in Battle finds its end,
May it be a shield, your path to defend.
In the realm of battle, both near and far,
May this incantation's magic guide you like a shining star.

164.   Spell for Creativity and Inspiration

In the realm of boundless imagination's sway,
I seek the spell to unleash creative display.
With open heart and mind, I call forth inspiration's fire,
Igniting the spark within, taking me higher.

Preparation:

Find a quiet and inspiring space where you can focus on the spell.
Gather materials that symbolize creativity, such as art supplies, musical instruments, or writing tools.
Centering and Focus:

Take a moment to center your energy and clear your mind.
Close your eyes and breathe deeply, allowing any stress or distractions to fade away.
Invocation of the Muses:

Call upon the Muses, the ancient goddesses of inspiration and creativity.
Speak their names aloud or silently, inviting their presence and guidance.
Opening the Creative Channels:

Visualize a brilliant light at the center of your being, representing your creative essence.
Imagine this light expanding and radiating throughout your entire body, unlocking your creative channels.
Affirmation of Creative Power:

Repeat affirmations that affirm your creative abilities and potential.
Speak words such as, "I am a vessel of creative energy. My mind and spirit are open to inspiration and innovation."
Symbolic Action:

Engage in a creative act that resonates with you, such as painting, writing, or playing music.
Let the energy flow through you as you immerse yourself in the act of creation.
Connection with the Divine:

Tune into the divine source of inspiration, whether you perceive it as a higher power, the universe, or your own inner wisdom.
Feel a deep connection with this source, knowing that it is flowing through you and guiding your creative expression.

Gratitude and Release:

Express gratitude to the Muses and the divine source of inspiration for their presence and guidance.
Release any expectations or self-judgment, allowing your creativity to flow freely and authentically.
In the realm of boundless imagination's sway,
May this spell ignite your creative display.
Inspired and free, your creations will aspire,
Revealing the beauty of your creative fire.

Thus, the Spell for Creativity and Inspiration finds its end,
May it kindle the spark, your creativity to transcend.
In the realm of artistic expression, both near and far,
May this spell's magic guide you like a shining star.

165.　　Ritual of Offering to the Nile

In the realm of life's eternal flow,
We gather by the Nile's sacred glow.
With reverence and gratitude, we stand,
Offering our gifts, as we understand.

Preparation:

Choose a spot along the banks of the Nile where you can perform the ritual.
Bring offerings such as flowers, fruits, or small objects that represent abundance and gratitude.
Centering and Focus:

Stand by the river's edge and take a moment to connect with the energy of the Nile.
Close your eyes, breathe deeply, and listen to the gentle sounds of the flowing water.
Invocation of the Nile Deity:

Call upon the deity associated with the Nile, such as Hapi or Osiris.
Offer prayers or invocations, inviting their presence and blessings for the ritual.
Offering and Gratitude:

Select one of the offerings and hold it in your hands.
Express your gratitude to the Nile for its life-giving and nourishing qualities.
Place the offering gently into the water, symbolically giving back and honoring its importance.
Chanting and Blessing:

Begin chanting or reciting words of blessing for the Nile.
Speak words that convey appreciation, abundance, and reverence for the Nile's essential role in sustaining life.
Unity and Oneness:

Extend your arms out towards the river, visualizing a connection between your energy and the Nile's energy.
Feel the unity and oneness with the river, recognizing that it is a vital part of the natural world and our interconnectedness.
Reflection and Meditation:

Take a moment of silence to reflect on the significance of the Nile in ancient Egyptian culture and its continued importance in the present.

Meditate on the blessings and abundance that the Nile brings to the land and its people.
Closing and Gratitude:

Offer a final prayer of gratitude to the Nile and the deity invoked.
Thank them for their presence and blessings, and express your commitment to honor and protect the Nile in your daily life.
In the realm of life's eternal flow,
May this offering to the Nile's sacred glow,
Express gratitude and reverence so grand,
Honoring the river, a gift from the divine hand.

Thus, the Ritual of Offering to the Nile finds its end,
May it forever the river's essence transcend.
In the realm of flowing waters, both near and far,
May this ritual's magic guide us like a shining star.

166. Incantation for Protection of Livestock

In the realm where beasts of field do roam,
I call upon the powers to protect their home.
With words of power and intention strong,
Shield our livestock from harm and wrong.

Preparation:

Find a quiet and open space near the livestock's shelter or grazing area.
Gather symbols of protection, such as a small figurine or an amulet representing animals.
Centering and Focus:

Stand amidst the presence of the livestock and take a moment to ground yourself.
Close your eyes and breathe deeply, allowing your energy to align with the natural world around you.
Invocation of Protective Deities:

Call upon the deities associated with animal protection, such as Hathor or Bes.
Offer prayers or invocations, inviting their presence and assistance in safeguarding the livestock.
Incantation:

Speak the words of power with conviction and clarity,
invoking the protective forces to keep the livestock free.
"By ancient might and cosmic grace,
I invoke protection for these creatures' space.
From harm and danger, I bid them stay,
Safeguarded and guided, night and day."
Visualization:

Envision a radiant shield of light surrounding the livestock and their habitat.
See this shield repelling any negative influences, diseases, or predators that may pose a threat.
Symbolic Action:

Take a symbolic action to enhance the incantation's power.

For example, sprinkle a handful of grain or herbs around the livestock's area as an offering of protection.
Assurance and Blessing:

Speak words of assurance and blessing to the livestock, acknowledging their importance and value.
Express wishes for their well-being, health, and safety as they graze and thrive.
Gratitude and Farewell:

Express gratitude to the protective deities for their presence and assistance.
Thank them for their guardianship and bid them farewell, knowing that their protective energies continue to surround the livestock.
In the realm where beasts of field do roam,
May this incantation protect their home.
Shielded and guided, safe from harm's strife,
May our livestock thrive, a cherished part of life.

Thus, the Incantation for Protection of Livestock finds its end,
May it safeguard the creatures, their well-being to transcend.
In the realm of animal guardianship, both near and far,
May this incantation's magic guide us like a shining star.

167.   Spell for Banishing Nightmares

In the realm where dreams hold sway,
I cast a spell to keep nightmares at bay.
With words of power and sacred light,
I banish fear that haunts the night.

Preparation:

Find a quiet and comfortable space where you can relax and focus.
Gather a small white candle, a piece of paper, and a pen.
Centering and Focus:

Sit or lie down in a relaxed position.
Close your eyes, take deep breaths, and let go of any tension or thoughts.
Invocation of Divine Protection:

Call upon a deity or spirit that represents protection and light, such as Isis or Ra.
Offer a brief prayer or invocation, inviting their presence and assistance.
Writing the Nightmare:

Take the piece of paper and write down a brief description or symbol of the
nightmare that troubles you.
Visualize transferring the energy of the nightmare onto the paper.
Affirmation of Power:

Hold the paper in your hands and repeat an affirmation that affirms your power over
your dreams and subconscious.
Example affirmation: "By the light within me, I release this fear. Nightmares hold no
power over me. I reclaim my peace and sleep peacefully."
Lighting the Candle:

Light the white candle as a symbol of purity and divine light.
Visualize the flame growing brighter, illuminating the space around you with positive
energy.
Burning the Nightmare:

Use the candle flame to burn the paper with the description of the nightmare.
As it burns, imagine the nightmare dissipating, transforming into ashes, and being
carried away by the cleansing power of the flame.
Visualization and Protection:

Close your eyes and visualize a serene and safe place, like a peaceful meadow or a calming ocean.

Imagine yourself surrounded by a radiant sphere of protective light, shielding you from any negative energies or nightmares.

Gratitude and Closure:

Express gratitude to the deity or spirit you invoked for their guidance and assistance.

Thank them for their protection and support in banishing the nightmares.

In the realm where dreams hold sway,

May this spell keep nightmares away.

By sacred light and empowered will,

I reclaim my dreams, serene and still.

Thus, the Spell for Banishing Nightmares finds its end,

May it bring peaceful sleep, to dreams we transcend.

In the realm of restful nights, both near and far,

May this spell's magic guide us like a shining star.

168.   Ritual of Sun Salutation

In the realm where sunlight's rays abound,
We honor the sun, its warmth profound.
With a ritual of movement and devotion,
We greet the day with heartfelt emotion.

Preparation:

Find a quiet and open space where you can perform the ritual.
Wear loose and comfortable clothing that allows freedom of movement.
Centering and Focus:

Stand with your feet hip-width apart, facing the direction of the rising sun.
Close your eyes, take deep breaths, and allow your body to relax.
Invocation of Solar Energy:

Raise your hands above your head, palms facing upward, and visualize the radiant
energy of the sun pouring into your body.
Offer a prayer or invocation to the sun, expressing gratitude for its life-giving energy
and blessings.
Sun Salutation Movements:

Begin with the Mountain Pose: Stand tall, with your feet rooted to the ground and
your arms relaxed by your sides.
Inhale deeply and raise your arms overhead, arching your back gently.
Exhale as you bend forward, bringing your hands to the ground or resting them on
your shins in a Forward Fold.
Inhale and step your left foot back into a lunge position, while lifting your chest and
raising your gaze in the Low Lunge.
Exhale and step your right foot back into a plank position, aligning your body in a
straight line.
Inhale and lower your body into a Chaturanga, keeping your elbows close to your
sides.
Exhale and lower your hips while lifting your chest into the Upward-Facing Dog pose,
gazing upward.
Inhale and lift your hips, coming into a Downward-Facing Dog pose, with your body
forming an inverted "V" shape.
Exhale and step your left foot forward into a lunge position, repeating the Low Lunge
on the other side.

Inhale and rise up, extending your arms overhead, coming back to the Mountain Pose.

Repeat the sequence, starting with the opposite foot in the lunge position.

Mindful Breathing:

Throughout the Sun Salutation movements, synchronize your breath with each movement.

Inhale deeply during the upward movements and exhale fully during the downward movements.

Focus on the sensation of the breath flowing in and out, grounding you in the present moment.

Gratitude and Closing:

As you complete the last repetition of the Sun Salutation, stand tall in the Mountain Pose.

Offer a final prayer or expression of gratitude to the sun for its nourishing energy and the blessings of the new day.

Take a moment to bask in the warmth and energy of the sun, feeling its vitality infusing your body and spirit.

In the realm where sunlight's rays abound,

We greet the day with movements profound.

With each Sun Salutation, we embrace,

The sun's energy, its life-giving grace.

Thus, the Ritual of Sun Salutation finds its end,

May it illuminate our path, our spirits ascend.

In the realm of radiant light, both near and far,

May this ritual's magic guide us like a shining star.

169.   Incantation for Safe Sea Voyage

In the realm where waves embrace the shore,
I call upon the powers to safeguard and restore.
With words of power and the ocean's might,
I invoke protection for a voyage, day or night.

Preparation:

Find a calm and quiet place where you can focus your energy.
Close your eyes, take deep breaths, and visualize the vast expanse of the sea.
Invocation of Marine Deities:

Call upon the deities associated with the sea, such as Poseidon or Isis.
Offer a prayer or invocation, inviting their presence and assistance in ensuring a safe
sea voyage.
Connection to the Elements:

Connect with the elements of water and air, visualizing their harmonious union.
Feel the ebb and flow of the tides, and the gentle breeze guiding the ship's course.
Incantation:

Speak the words of power with confidence and clarity, invoking the protective forces
of the sea.
"By the power of the ocean deep,
I call upon its watchful keep.
With wind and wave, guide this ship true,
Safeguard us, our voyage renew."
Symbolic Action:

Take a small object that represents the sea or sailing, such as a seashell or a piece of
nautical rope.
Hold it in your hands and infuse it with your intention of safe travel and protection.
Visualization of Safe Voyage:

Close your eyes and envision the ship sailing upon calm and clear waters.
See the vessel guided by gentle winds, surrounded by a protective aura that shields it
from storms and hazards.
Blessing of the Crew and Ship:

Extend your intention of protection and safety to the captain, crew, and all those on board the ship.
Envision them surrounded by a sphere of light, shielding them from harm and ensuring their safe return.
Gratitude and Farewell:

Express gratitude to the marine deities for their presence and protection.
Thank them for their watchful guidance and bid them farewell, knowing that their blessings continue to safeguard the sea voyage.
In the realm where waves embrace the shore,
May this incantation protect forevermore.
Guided and guarded by the ocean's might,
A safe sea voyage, both day and night.

Thus, the Incantation for Safe Sea Voyage finds its end,
May it bring protection, on the ocean's path we wend.
In the realm of maritime travels, both near and far,
May this incantation's magic guide us like a shining star.

170.　　Spell for Enhancing Intuition

In the realm where inner wisdom resides,
I seek to enhance intuition's tides.
With a spell of clarity and insight,
I awaken the senses, shining bright.

Preparation:

Find a quiet and peaceful space where you can focus your energy.
Create an atmosphere conducive to relaxation, such as lighting candles or playing soft instrumental music.
Centering and Grounding:

Sit or lie down in a comfortable position.
Close your eyes, take deep breaths, and imagine roots growing from your body, anchoring you to the earth.
Invocation of Higher Guidance:

Call upon your chosen deity or spirit guide associated with intuition and insight, such as Thoth or Isis.
Offer a prayer or invocation, inviting their presence and assistance in enhancing your intuitive abilities.
Visualization of Clear Waters:

Imagine a calm and clear pool of water in your mind's eye.
See yourself standing at the edge of the pool, ready to immerse yourself in its clarity.
Incantation:

Speak the following words with intention and belief in their power:
"By the wisdom deep within,
I awaken intuition, let it begin.
Clear the fog, open the way,
Enhance my senses, day by day."
Activation of the Senses:

Focus on each of your senses, one at a time, and imagine them becoming heightened and attuned.
Visualize your eyes seeing with clarity, your ears hearing subtle whispers of insight, your nose detecting the subtlest of scents, your skin feeling the energy of the world, and your taste buds savoring the flavors of intuition.

Receptive State:

Allow your mind to relax and become receptive to intuitive messages.
Release any expectations or judgments, and simply be open to whatever insights may come.
Journaling and Reflection:

After the spell, take a moment to write down any thoughts, impressions, or messages that came to you during the ritual.
Reflect on these insights and trust in your intuition's guidance.
Gratitude and Closure:

Express gratitude to the deity or spirit guide you invoked for their presence and assistance.
Thank them for their guidance in enhancing your intuition and bid them farewell, knowing that their wisdom remains with you.
In the realm where inner wisdom resides,
May this spell enhance intuition's tides.
Awakened senses, shining bright,
Guided by intuition's insightful light.

Thus, the Spell for Enhancing Intuition finds its end,
May it guide us to truths, on intuition we depend.
In the realm of heightened perception, both near and far,
May this spell's magic guide us like a shining star.

171. Ritual of Temple Cleansing

In the sacred space where spirits dwell,
I invoke the ritual to cleanse and dispel.
With purifying energies, pure and strong,
I restore the temple where gods belong.

Preparation:

Gather the necessary tools for the ritual, such as a bowl of purified water, incense, and a feather for sweeping.
Enter the temple space with a focused and reverent mindset.
Setting the Intention:

Stand at the entrance of the temple and set your intention for the ritual.
Visualize the space being cleansed of stagnant energy, impurities, and any negative influences.
Sacred Smoke Purification:

Light the incense and let its fragrant smoke fill the air.
Move throughout the temple, wafting the smoke in each corner, alcove, and sacred object.
Visualize the smoke purifying the space, cleansing it of any lingering negativity.
Water Cleansing:

Dip the feather into the bowl of purified water.
Starting from the entrance, lightly flick the feather to sprinkle droplets of water throughout the temple.
As you do so, envision the water washing away any residual impurities, leaving the space pristine and renewed.
Chanting and Invocation:

Recite a sacred chant or invocation, calling upon the deities associated with the temple.
Invoke their presence, wisdom, and blessings to purify and restore the sanctity of the space.
Allow the sound of your voice to resonate within the temple, infusing it with positive vibrations.
Energy Clearing:

Stand at the center of the temple and raise your hands towards the ceiling.

Visualize pure, radiant light flowing down from above, filling the space with divine energy.
Imagine this light penetrating every corner, crevice, and surface, driving out any lingering negative energy.
Gratitude and Closing:

Offer gratitude to the deities for their presence and assistance in the temple cleansing.
Express appreciation for the renewed energy and sanctity of the space.
Close the ritual by bowing or offering a prayer, acknowledging the sacredness of the temple.
In the sacred space where spirits dwell,
May this ritual cleanse and dispel.
Purifying energies, pure and strong,
Restore the temple where gods belong.

Thus, the Ritual of Temple Cleansing finds its end,
May it bring purity and blessings, around every bend.
In the realm of sacred spaces, both near and far,
May this ritual's magic guide us like a shining star.

172.   Incantation for Protection of Children

In the realm where innocence and wonder reside,
I call upon the powers to protect and guide.
With words of power and love's pure light,
I invoke protection for children day and night.

Preparation:

Find a calm and quiet space where you can focus your energy.
Clear your mind and center yourself, connecting with the loving energy within.
Invocation of Protective Deities:

Call upon the deities associated with child protection, such as Bes or Taweret.
Offer a prayer or invocation, inviting their presence and assistance in safeguarding
children from harm.
Visualization of Protective Light:

Envision a warm, golden light surrounding and permeating the space around you.
Visualize this light expanding to encompass all children, forming a protective shield
around them.
Incantation:

Speak the following words with intention and love:
"By the power of love and light divine,
I invoke protection for children, mine.
Shield them from harm, both seen and unseen,
Embrace them with love, keep them serene."
Connection to Universal Love:

Visualize a beam of radiant love energy flowing from your heart to the hearts of all
children.
See this love energy enveloping them, fostering a sense of safety, joy, and well-being.
Affirmation of Safety:

Repeat affirmations such as:
"Children are protected, safe, and secure."
"Divine love surrounds them, now and forever."
"They are guided and watched over, day and night."
Gratitude and Closure:

Express gratitude to the protective deities for their presence and assistance.
Thank them for their loving care and bid them farewell, knowing that their watchful guardianship remains.
In the realm where innocence and wonder reside,
May this incantation protect and guide.
Children embraced by love's pure light,
Protected day and night.

Thus, the Incantation for Protection of Children finds its end,
May it bring comfort and safety, on children it attend.
In the realm of cherished little ones, both near and far,
May this incantation's magic guide them like a shining star.

173.   Spell for Success in Exams

In the realm where knowledge and wisdom intertwine,
I call upon powers to aid this quest of mine.
With focused mind and unwavering will,
I summon success in exams, my mind to fill.

Preparation:

Find a quiet and comfortable space where you can concentrate without distractions.
Gather your study materials and any items that bring you a sense of focus and
confidence.
Centering and Focus:

Take a few deep breaths to calm your mind and body.
Close your eyes and visualize a clear and focused mental state, ready to absorb
knowledge.
Invocation of Intellect:

Call upon the deities associated with wisdom and intellect, such as Thoth or Seshat.
Offer a prayer or invocation, inviting their presence and guidance in your studies and
exams.
Visualization of Success:

Visualize yourself sitting in the exam room, feeling calm and confident.
See yourself answering questions with ease, recalling information effortlessly, and
achieving a successful outcome.
Incantation:

Speak the following words with conviction and belief:
"By the power of knowledge and mind's clarity,
I summon success in exams, so mote it be.
My mind is focused, my memory sharp,
I navigate the questions, never to falter or harp."
Study and Preparation:

Engage in diligent study and preparation, focusing on the subjects and topics at hand.
Utilize effective study techniques, such as organizing information, creating mnemonic
devices, and practicing with sample questions.
Confidence Boosting:

Repeat affirmations to boost your confidence, such as:
"I am well-prepared and capable of succeeding in exams."
"I retain knowledge easily and recall it effortlessly."
"I am calm, focused, and confident during exams."
Gratitude and Closure:

Express gratitude to the deities for their presence and assistance in your studies and exams.
Thank them for their guidance and bid them farewell, knowing that their wisdom and support remain with you.
In the realm where knowledge and wisdom intertwine,
May this spell aid success in exams, this quest of mine.
Focused mind and unwavering will,
Summoning success in exams, my mind to fill.

Thus, the Spell for Success in Exams finds its end,
May it guide you to triumph, around every bend.
In the realm of knowledge's pursuit, both near and far,
May this spell's magic shine like a guiding star.

174. Ritual of Full Moon Celebration

In the realm where moonlight's glow enchants,
We gather under the celestial expanse.
With joyful hearts and spirits soaring high,
We celebrate the Full Moon's presence in the sky.

Preparation:

Choose an outdoor location where you have a clear view of the Full Moon.
Decorate the space with lanterns, candles, and flowers, creating a festive atmosphere.
Opening Invocation:

Begin by standing under the open sky, facing the Full Moon.
Raise your hands towards the moon and speak an invocation, welcoming its energy and blessings.
Music and Dance:

Play enchanting music that resonates with the essence of the Full Moon.
Dance and move freely, allowing the moonlight to inspire and energize your movements.
Gratitude and Reflection:

Take a moment to express gratitude for the moon's radiant presence and its influence on nature and tides.
Reflect on the cycles of life, acknowledging the changes and transformations you have experienced.
Moonlight Meditation:

Find a comfortable spot to sit or lie down, facing the moon.
Close your eyes and allow the moon's gentle glow to wash over you.
Engage in a guided meditation or simply immerse yourself in the tranquil energy of the moonlit night.
Moon Blessing:

Raise your hands towards the moon, palms open and facing upwards.
Silently or aloud, offer a prayer or blessing, asking for the moon's guidance, inspiration, and protection.
Sharing and Nourishment:

Gather with friends or fellow participants and share a meal or snacks.

Reflect on the symbolism of nourishment and the interconnectedness of all beings under the moon's watchful gaze.
Closing:

Offer a final expression of gratitude to the Full Moon for its presence and blessings.
Lower your hands and take a moment to absorb the peaceful and harmonious energy of the evening.
In the realm where moonlight's glow enchants,
We celebrate the Full Moon's luminous dance.
With joyful hearts and spirits soaring high,
We honor the moon, lighting up the sky.

Thus, the Ritual of Full Moon Celebration finds its end,
May its magic and blessings to you extend.
In the realm of moonlit gatherings, both near and far,
May this ritual's enchantment be your guiding star.

175.   Incantation for Protection of the Pharaoh

In the realm where royalty holds divine sway,
I call upon ancient powers to protect and stay.
With reverence and honor, we invoke their might,
To shield the Pharaoh, the beacon of light.

Preparation:

Create a sacred space, adorned with symbols of power and royalty.
Place an image or representation of the Pharaoh at the center of the space.
Invocation of Protective Deities:

Call upon the deities associated with the protection of royalty, such as Horus or Isis.
Offer a prayer or invocation, inviting their presence and guardianship over the
Pharaoh.
Symbolic Gesture:

Extend your hands towards the image of the Pharaoh, palms facing outward.
Visualize a golden light emanating from your hands, enveloping the Pharaoh in a
protective aura.
Incantation:

Speak the following words with reverence and conviction:
"By the ancient powers that govern the land,
I invoke protection for Pharaoh, mighty and grand.
Shielded from harm, crowned in glory divine,
Safe and secure, in rulership's sacred line."
Visualization of Protection:

Envision a radiant shield of golden light surrounding the Pharaoh, impenetrable by
any harm or ill-intention.
See this shield growing stronger and more luminous, fortifying the Pharaoh's position
and authority.
Offerings of Protection:

Present offerings of incense, flowers, or symbolic objects associated with protection
and royalty.
Express gratitude for the guidance and guardianship bestowed upon the Pharaoh.

Gratitude and Closure:

Express gratitude to the protective deities for their presence and assistance.
Thank them for their watchful care over the Pharaoh, ensuring their safety and prosperity.
In the realm where royalty holds divine sway,
May this incantation protect and stay.
The Pharaoh, guided by powers ancient and true,
Shielded from harm, their reign renewed.

Thus, the Incantation for Protection of the Pharaoh finds its end,
May it safeguard the ruler, their realm to transcend.
In the realm of regal authority, both near and far,
May this incantation's magic shine like a guiding star.

176.   Spell for Finding Lost Objects

In the realm where lost things are waiting to be found,
I call upon powers to help me, to astound.
With focused intent and the energy of the divine,
I summon the return of what once was mine.

Preparation:

Find a quiet space where you can concentrate without distractions.
Gather any items that are associated with the lost object or have a personal
connection to it.
Centering and Focus:

Take a few deep breaths to calm your mind and center yourself.
Visualize the lost object clearly in your mind, holding the image with unwavering
focus.
Invocation of Assistance:

Call upon the energies and spirits that can aid in the retrieval of lost objects.
Speak an invocation, requesting their guidance and intervention in locating the item.
Incantation:

Speak the following words with belief and determination:
"Lost and hidden, I seek what was mine,
With this spell, its whereabouts I define.
Guides of the unseen, aid me in my quest,
Unveil the path, let the lost object manifest."
Sensory Connection:

Hold the associated items or objects in your hands.
Close your eyes and focus on the sensations they evoke, allowing your intuition to
guide you.
Search and Awareness:

Begin your search with a clear and open mind, paying attention to any intuitive
nudges or sudden thoughts.
Follow your instincts and be open to unexpected places or clues that may lead you to
the lost object.
Gratitude and Closure:

Whether you find the object or not, express gratitude to the energies and spirits invoked for their assistance.
Thank them for their guidance and acknowledge their presence, knowing that their support remains with you.
In the realm where lost things are waiting to be found,
May this spell bring what's lost back around.
With focused intent and energy divine,
May the lost object return, a treasure once mine.

Thus, the Spell for Finding Lost Objects finds its end,
May it aid you in locating what was lost, on which you depend.
In the realm of lost and found, both near and far,
May this spell's magic guide you, like a guiding star.

177. Ritual of Celestial Alignment

In the realm where stars and planets align,
We gather to commune with the cosmic design.
With reverence and awe, we seek harmony's flow,
To align our beings with the celestial glow.

Preparation:

Choose an outdoor location with a clear view of the night sky.
Set up a sacred space with candles, crystals, and symbols representing celestial bodies.
Grounding and Centering:

Stand barefoot on the earth, feeling its energy beneath your feet.
Take deep breaths, inhaling the cosmic energy above and exhaling any tension or distractions.
Invocation of Celestial Beings:

Call upon the celestial beings and energies that resonate with your intention.
Speak an invocation, inviting their presence and guidance in the ritual.
Starlight Meditation:

Find a comfortable position, facing the vast expanse of the night sky.
Close your eyes and visualize the stars and planets shining brightly above you.
Allow their celestial light to permeate your being, illuminating your inner landscape.
Sacred Movements:

Begin to move your body in a fluid and graceful manner, inspired by the celestial dance.
Reach your arms towards the sky, stretching and embracing the cosmic energy around you.
Let your movements flow, embodying the harmony and balance of the celestial realms.
Affirmations and Intentions:

Speak affirmations or set intentions aligned with the celestial energies.
Express gratitude for the guidance and blessings that the cosmos bestows upon you.
Celestial Connection:

Raise your arms towards the heavens, palms open and facing upwards.

Visualize a beam of radiant light descending from the stars, connecting you with the celestial realm.
Closing and Gratitude:

Lower your arms and take a moment to express gratitude to the celestial beings and energies.
Thank them for their presence, guidance, and the alignment they have brought to your being.
In the realm where stars and planets align,
May this ritual bring celestial harmony divine.
Aligned with the cosmic flow, we find our place,
Connected to the celestial, in infinite grace.

Thus, the Ritual of Celestial Alignment finds its end,
May its magic and harmony within you transcend.
In the realm of celestial communion, both near and far,
May this ritual's enchantment guide you, like a guiding star.

178.   Incantation for Protection of the Royal Family

In the realm where royal lineage holds divine sway,
I call upon ancient powers to protect and stay.
With reverence and devotion, we seek their divine might,
To safeguard the royal family, radiant in their light.

Preparation:

Create a sacred space adorned with symbols of royalty and protection.
Place an image or representation of the royal family at the center of the space.
Invocation of Protective Deities:

Call upon the deities associated with protection and royal lineage, such as Isis or Horus.
Offer a prayer or invocation, inviting their presence and guardianship over the royal family.
Symbolic Gesture:

Extend your hands towards the image of the royal family, palms facing outward.
Visualize a shield of golden light emanating from your hands, enveloping the royal family in a protective aura.
Incantation:

Speak the following words with reverence and certainty:
"By the ancient powers that govern this land,
I invoke protection for the royal family, majestic and grand.
Shielded from harm, crowned in divine might,
Their radiance shines, casting darkness to flight."
Visualization of Protection:

Envision a radiant shield of golden light surrounding the royal family, impenetrable by any harm or ill-intention.
See this shield growing stronger and more luminous, fortifying their position and safeguarding their well-being.
Offerings of Protection:

Present offerings of incense, flowers, or symbolic objects associated with protection and royalty.

Express gratitude for the guidance and guardianship bestowed upon the royal family.
Gratitude and Closure:

Express gratitude to the protective deities for their presence and assistance.
Thank them for their watchful care over the royal family, ensuring their safety,
prosperity, and continued reign.
In the realm where royal lineage holds divine sway,
May this incantation protect and stay.
The royal family, guided by powers ancient and true,
Shielded from harm, their radiance ever anew.

Thus, the Incantation for Protection of the Royal Family finds its end,
May it safeguard the rulers, their realm to transcend.
In the realm of regal authority, both near and far,
May this incantation's magic shine like a guiding star.

179.   Spell for Healing Relationships

In the realm where hearts are wounded and estranged,
I call upon divine forces to bring love's change.
With compassion and forgiveness, we seek to mend,
To heal relationships and bring harmony, our intent.

Preparation:

Find a quiet and serene space where you can focus without interruptions.
Gather a pink candle, a small piece of paper, and a pen.
Centering and Calming:

Sit comfortably and take a few deep breaths to center your mind and body.
Release any tension or negative emotions, allowing yourself to enter a state of calm.
Writing the Names:

Take the small piece of paper and write the names of the individuals involved in the strained relationship.
Visualize their faces as you write their names, connecting with their energy and the bond you once shared.
Candle Blessing:

Hold the pink candle in your hands and imbue it with your intentions for healing and reconciliation.
Visualize the flame representing the warm and gentle energy of love, soothing and healing any wounds.
Incantation:

Light the pink candle and say the following words with sincerity and conviction:
"By the sacred flame, love's power ignite,
Let healing flow, bringing darkness to light.
Hearts once divided, now let them mend,
Restore love's bond, may this spell transcend."
Visualizing Reconciliation:

Close your eyes and visualize the individuals involved in the relationship coming together in a peaceful and harmonious manner.
See them engaged in positive communication, understanding, and embracing forgiveness.
Letting Go and Forgiving:

Release any resentment or negative feelings you may hold towards the other person.
Offer forgiveness from your heart, both for yourself and for the other person involved.
Burning the Paper:

Hold the piece of paper with the names over the flame of the pink candle.
As it catches fire, visualize any negative energy or past wounds being transformed into love and healing.
Gratitude and Closure:

Express gratitude for the healing and reconciliation that is taking place.
Thank the divine forces and energies for their guidance and assistance in bringing about positive change.
In the realm where hearts are wounded and estranged,
May this spell bring healing, love's power exchanged.
Relationships restored, wounds now on the mend,
Harmony and forgiveness, a new chapter to transcend.

Thus, the Spell for Healing Relationships finds its end,
May it bring forth healing, love's magic to extend.
In the realm of interconnectedness, both near and far,
May this spell's enchantment guide you, like a guiding star.

180.   Ritual of Offering to the Sky Goddess Nut

In the realm where heavens embrace the earth,
We offer homage to the Sky Goddess' birth.
With reverence and gratitude, we present our gift,
To the celestial deity, whose beauty and grace uplift.

Preparation:

Find an open space outdoors where you can see the sky clearly.
Set up a sacred space with symbols or images representing the Sky Goddess Nut.
Invocation of Nut:

Stand facing the sky, raise your arms towards the heavens.
Speak an invocation to the Sky Goddess Nut, expressing your reverence and calling upon her presence.
Offering:

Choose an offering that represents abundance and nourishment, such as fruits or grains.
Hold the offering in your hands and infuse it with your gratitude and intentions.
Blessing and Prayer:

Speak a prayer or blessing, dedicating the offering to the Sky Goddess Nut.
Express gratitude for her guidance, protection, and the boundless expanse of the sky.
Raising the Offering:

Extend your arms towards the sky, presenting the offering to the celestial realm.
Visualize the energy of your offering ascending to the heavens, reaching the domain of the Sky Goddess.
Connection with the Divine:

Close your eyes and feel the presence of the Sky Goddess Nut enveloping you.
Experience the vastness and boundless energy of the sky flowing through your being.
Gratitude and Closure:

Express gratitude to the Sky Goddess Nut for her blessings and the connection established.
Thank her for her continued presence and guidance in your life.

In the realm where heavens embrace the earth,
We offer homage to the Sky Goddess' birth.
May this ritual's offering be received with delight,
By the celestial deity, radiant in her celestial light.

Thus, the Ritual of Offering to the Sky Goddess Nut finds its end,
May its devotion and gratitude forever transcend.
In the realm of celestial embrace, both near and far,
May this ritual's enchantment guide you, like a guiding star.

181.   Incantation for Protection Against Natural Disasters

In the realm where nature's forces unleash their might,
I call upon ancient powers to guard us day and night.
With reverence and plea, we seek protection from above,
Shield us from the fury, bring safety, peace, and love.

Centering and Grounding:

Find a quiet and calm space where you can focus your energy.
Take deep breaths, centering yourself and connecting with the earth beneath you.
Invocation of Divine Forces:

Call upon the deities associated with protection and natural elements, such as Ra or Hathor.
Speak their names with respect, inviting their presence and assistance in safeguarding against disasters.
Incantation:

Recite the following words with conviction and belief:
"By the ancient powers that shape the land,
I invoke protection, a divine command.
Shield us from tempests, from nature's wrath,
Bring safety and calm, on the destined path."
Visualizing Protection:

Close your eyes and envision a shield of radiant light forming around you and your surroundings.
Visualize this shield growing stronger and more resilient, capable of repelling any natural disaster.
Offering of Gratitude:

Express gratitude to the divine forces for their protection and guidance.
Offer a token of appreciation, such as a small offering of water or a symbolic object representing nature.
Empowering the Incantation:

Repeat the incantation, infusing it with your intention for protection and safety.

Feel the words resonating within you and reverberating out into the world, strengthening the protective shield.
Closing and Grounding:

Slowly bring your awareness back to the present moment.
Express thanks to the deities and the earth for their presence and support.
In the realm where nature's forces unleash their might,
May this incantation protect us day and night.
Shielded from disasters, by ancient powers above,
Bringing safety, peace, and love.

Thus, the Incantation for Protection Against Natural Disasters finds its end,
May its enchantment guide and defend.
In the realm of elemental forces, both near and far,
May this incantation's magic shine like a guiding star.

182.   Spell for Restful Sleep

In the realm of dreams where tranquility resides,
I call upon soothing energies to subside.
With gentle embrace, I bid rest to unfold,
Granting peaceful slumber, a respite from the world.

Creating a Serene Environment:

Prepare your sleeping space by tidying up and removing any distractions.
Dim the lights and create a calming atmosphere with soft music or natural sounds.
Cleansing Ritual:

Take a warm bath or shower before bedtime, visualizing any stress or tension being washed away.
Light a white candle to symbolize purity and clarity.
Calming Aromatherapy:

Place a few drops of lavender essential oil on a cloth or in a diffuser near your bed.
Inhale the soothing scent and let it relax your mind and body.
Bedtime Affirmations:

Repeat positive affirmations related to restful sleep, such as:
"I am calm and relaxed, ready for a peaceful night's sleep."
"My mind and body are at ease, inviting deep rest and rejuvenation."
Visualization and Relaxation:

Lie down in bed and close your eyes.
Visualize a serene landscape or a peaceful scene that brings you a sense of calmness and tranquility.
Relax each part of your body, starting from your toes and moving upward, releasing any tension or tightness.
Sleep Incantation:

Repeat the following words softly or in your mind, allowing their soothing vibrations to guide you:
"By the moon's gentle glow and stars above,
I invoke restful sleep, a night filled with love.
Peace envelops me, dreams caress my mind,
A blissful slumber, the solace I find."
Gratitude and Surrender:

Express gratitude for the opportunity to rest and rejuvenate.
Surrender any worries or thoughts to the universe, trusting that they will be resolved in due time.
In the realm of dreams where tranquility resides,
May this spell bring rest that gently guides.
Peaceful slumber, a respite from the world,
A rejuvenating sleep, its blessings unfurled.

Thus, the Spell for Restful Sleep finds its end,
May its enchantment your nights transcend.
In the realm of tranquil dreams, both near and far,
May this spell's magic guide you, like a guiding star.

183. Ritual of Temple Construction

In the realm where divine presence shall reside,
We embark on a sacred task with hearts unified.
With reverence and purpose, we build a holy abode,
A temple to honor the gods, a dwelling for their bestowed.

Ground Blessing:

Begin the ritual by seeking a suitable location for the temple.
Perform a ground blessing, purifying the site and invoking the blessings of the earth.
Foundation Ceremony:

Gather the necessary materials for the temple construction.
Lay the foundation stones, symbolizing the solid base upon which the temple shall rise.
Sacred Geometry:

Envision and mark the sacred geometrical proportions of the temple's design.
Incorporate symbolic shapes and patterns that hold significance to the deities being honored.
Invocation of Deities:

Invoke the deities associated with the temple, calling upon their presence and blessings.
Offer prayers and incantations to invite their guidance and protection throughout the construction process.
Construction:

Begin the physical construction of the temple, following the predetermined design and architectural plans.
Each member of the construction team contributes with reverence and dedication, understanding the sacredness of their work.
Offering and Blessing:

Once the temple structure is complete, hold a ceremony of offering and blessing.
Present offerings of incense, flowers, and sacred items to consecrate the temple and invite divine energies to dwell within.
Inauguration and Celebration:

Hold a grand inauguration ceremony to mark the completion of the temple.

Perform rituals, prayers, and ceremonies to activate the sacred space and invite worshippers to experience its divine presence.
In the realm where divine presence shall reside,
May this ritual of temple construction be our guide.
With reverence and purpose, a sacred abode we create,
A dwelling for the gods, their blessings to resonate.

Thus, the Ritual of Temple Construction finds its end,
May its sanctity and devotion forever transcend.
In the realm of divine worship, both near and far,
May this temple stand as a guiding star.

184. Incantation for Protection of Sacred Sites

In the realm where ancient spirits reside,
I invoke protection for sites sanctified.
With reverence and honor, we guard the sacred ground,
Preserving its power, its wisdom profound.

Grounding and Centering:

Find a quiet and peaceful place near the sacred site.
Take deep breaths, grounding yourself in the present moment and connecting with
the earth beneath you.
Invocation of Guardians:

Call upon the guardians of the sacred site, the ancient spirits and deities who watch
over its sanctity.
Speak their names with respect, inviting their presence and assistance in safeguarding
the site.
Incantation:

Recite the following words with intention and belief:
"By ancient spirits, I call upon your might,
Protect this sacred site, both day and night.
Ward off any harm, preserve its sacred power,
Let only reverence and wisdom here flower."
Visualizing Protective Light:

Close your eyes and envision a brilliant light surrounding the sacred site, forming a
protective shield.
See this light growing brighter and stronger, repelling any negative energies or
intentions.
Offering of Gratitude:

Express gratitude to the guardians and spirits for their protection and guidance.
Offer a small token of appreciation, such as water, flowers, or a symbolic object
representing the sacred site.
Empowering the Incantation:

Repeat the incantation, infusing it with your intention for protection and preservation.

Feel the words resonating within you and radiating out into the world, strengthening the protective shield.
Closing and Grounding:

Slowly bring your awareness back to the present moment.
Express thanks to the guardians and spirits for their presence and watchful care.
In the realm where ancient spirits reside,
May this incantation protect sites sanctified.
Preserving their power, their wisdom profound,
Guarding the sacred ground, forever bound.

Thus, the Incantation for Protection of Sacred Sites finds its end,
May its enchantment to the spirits ascend.
In the realm of sanctity and reverence, both near and far,
May this incantation's magic shine like a guiding star.

185. Spell for Confidence and Self-Empowerment

In the realm where inner strength resides,
I invoke the spell to empower and provide.
With unwavering belief in my own worth,
I embrace confidence, stepping forth.

Preparation:

Find a quiet and sacred space where you can focus without distractions.
Light a yellow or gold candle to symbolize confidence and self-empowerment.
Centering and Grounding:

Take deep breaths and visualize roots extending from your feet, grounding you to the earth.
Feel your connection to the energy of the earth, allowing it to stabilize and support you.
Affirmations:

Repeat positive affirmations that resonate with you, such as:
"I am worthy of love, success, and happiness."
"I embrace my unique strengths and talents."
"I radiate confidence and self-assurance."
Visualization:

Close your eyes and imagine a bright golden light surrounding your body.
See this light growing stronger and brighter with each breath, filling you with confidence and self-empowerment.
Visualize yourself accomplishing your goals and facing challenges with grace and determination.
Incantation:

Repeat the following words with conviction and belief:
"By the power within, I reclaim my might,
Confidence and self-empowerment ignite.
I release self-doubt and embrace my worth,
With inner strength, I conquer the earth."
Embracing the Spell:

Embrace the energy and intention of the spell, allowing it to infuse every part of your being.

Stand tall and feel the surge of confidence flowing through you, empowering your thoughts and actions.

Gratitude and Closing:

Express gratitude for the newfound confidence and self-empowerment.

Blow out the candle, symbolizing the completion of the spell.

In the realm where inner strength resides,

May this spell empower and provide.

With confidence and self-empowerment, I arise,

Stepping forth with conviction, to reach the skies.

Thus, the Spell for Confidence and Self-Empowerment finds its end,

May its enchantment within you transcend.

In the realm of inner power and resilience, both near and far,

May this spell's magic guide you like a guiding star.

186.   Ritual of Offering to the God Osiris

In the realm where Osiris reigns supreme,
We gather to honor, to worship, and to dream.
With offerings of reverence and heartfelt praise,
We invoke the presence of the god who conveys.

Preparation:

Find a quiet and sacred space to perform the ritual.
Gather offerings such as incense, flowers, fruits, and a cup of cool water.
Invocation:

Stand before an image or representation of Osiris.
Begin by reciting a prayer or invocation, calling upon Osiris to grace the ritual with
his divine presence.
Offering of Incense:

Light the incense and hold it before you as a symbol of purification and devotion.
Waft the incense smoke towards the image of Osiris, allowing its fragrance to reach
him.
Offering of Flowers:

Place the flowers before the image of Osiris, symbolizing beauty, growth, and life.
Offer a heartfelt prayer or expression of gratitude for the blessings in your life.
Offering of Fruits:

Present the fruits as an offering to Osiris, representing abundance and sustenance.
Speak words of appreciation for the nourishment and blessings provided by the earth.
Offering of Water:

Pour the cool water into a cup and hold it before you.
Offer the water to Osiris, expressing a desire for purification, renewal, and spiritual
nourishment.
Closing:

Conclude the ritual by expressing gratitude to Osiris for his presence and blessings.
Offer a final prayer or blessing, expressing your devotion and asking for Osiris's
continued guidance and protection.
In the realm where Osiris reigns supreme,
May this ritual honor his eternal gleam.

With offerings of reverence and heartfelt praise,
We invoke his presence, throughout our days.

Thus, the Ritual of Offering to the God Osiris finds its end,
May its devotion and grace forever transcend.
In the realm of divine worship, both near and far,
May Osiris's blessings shine like a guiding star.

187. Incantation for Protection Against Snake Bites

In the realm where danger may arise,
I call upon protection, swift and wise.
Shield me from venomous fangs that may strike,
Grant me safety and courage, day and night.

Centering and Focus:

Find a quiet and calm space where you can focus your energy.
Take deep breaths, grounding yourself in the present moment.
Visualization:

Close your eyes and visualize a shield of shimmering golden light surrounding your body.
See this shield growing stronger and impenetrable, forming a protective barrier against snake bites.
Incantation:

Repeat the following words with conviction and belief:
"By ancient power and sacred decree,
I am shielded from serpents, wild and free.
Venomous fangs, keep your distance away,
I walk unharmed, protected each day."
Symbolic Gesture:

Create a symbolic gesture using your hands, mimicking a shield or a protective barrier.
As you perform the gesture, imagine the energy flowing from your hands, reinforcing the protective shield.
Calling upon the Divine:

Invoke the aid of a deity associated with protection, such as Wadjet, the snake goddess.
Offer a prayer or invocation, requesting their assistance in keeping you safe from snake bites.
Gratitude and Closing:

Express gratitude to the deity and the forces of protection for their watchful care.

Slowly bring your awareness back to the present moment, feeling the strength and protection of the incantation.
In the realm where danger may arise,
May this incantation protect from snake bites.
Shielded from venomous fangs that may strike,
Safety and courage accompany me, day and night.

Thus, the Incantation for Protection Against Snake Bites finds its end,
May its enchantment to safety forever transcend.
In the realm of serpents and protection, both near and far,
May this incantation's magic shine like a guiding star.

188.   Spell for Reconciliation

In the realm of fractured bonds and strife,
I seek the spell to mend and bring back life.
With words of healing and a heart sincere,
May reconciliation now draw near.

Preparation:

Find a quiet and peaceful space where you can focus your energy.
Light a white or pink candle to symbolize love, healing, and harmony.
Centering and Intent:

Take a few deep breaths to calm your mind and focus your intention on
reconciliation.
Clear your thoughts and open your heart to forgiveness and understanding.
Invocation:

Call upon the presence of the higher powers or deities associated with love and
reconciliation, such as Hathor or Ma'at.
Speak their names and invite their guidance and assistance in the process of
reconciliation.
Reflection and Empathy:

Reflect on the situation and the perspective of the other person involved.
Put yourself in their shoes and try to understand their feelings and motivations.
Healing Words:

Write down or speak a heartfelt letter or message expressing your desire for
reconciliation.
Pour out your emotions, expressing regret, understanding, and a genuine willingness
to mend the relationship.
Symbolic Gesture:

Hold the letter or message in your hands and visualize the negative energy and
barriers dissolving.
Imagine a golden light enveloping the words, infusing them with love and healing.
Release and Letting Go:

Burn the letter or message, symbolizing the release of negative emotions and past
grievances.

As the flames consume the paper, imagine the energy transforming into love and healing.
Closing and Forgiveness:

Offer a prayer or affirmation, expressing your willingness to forgive and let go of any resentment or anger.
Embrace a sense of peace and openness to reconciliation, allowing healing to begin.
In the realm of fractured bonds and strife,
May this spell bring back harmony and life.
With words of healing and a heart sincere,
May reconciliation now draw near.

Thus, the Spell for Reconciliation finds its end,
May its enchantment of peace forever transcend.
In the realm of healing and forgiveness, both near and far,
May this spell's magic shine like a guiding star.

189.   Ritual of Star Invocation

In the realm of celestial wonders above,
We gather to honor the stars we love.
With awe and reverence, our spirits rise,
To invoke their guidance in the darkened skies.

Preparation:

Find a quiet and open space outdoors, away from city lights.
Choose a clear night when the stars are visible.
Centering and Connection:

Stand or sit comfortably, grounding yourself with deep breaths.
Close your eyes and connect with the Earth beneath you.
Star Gazing:

Open your eyes and gaze up at the night sky.
Observe the patterns and constellations, feeling the vastness of the universe.
Invocation:

Raise your hands towards the stars, palms open and facing upward.
Speak words of invitation, calling upon the celestial energies:
"O radiant stars, guides of the night,
I invoke your wisdom, shining bright.
Illuminate my path with your cosmic light,
And bless my journey with celestial insight."
Personal Intention:

Reflect on your desires, aspirations, or questions you seek answers to.
Silently or aloud, state your intention and ask for guidance from the stars.
Communion:

Meditate in silence, opening your heart and mind to receive the messages and
energies of the stars.
Be open to any sensations, visions, or insights that may come to you during this
connection.
Gratitude and Farewell:

Express gratitude to the stars for their presence and guidance.
Thank them for the insights received and the blessings bestowed upon you.

Closing:

Lower your hands and take a moment to ground yourself once more.
Offer a final prayer or affirmation, expressing your appreciation for the celestial realm.
In the realm of celestial wonders above,
We honor the stars we deeply love.
With awe and reverence, our spirits rise,
As we invoke their guidance in the darkened skies.

Thus, the Ritual of Star Invocation finds its end,
May its connection to the stars forever transcend.
In the realm of cosmic energies, both near and far,
May the guidance of the stars shine like a guiding star.

190. Incantation for Protection of Sacred Animals

In the realm of creatures divine and pure,
I call upon the power to endure.
Guard and shield the sacred ones so dear,
Protect them from harm, forever near.

Centering and Focus:

Find a quiet and serene space where you can connect with the energy of nature.
Take deep breaths, grounding yourself in the present moment.
Invocation:

Call upon the presence of the divine forces or deities associated with the protection
of animals, such as Bastet or Horus.
Speak their names and invite their guidance and guardianship over the sacred
animals.
Connection with Nature:

Visualize a lush and vibrant natural setting, filled with the presence of the sacred
animals.
Feel a sense of unity with the animal kingdom, recognizing their sacredness and
significance.
Incantation:

Repeat the following words with reverence and intention:
"By ancient power and sacred decree,
I invoke protection, for creatures wild and free.
From harm and danger, I shield their way,
Sacred animals, guarded night and day."
Symbolic Gesture:

Hold your hands outstretched, palms facing upward, as a symbolic gesture of offering
and protection.
Visualize a radiant energy emanating from your hands, forming a shield of light
around the sacred animals.
Gratitude and Blessing:

Offer a prayer or blessing, expressing gratitude for the presence of sacred animals and their role in the natural world.

Ask for their continued well-being and protection, sending love and positive energy their way.

Closing:

Slowly bring your awareness back to the present moment, feeling the connection and energy of the incantation within you.

Carry the intention of protecting sacred animals in your heart and actions, honoring their place in the divine order.

In the realm of creatures divine and pure,
May this incantation's magic endure.
Guard and shield the sacred ones so dear,
Protect them from harm, forever near.

Thus, the Incantation for Protection of Sacred Animals finds its end,
May its enchantment of safeguarding forever transcend.
In the realm of animals sacred and wise,
May their protection be seen through compassionate eyes.

191. Spell for Finding a Soul Mate

In the realm of love's eternal quest,
I seek a soul mate, the one who's best.
With this spell, I call forth destiny's hand,
To guide me to love's sacred land.

Setting the Intention:

Find a quiet and peaceful space where you can focus your energy.
Light a pink or red candle to symbolize love and passion.
Centering and Alignment:

Take deep breaths to center yourself and align your intentions with your heart's desires.
Visualize yourself surrounded by a loving and supportive energy.
Invocation:

Call upon the presence of the divine forces associated with love and destiny, such as Isis or Aphrodite.
Speak their names and invite their guidance in finding your soul mate.
Personal Affirmation:

State your intention clearly and confidently, affirming your readiness and openness to receive love.
Repeat a positive affirmation, such as:
"I am deserving of a loving and fulfilling relationship.
I am open and ready to meet my soul mate.
I attract love and partnership into my life."
Visualization:

Close your eyes and visualize yourself in a loving and harmonious relationship.
Imagine the qualities and attributes you desire in your soul mate, envisioning them by your side.
Love Attraction Ritual:

Write down a list of the qualities you seek in a soul mate, focusing on love, compatibility, and shared values.
Place the list under the candle, symbolizing your intention to attract these qualities into your life.
Gratitude and Release:

Express gratitude for the love that is coming into your life, even before it manifests physically.

Release any doubts or fears, trusting in the divine timing and the universe's ability to bring love to you.

Closing:

Thank the divine forces for their guidance and assistance in your journey to find a soul mate.

Blow out the candle, symbolizing the completion of the spell.

In the realm of love's eternal quest,

May this spell bring forth what's best.

With destiny's hand, my soul mate I shall find,

Love's sacred land, together we'll bind.

Thus, the Spell for Finding a Soul Mate finds its end,

May its enchantment of love forever transcend.

In the realm of heartfelt connections, both near and far,

May the path to your soul mate be guided by love's guiding star.

192. Ritual of Offering to the Goddess Hathor

In the presence of Hathor, goddess divine,
We gather to offer, to honor your shrine.
With reverence and gratitude, our hearts do entwine,
As we invoke your blessings, O goddess sublime.

Setting the Sacred Space:

Find a peaceful and quiet space where you can create a sacred atmosphere.
Arrange a small altar with images or statues representing Hathor and other symbolic items.
Purification and Centering:

Begin by purifying yourself and the sacred space through a ritual cleansing, such as washing your hands or lighting incense.
Take deep breaths, centering yourself and focusing your mind on the presence of Hathor.
Invocation:

Light candles or incense as offerings and symbols of divine presence.
Call upon the presence of Hathor with heartfelt words, such as:
"Hathor, radiant goddess of joy and love,
We invoke your presence from realms above.
Join us in this sacred space we create,
Bless us with your grace, O deity great."
Offering:

Prepare an offering for Hathor, such as flowers, milk, honey, or sweet treats.
Place the offering on the altar, expressing your gratitude and devotion.
Prayer and Devotion:

Offer prayers, expressing your intentions, desires, or gratitude to Hathor.
Speak from the heart, sharing your deepest thoughts and feelings.
Communion and Celebration:

Take a moment to meditate or contemplate, allowing yourself to connect with the energy of Hathor.
Feel her presence surrounding you, filling your heart with joy and love.

Closing:

Express gratitude to Hathor for her presence and blessings.
Blow out the candles or extinguish the incense as a symbolic closing of the ritual.
In the presence of Hathor, goddess divine,
We offer our reverence at your sacred shrine.
With joy and love, our spirits entwine,
As we receive your blessings, O goddess sublime.

Thus, the Ritual of Offering to the Goddess Hathor finds its end,
May its enchantment of devotion forever transcend.
In the realm of Hathor's grace, may we be blessed,
With joy and love, by her presence, forever impressed.

193.   Incantation for Protection Against Scorpions

Oh mighty gods, I call upon your might,
To shield me from scorpions with your divine light.
With this incantation, I seek your protection,
Guard me from danger with your divine reflection.

Setting the Intention:

Find a calm and quiet space where you can focus your energy.
Light a candle or incense to symbolize divine presence and protection.
Centering and Grounding:

Take deep breaths, grounding yourself and connecting with the earth's energy.
Visualize a protective shield surrounding you, impenetrable to scorpions.
Invocation of Deities:

Call upon the deities associated with protection and divine guardianship, such as Isis or Serket.
Speak their names with reverence, inviting their assistance in warding off scorpions.
Incantation:

Recite the following incantation or create your own, speaking with confidence and belief:
"By the power of the gods, I am shielded and strong,
From scorpions' venom, I am kept safe and long.
With divine protection, I am surrounded and blessed,
No harm shall befall me, I am divinely addressed."
Visualization:

Close your eyes and visualize a glowing aura of light enveloping your body.
See this protective light extending outward, forming a barrier against scorpions.
Protective Gesture:

Make a sweeping motion around your body with your hands, as if creating a shield.
Imagine this gesture sealing the protective energy around you.
Gratitude and Release:

Express gratitude to the deities for their protection and assistance.

Release any fears or anxieties, knowing that you are divinely protected.
Closing:

Blow out the candle or let the incense burn out, symbolizing the completion of the incantation.
Oh mighty gods, your protection I embrace,
Shielded from scorpions' venomous embrace.
With this incantation, I am kept secure and free,
Protected by divine power, for eternity.

Thus, the Incantation for Protection Against Scorpions finds its end,
May its power and protection forever transcend.
In the realm of safety and divine grace,
May scorpions' harm never find a place.

194.   Spell for Emotional Release

In the depths of our emotions, we seek release,
A spell to bring comfort, to find inner peace.
With the power of words and intentions aligned,
We let go of burdens that weigh on the mind.

Preparation:

Find a quiet and serene space where you can focus on your emotions.
Light a candle or incense to create a sacred atmosphere.
Centering and Grounding:

Take deep breaths, allowing yourself to relax and find inner calm.
Feel your connection to the earth, grounding yourself in its stability.
Invocation:

Call upon the divine forces of healing and emotional support.
Speak their names with reverence and sincerity, inviting their presence.
Release:

Reflect on the emotions that burden your heart and mind.
Write down or speak aloud the emotions you wish to release.
Visualize these emotions transforming into energy that no longer serves you.
Incantation:

Recite the following spell or create your own, speaking with intent and conviction:
"Emotions deep, I set you free,
Release your hold, let me be.
Transform and flow, no longer bind,
Inner peace and clarity I find."
Symbolic Action:

Tear or burn the written representation of the emotions, symbolizing their release.
Visualize the energy of the emotions dissipating into the universe.
Healing Visualization:

Close your eyes and imagine a soothing light surrounding you.
Visualize this light gently healing and comforting the places where the emotions
resided.
Gratitude and Closure:

Express gratitude to the divine forces for their presence and assistance.
Take a few moments to breathe deeply and feel the newfound sense of emotional release.
In the depths of our emotions, we find solace and peace,
With this spell's power, our burdens release.
Emotional healing, a path we now tread,
Free from the weight that once filled us with dread.

Thus, the Spell for Emotional Release finds its end,
May its healing energy forever transcend.
In the realm of emotional well-being and grace,
May peace and serenity find a permanent place.

195.   Ritual of Lunar Devotion

When the moon shines bright in the darkened sky,
We gather in reverence as time passes by.
With hearts open wide and spirits aligned,
We honor the lunar goddess, divine and kind.

Preparation:

Choose a clear night when the moon is visible.
Find a quiet outdoor space where you can witness the moon's presence.
Cleansing and Grounding:

Take a few deep breaths to center yourself.
Visualize any negativity or distractions leaving your body as you exhale.
Imagine roots extending from your feet, grounding you to the earth.
Moon Gazing:

Face the moon and gaze upon its luminous beauty.
Absorb its gentle radiance and allow yourself to be filled with its energy.
Feel a connection growing between you and the lunar realm.
Invocation:

Speak aloud or silently call upon the lunar goddess or deities associated with the moon, such as Isis or Thoth.
Invite their presence and guidance in your lunar devotion.
Lunar Affirmations:

Recite affirmations or words of praise dedicated to the moon, expressing gratitude and admiration for its influence and power.
Speak from your heart, allowing your words to flow with sincerity and reverence.
Offerings:

Prepare offerings that symbolize the moon's attributes, such as silver-colored items, white flowers, or moon-shaped objects.
Place the offerings on a small altar or directly on the ground, facing the moon.
Meditation and Connection:

Close your eyes and enter into a meditative state.
Visualize yourself merging with the lunar energy, becoming one with its gentle yet transformative essence.

Listen to the whispers of the moon, allowing its wisdom to flow through your being.
Gratitude and Closing:

Express gratitude to the lunar goddess and deities for their presence and blessings.
Slowly open your eyes and take a moment to absorb the energy and serenity of the
moonlit surroundings.
In the moon's gentle glow, our devotion takes flight,
A sacred connection, shining in the night.
With this ritual, we honor the lunar way,
Guided by its luminous and mystical display.

Thus, the Ritual of Lunar Devotion finds its end,
May its lunar energy forever transcend.
In the realm of celestial beauty and grace,
May the moon's presence light our sacred space.

196.   Incantation for Protection of Agricultural Crops

By the power of the earth and the sun's golden light,
I call upon the spirits, guardians of growth and might.
Protect these fields, blessed with life's abundant grace,
Shield our crops from harm and ensure their thriving embrace.

Preparation:

Stand in the center of the agricultural field or garden.
Take a moment to ground yourself, feeling your connection to the earth beneath your feet.
Invocation:

Raise your arms to the sky, palms open, and speak the following invocation:
"Spirits of the land, guardians of growth,
I beseech you now, protect this field and both.
With reverence, I call upon your power and might,
Guard our crops day and night."
Connection to the Elements:

Touch the earth with your hands and feel its fertile energy.
Envision roots extending from your feet, tapping into the nourishing soil.
Feel the warmth of the sun on your face, acknowledging its vital role in plant growth.
Protection Incantation:

Recite the following incantation or create your own, speaking with conviction:
"Fields of green and crops so dear,
I call upon the spirits, draw them near.
Protect this land, shield it from harm,
Guard our crops with your powerful charm.
May pests and disease be cast away,
So our harvest thrives, day by day."
Visualization:

Close your eyes and visualize a radiant, protective energy enveloping the entire field.
See it forming a shield, warding off pests, disease, and any harmful influences.
Imagine the crops growing strong and healthy, flourishing under the watchful care of the spirits.

Gratitude and Closure:

Lower your arms, bringing your focus back to the present.
Express gratitude to the spirits and the elements for their assistance and protection.
Offer a small token of appreciation, such as a handful of grains or a leaf, to the earth.
In this sacred space, we ask for protection divine,
May the spirits guard our crops, for they are thine.
With this incantation, we seek nature's gentle embrace,
Agricultural bounty, blessed by the spirits' grace.

Thus, the Incantation for Protection of Agricultural Crops finds its end,
May its magic and guardianship forever transcend.
In the realm of fertile lands and nature's embrace,
May our crops thrive and flourish, with abundance and grace.

197. Spell for Spiritual Awakening

In the realm of higher consciousness and divine light,
I seek awakening, to expand my spiritual sight.
With this spell, I call upon the sacred forces above,
To guide me on a path of enlightenment and love.

Preparation:

Find a quiet and peaceful space where you can focus without distractions.
Light a candle or incense to create a sacred atmosphere.
Centering and Grounding:

Sit or stand comfortably, closing your eyes and taking a deep breath.
Feel the earth beneath your feet, grounding yourself in its stability.
Visualize a pillar of light extending from the crown of your head to the core of the earth, anchoring you.
Invocation:

Speak the following invocation or adapt it to your personal beliefs:
"Divine spirits and celestial guides,
Hear my call as I seek the tides.
Awaken within me a higher sight,
Illuminate my path with radiant light."
Affirmations:

State affirmations that align with your intention for spiritual awakening.
Speak them aloud with conviction, feeling their truth resonate within you.
Examples include: "I am open to receiving divine wisdom," "I embrace my spiritual journey with love and courage," or "I am connected to the divine within and around me."
Visualization:

Envision a brilliant light entering your being, filling you with radiant energy.
See this light expanding and illuminating every aspect of your being, awakening dormant spiritual faculties.
Imagine yourself surrounded by a cocoon of divine light, protected and guided on your spiritual journey.
Gratitude and Closing:

Express gratitude to the divine forces and guides for their presence and assistance.

Slowly open your eyes, carrying the awareness of your spiritual awakening with you.
In this sacred moment, my spirit takes flight,
A spell of awakening, in the realm of divine light.
May the path of enlightenment unfold with grace,
Guided by celestial forces, in this sacred space.

Thus, the Spell for Spiritual Awakening finds its end,
May its power and wisdom forever transcend.
In the realm of expanded consciousness and divine embrace,
May your spirit awaken, in love and cosmic grace.

198. Ritual of Opening the Gates of the Underworld

In the ancient realm where darkness holds sway,
We invoke the sacred rites to open the way.
To the mysterious realm where spirits reside,
We call upon the gates of the Underworld wide.

Preparation:

Choose a secluded and quiet location for the ritual.
Create an altar with representations of the underworld, such as images of deities
associated with the afterlife or symbols of death and rebirth.
Invocation:

Light a black candle as a symbol of the underworld's darkness and the gateway to the
realm of spirits.
Speak the following invocation or compose your own, with reverence and respect:
"Oh, gatekeeper of the Underworld's might,
I call upon you on this sacred night.
Open the gates, reveal the unseen,
Let the spirits emerge and the realms convene."
Offerings:

Prepare offerings for the spirits, such as water, food, or incense.
Place the offerings on the altar, symbolically inviting the spirits to partake in the ritual.
Incantation:

Recite the incantation with clarity and intention, reaching out to the spirits:
"By the power of ancient rites and sacred lore,
I open the gates to the Underworld's door.
Spirits of the departed, hear my call,
Cross over now, into this mortal thrall."
Stillness and Listening:

Sit or stand in silence, opening yourself to the presence of the spirits.
Listen with your inner senses, being receptive to any messages or signs they may
convey.
Remain patient and respectful, allowing the spirits to make their presence known.
Closing and Farewell:

Express gratitude to the spirits for their presence and guidance.
Extinguish the black candle, symbolizing the closing of the gates.
Safely dispose of the offerings, either by burying them in the earth or leaving them in a designated outdoor space.
In this sacred space, the gates have been unsealed,
The realm of spirits revealed, their presence congealed.
May the wisdom and guidance of the departed be found,
In the realm of the Underworld, forever profound.

Thus, the Ritual of Opening the Gates of the Underworld finds its end,
May its connection to the spirit realm forever transcend.
In the realm where darkness and spirits reside,
May you find wisdom and guidance, with spirits by your side.